Celebrations that Stick!

Ideas for Old/Independent Catholic Communities
during the Year of Mark 2021

Hon. Rev. Dr. Jayme Mathias

Extraordinary Catholics Press
Austin, Texas

Extraordinary Catholics Press
P.O. Box 2386
Austin, Texas 78768

Cover design: Luis Armando Ordaz Gutiérrez

Printed in the United States of America

ISBN 979-8-57-167652-6

Table of Contents

Preface

I take great pride in self-identifying as Independent Catholic, and, when asked what it means to be Independent Catholic, I summarize that I am "Catholic, but not Roman Catholic." I know: Some of our sisters and brothers take offense at this, arguing that we should not measure ourselves with a Roman "yardstick," but, in a world filled with over one billion Roman Catholics, we, as Independent Catholics, pique the curiosity of others when we suggest that we are...Catholic, but not Roman Catholic.

Birds of many feathers fill the Independent Catholic movement, and we self-identify in numerous ways: as Independent Catholic, American Catholic, Apostolic Catholic, Ecumenical Catholic, Free Catholic, Liberal Catholic, Old Catholic, Old Roman Catholic, Orthodox Catholic, Reformed Catholic, Synodal Catholic—and so many other names that express our self-identity and our desire to be viewed in connection to the Catholic tradition. This book is an attempt to help us "bind ourselves back"—ultimately the root of any *re-ligio*—with our Old and Independent Catholic roots, introducing us to the people and events that we might celebrate as Independent Catholics.

As Independent Catholics, we have much to offer the world. We offer people freedom from the structures and strictures of other traditions, and our sense of "sacramental justice" allows us to offer the sacraments of the Church more liberally than others. We do well to ask ourselves: Why aren't people flocking to us in droves?

Last year, in the first edition of this work, I offered a theoretical framework for the five stages of growth for Independent Catholic communities. Many of us struggle alone, as "sheepless shepherds," with no one drawn to our "work," our *leitourgia*. Others lead communities too small to sustain them and their families.

This book challenges us to reflect on our own situations. It is a call to introspection. Be honest: What would it take for people to take more interest in you and your ministry, to feel nourished by you, to more generously share of themselves with you and your efforts, and to contribute to the growth of your ministry? Make 2021 be the year that you work to strengthen your ministry—for your sake and for the sake of our entire Independent Catholic movement!

Creating Celebrations that "Stick"

A number of recent works have built on the themes of Chip and Dan Heath's 2007 work, *Made to Stick*. Using the acronym SUCCESs, they suggest that ideas are "stickier" when they are expressed in Simple, Unexpected, Concrete, Credible, Emotional Stories.

There's a story in my head that I just can't shake, and—warning!—if you read it, you likely won't shake it either. When I was a young Conventual Franciscan Friar, Brother Randy Kin told a story, which went something like this:

> One dark night, John was speeding down the roads of rural Ohio in his pickup, when he struck a deer so hard that the deer came up, over the hood of his truck, and smashed through the windshield. The deer kicked John to death.

Thirty-five years later, I can't get this story out of my head! Chip and Dan Heath help us to understand why.

First, it's a **story**. You won't change my behavior by telling me not to speed. Give me a good story, though, and there's a chance that your message will "stick," that it will modify my behavior. Brother Randy drew me into his story, and, ever since, I've not wanted to end up like his friend, John!

Second, it's **simple**. Brother Randy told that story in a sentence or two. I lived with Brother Randy for two years—and I remember nothing he said in the same way that I remember that simple story. There was nothing complicated about it. The simple message: If you speed at night, you risk being kicked to death by a deer!

Third, it's **unexpected**. I've heard many predictable stories in my life, but I didn't expect the ending to Brother Randy's story. I didn't expect John to die in that collision; even less did I expect him to be kicked to death by a deer!

Fourth, it's **concrete**. There is nothing abstract about this story. You hear the story, and you imagine John's demise in vivid detail!

Fifth, it's **credible**. As a young man, I believed it—and, even today, I have no reason to doubt that such an event could happen. If you hit a deer at a high velocity, it seems plausible that the deer could end up in your car!

Finally, it's **emotional**. You feel for John, and your body viscerally reacts as you imagine what it would be like to experience such a death.

Yes, Brother Randy's story was a story that "sticks"!

Now, be honest: How many of your homilies and celebrations might be said to "stick"? Do the folks who come to you for sacraments and celebrations remember you and your words? Likely not. Do they remember the way you made them feel? Definitely! As human beings, that's how we're wired.

Let's attempt to enumerate a few lessons for Independent Catholic clergy and lay leaders:

1. **Speak more simply!** Why speak of Jesus' "disciples" or "apostles," when you can more simply refer to them as Jesus' friends? Yes, the Church has an entire vocabulary that is largely unintelligible to most folks. Journalists learn to write at an eighth-grade level; they learn the KISS method: Keep It Simple, Sister!

2. **Speak and act in good, unexpected ways!** Never begin your preaching with "In today's gospel..." It's an instant recipe for lulling people into temporary coma. Create a "hook" instead, to grab your listeners attention from the start. Better yet, share a joke with an unexpected twist. Break into song as you tie popular lyrics to the message you're preaching. Engage your listeners in ways they don't expect to be engaged. John Maxwell speaks of the need to constantly "spike" listeners' attention; one way to grab their attention is by saying or doing the (good, appropriate)things they least expect. These are the things that "stick"!

3. **Be concrete!** Using a technique I learned from John Maxwell a few years ago, I invited our local clergy to evaluate their preaching by parsing their homilies into their parts: stories/jokes, scripture, ties to the liturgy, prayer, etc. One "bucket" into which we parsed homilies was "abstract concepts." Be honest: When we preach about "salvation," "incarnation," and the "Trinity," our listeners tune us out. These things aren't part of their daily experience. When I was a young priest, folks called me "Father Show-and-Tell"; I always had an object lesson to share. Most people are visual learners: they'll remember what they see far longer than anything they heard. Take advantage of this! Parishioners recently reminisced about my "apple homily," my "chocolate milk homily" and my "mustard seed" homily. People remember such visuals; if we can successfully tie a memorable message to such objects, those message will "stick" for a long time!

4. **Speak credibly!** Be honest: What are the things that diminish the credibility of your message? I confess that I often rehearse my homilies, jokes and stories, so they might come off as less authentic. Even my mode of dress might keep people from

connecting with me. Credibility is all about connection, and one way to increase our credibility is to connect people with the riches of our Old/Independent Catholic tradition!

5. **Touch their emotions!** On the emotional roller coaster of ministry—a funeral one hour and a wedding the next—we, as clergy, sometimes find it difficult to connect with feelings; as a result, our liturgies and homilies become mental exercises void of the emotional content that engages others. People don't come to you to connect with a robot; they want to bond with a thinking, feeling creature like themselves. Acknowledge your emotions and theirs, and build bridges between the two!

6. **Tell a story!** If given the opportunity to introduce a saint through a narration of facts, or through an anecdote or story, remember that the latter will be remembered longer. Stories involve and "transport" us, causing us to suspend judgment as we absorb information and values. They contain layers of information and coding, which engage us and even shape our brains! In short, stories "stick"!

7. Finally, Chip and Dan Heath didn't say it, so I will: **Be brief.** That was the wisdom my mother shared with me when I was preparing to preach my first homily as a young priest. It was as if she was channeling St. Francis of Assisi, who told his friars to preach "with brevity, because our Lord when on earth kept his word brief." I don't understand Francis' logic, but I agree with his sentiment: Why preach for 20 minutes, when you can say the same in four? At my former parish, which we grew to be Austin's largest Spanish-language Roman Catholic community, I was known as the "King of the Four-Minute Homily." The people who come to you are being generous; don't waste their time or anesthetize them with a long, meandering message they won't remember!

Consider other ways to create experiences that "stick." A warm word of welcome, a hospitable environment, and a sense of connection and belonging will all likely go far in causing others to "stick" around. Remember the adage: They won't care how much you know, until they know how much you care. Let's make 2021 a year of caring connection!

For the sake of all to whom we minister, we invite you—we challenge you—to use this resource for your own creation of celebrations that "stick"!

Sunday, November 29, 2020
FIRST SUNDAY OF ADVENT
(blue or violet)

It's the **Year of Mark** (Year B): Be sure to provide some catechesis and/or an overview of this first gospel and its very low Christology. Be sure to situate this gospel as being written by one who was not an eyewitness of Jesus' ministry—evidenced by the author's lack of knowledge about Palestinian geography—likely by an unknown Christian in the name and spirit of Peter's interpreter, John Mark.

Advent has arrived! Be sure to share a brief lesson on this **season of joyful hope**—and to speak of **Christ's three comings**: in flesh 2,000 years ago, at the end of time, and in the liturgy your community celebrates!

Now that Thanksgiving is over, some radio stations are already playing Christmas music 24/7. Challenge congregants to **respect the integrity of the Advent season** and to **"fast" from Christmas music and decorations until December 24**. For more ideas on how congregants might honor the Advent season, visit https://adventconspiracy.org!

Think about your worship environment!

- The beginning of a new liturgical year might be an ideal time to try out a **new placement for your liturgical furniture**.
- In place of the penitential color of violet (*violaceus*), **consider using blue this year**—a beautiful winter color that calls to mind Mary during these weeks leading up to the birth of her son! If you stick with violet, consider a shade that's toward the blue end of the spectrum, reminiscent of the night sky before the dawn, and use complementary violets that vary, like the shades of the sky.
- Be sure to steam or iron your **Advent vestments**—and to coordinate the color of your vestments with any other touches of blue or violet in your worship space!
- Plan how you might tie the **Advent décor** of your worship environment to the décor of the Christmas season, so as to lessen the load of Christmas decorating on December 24 and to provide a smoother transition from one season to the other—or, even better, to show a more seamless joining of the Advent and Christmas seasons! Consider pulling out the **garland and Christmas trees** and decorating them with touches of your Advent color, which can be replaced with touches of Christmas color on December 24.

- Bring a touch of **Advent color and/or accents** to other places outside your worship space: to outdoor areas, the entrance into your worship space, your Blessed Sacrament chapel, your parish hall and/or classrooms, etc. Try an outdoor banner and/or place an evergreen wreath on the front door!

- Dust off your **Advent wreath,** or create a new arrangement this year—perhaps even a "deconstructed wreath" consisting of four candles in four places. If you have a smaller space and are trying for a more contemporary look, try adding a floating candle to a large glass bowl of water on each Sunday of Advent. Want to try a vintage look? Suspend a wagon wheel from the ceiling: Early American pioneers hung their wagon wheels indoors during the winter (to keep them from warping), and they decorated them with evergreens and lights to ward off the winter darkness. Instead of colored candles, consider colored glass globes that can be placed over candles; the globes can be taken off at Christmas to expose white candles. Be sure the Advent wreath is a focal point during prayer—but that it doesn't overshadow or overpower the primary liturgical objects of the altar and ambo. Consider placing it in the spot where you'll have your creche on Christmas (to make the connection of Christ coming as the Light of the world), or consider keeping the wreath throughout the Christmas season, but with white candles and white/gold ribbon. Always consider placing the Advent wreath and/or creche in a place where people can be drawn into prayer—a "shrine" within your worship space—perhaps in a place where parents and grandparents can conveniently share a lesson with their children or grandchildren.

- Do you have any large icons of **St. John the Baptist** and/or of the **Visitation of Mary**? Think of incorporating them into the worship environment when the scriptures speak of them.

- Consider whether you'll keep the nativity scene out of the worship space until Christmas (which many liturgists recommend), or whether you'll **heighten the anticipation with a gradual addition of figures to the creche** over the four weeks of Advent. Remember: when you place the nativity scene in your worship space, **the manger is left empty until Christmas!**

Need help decorating your worship space? Don't be bashful: **Ask for volunteers!** Take leadership. Assign tasks and responsibilities. Play appropriate Advent music while you decorate. Then show your gratitude with hot chocolate and cookies, or some other appropriate winter food and drink!

The Advent wreath is an important liturgical symbol. **Bless your Advent wreath** on this first Sunday of Advent. **Involve a parish family by inviting them to carry the first, lighted, blue or violet candle in procession, or to light it at the appropriate moment.** Be sure to speak of the symbolism of the increasing light that we'll see during these four Sundays! Send congregants home with a prayer of blessing for their own Advent wreaths and with ideas on how they might pray as a family during this season — perhaps before a daily family meal!

In some places, the **Jesse Tree** is a popular tradition that features symbols from the story of our salvation. Consider a Jesse Tree this year, or encourage families to create their own Jesse trees and/or Advent calendars at home!

Thinking of helping those in need at a time when much of the world is focused on consumerism? Create a **"giving tree"** with tags listing gift items that might be used by the homeless or desired by families and/or senior adults in need, and/or have a coat drive and invite families to donate gently-used coats, hats, gloves, boots and blankets. A local homeless shelter will surely welcome your generosity. Alternatively, since we find ourselves in the middle of a pandemic, consider a "giving tree" of items needed by local medical professionals and those suffering from this pandemic (e.g., masks, gloves, sanitizer).

Consider **restrained music** during Advent, building to a crescendo with the splendid music of the Christmas season!

To honor the penitential nature of Advent, consider singing the **Penitential Rite** and or using **Eucharistic Prayers for Reconciliation**. Think, too, of how you might better incorporate **moments of silence** into the liturgies of these dark, winter days — perhaps with longer pauses after the proclamations of scripture and/or after reception of the eucharist.

Remember: **The *Gloria* is *not* sung during the Advent season!**

Be mindful of the **exclusive language** in today's scriptures. The first reading twice speaks of God in masculine terms. The psalm contains two references to the "son of man," and the other instance of "man" can easily be replaced by "one."

The thread in today's scriptures: Trito-Isaiah prayed for God to return (Is. 63:17), and the psalmist prayed that God might "come to save us" (Ps. 80:3). Because we know not "the day of our Lord Jesus Christ" (1Cor. 1:8), Jesus urges us to "be watchful! Be alert!" (Mk. 13:33).

Holy humor: The story is told of the scrapyard that the U.S. government owned in the middle of the desert. Congress determined that someone might steal from the scrapyard, so they created the position of a watchperson to guard the yard. To provide instructions for the watchperson, the government created additional positions: one person to write instructions, another to train the watchperson, and another to perform time studies. To ensure that the watchperson correctly performed his/her job, government officials created another position: a report writer. To pay the watchperson, the government hired two more people: a timekeeper and a payroll officer. To manage the watchperson, they created a team of three people — an administrator, an administrative assistant, and a legal secretary. A year later, Congress received a report on the situation and learned that the project was over budget. They knew they needed to make cutbacks — so they laid off...the watchperson! [Segue to the importance of watchpeople in ancient and modern society — the watchperson was the most important person in that story after all! — and how it is that we, like the watchperson of the scrapyard, must be watchful and alert!]

Looking for a visual aid for your homily or object lesson? Consider a spyglass or a pair of binoculars! Twice warning us to "watch," Jesus calls to mind the image of sentinels, waiting "in the evening, [and] at midnight, [and] at cockcrow, [and] in the morning" (Mk 13:35). We must be alert and awake, watching and waiting for the coming of the Lord! Other possible object lessons: unclean rags (Is. 64:5), dead leaves (Is. 64:5), or clay (Is. 64:7).

For the intellectually-curious, consider sharing a lesson on the symbolism of the Advent wreath, its historical roots in sixteenth-century Germany, and the popular tradition of lighting the wreath before family meals in the "domestic church!"

It's Advent: Encourage congregants to find a way to **make this Advent special**! Here are a few ideas:

- Challenge congregants to commit themselves to a **special act of charity** during this Advent season.

- Invite them to consider the Advent tradition of choosing a **secret Christkindl** ("Christ Child"), a person for whom they might pray and/or secretly perform small acts of kindness during this Advent season!

- Host an activity in which families can create **Advent wreaths** and/or invite families to begin this season with **an empty manger in the home into which each member of the family can place a piece of straw for every good work performed in honor of the Baby Jesus** during these four weeks, so as to welcome the Christ Child at Christmas with a padded crib. Depending on the size of your congregation, consider doing this activity as a community in or outside of your worship space.

- Looking for other activities for children? Many children write letters to Santa during these weeks; encourage them to observe the Austrian tradition exercised by the von Trapp children of writing their own *"Christkindl* **Brief,"** a letter to the Baby Jesus that's placed on the window sill for their Guardian Angel to read to the Christ Child!

The First Sunday of Advent was traditionally known as **"Stir-up Sunday,"** due to the fact that the collect (or opening prayer) spoke of stirring up God's might. Many traditional Advent prayers contain the words: "Stir up your might, we beg you, and come...." Consider incorporating these words into your prayer today. If we were not in the middle of a pandemic, we might suggest involving congregants in stirring up a salad or a dessert—like a plum pudding—after Mass!

If we were not in the middle of a pandemic, we might suggest **a community-building event** this holiday season, like a parish trip to a local holiday light display and/or live nativity during the coming weeks. Alternatively, you could host a party in which parish families create Advent wreaths and/or holiday wreaths for their homes. This year, though, we likely do well to encourage families to engage in such practices on their own!

Social media is a great way to evangelize: Be sure to take advantage of social media for spreading word of the themes of this season! Think of creative ways to engage your congregants, perhaps through hashtags (#AdventLight #AdventHope #AdventJoy) and/or by inviting congregants to post photos and/or videos from their day to a **"digital Advent calendar"** of daily Advent themes!

On **November 30**, we celebrate **St. Andrew** (c. 5-60), referred to as one of Jesus' first disciples (Mt 4:18) and, in another place, as a disciple of John the Baptist who introduced his brother, Peter, to Jesus (Jn 1:40-42). Pause to celebrate the patron saint of those who fish and sing, and consider how you are bringing others to Jesus!

On **December 2**, we remember the passing of **Jan van Ruysbroeck** (1294-1381), the Augustinian priest and prominent Flemish mystic who penned 12 books on the spiritual life. Pause to consider where you are on the "spiritual ladder" — and what you might do to achieve the next "rung"!

On **December 2**, we remember the passing of **Pasquier Quesnel** (1634-1719), the French theologian banished from Paris for his Jansenist sympathies. The Roman church published a papal bull, *Unigenitus*, to condemn 101 sentences in his devotional commentary on the New Testament. In his memory, pray for all who continue to write and publish in an attempt to foster the devotion of others — and for all who are persecuted by the people they love!

On **December 2**, we remember the passing of **Thomas Forsyth "T.F." Torrance** (1913-2007), the Scottish Protestant theologian who was a pioneer in the study of science and theology and who edited the translations of hundreds of theological writings into English, including Karl Barth's six-million-word *Church Dogmatics*. Torrance was instrumental in drafting a joint statement on the doctrine of the Trinity for an historical agreement between the Reformed and Eastern Orthodox churches. In his memory, meditate on how generously you are sharing the gifts God has given you for the upbuilding of God's kingdom in this world!

On **December 3**, the Church celebrates **St. Francis Xavier** (1506-1552), the Jesuit ordained with St. Ignatius of Loyola and later sent to evangelize India. Often portrayed as a young, bearded Jesuit with a torch or flaming heart, he's the patron saint of navigators, missionaries, foreign missions and parish missions. If your community has any connection to the Jesuits and/or a desire to support the Church's missions, pray the Litany of St. Francis Xavier, provide a brief lesson and/or a call to action based on this "spiritual soldier," and/or meditate on the words of scripture shared with him by St. Ignatius: "What does it profit you to gain the whole world if you lose your soul?"

On **December 4**, the Church celebrates **St. John of Damascus** (c. 675-749), the first Christian Aristotelian, the last Greek Father, and the "Doctor of Christian Art." John was known for transmitting the teachings of the Greek Fathers and defending the veneration of images. In his memory, read of the iconoclasm that sprang up as a result of Christianity's interaction with Islam, host a religious art appreciation party, and/or reflect on the visual sacramentals of our Catholic tradition, which include statues, paintings and other images!

On **December 5**, the Church celebrates **St. Sabbas** (439-532), the fifth-century abbot, "Star of the Desert" and "Patriarch of Monks" who defended the faith at the Council of Chalcedon. Venerated by the Eastern Church, he's depicted as an abbot with an apple, since he overcame the temptation to eat an apple outside of prescribed meal times—and he vowed never to eat apples again. In Texas, he has a river, city, county and Spanish mission named for him. Take a moment to reflect on the greatest temptations you face in life—and ways in which you might better overcome them!

On **December 5**, we remember the passing of **Thomas Gallus of Vercelli** (c. 1200-1246), the French theologian and member of the School of St. Victor known for his commentaries on Pseudo-Dionysius. His schema for the relationship between love and knowledge in mystical ascent influenced Bonaventure and *The Cloud of Unknowing*. Reread one of Thomas' works and contemplate your own perspective on love and knowledge in achieving union with God!

On **December 5**, we remember the passing of **John Alan Lee** (1933-2013), the Canadian writer and LGBTQ activist known for his research on the sociological and psychological aspects of love and sexuality. The author of over 300 books and articles, he turned his attention later in life to the issues of assisted suicide and the right to die. In his memory, pray for "the flying boy" or girl you know, who might be addicted to such things as sex, work, pain and/or failure!

Sunday, December 6, 2020

SECOND SUNDAY OF ADVENT

(blue or violet)

Light two blue or violet candles of the Advent wreath!

Remember: **The *Gloria* is *not* sung during the Advent season!**

Note: **The introductory line of today's second reading is misleading.** The Letters of Peter are pseudonymous letters, written in Peter's name and spirit, but not written by Peter. You might find a way to clarify this confusion.

The thread in today's scriptures: Mark (1:3) is clear: John the Baptist is the one of whom Deutero-Isaiah spoke when he envisioned a voice crying out, "Prepare the way of the Lord" (Is. 40:3). Personified justice, too, shall…prepare the way of [God's] steps" (Ps. 85:14). Are you preparing yourself for the Lord's coming, by "conducting [yourself] in holiness and devotion" (2Pet. 3:11)?

Holy humor: The drunk man woke up, feeling repentant for drinking too much and getting into a bitter fight with his wife the night before. He noticed the box of beer bottles that caused the fight. Taking the box outside, he smashed one bottle against the brick wall of their home, saying, "You're the reason I fight with my wife!" Picking up another bottle, he smashed it against the wall, saying, "You're the reason my children don't feel loved!" He smashed a third bottle: "You're the reason I don't have a decent job!" When he picked up the fourth bottle, he noticed it was unopened and full of beer. He didn't hesitate: Setting it aside, he said, "You stand over here. I see you weren't involved." [Segue into our need to repent and to work on the "rugged land…[and] rough country" (Is. 40:4) in our lives!]

Looking for a visual aid for your homily or object lesson? Consider a paper airplane! Use it to simulate the landing of a plane. Do planes land on curved, hilly landing strips? Of course not. How are you smoothing the "hills" and filling the "valleys" of your life, so as to prepare for the Lord's smooth "landing" in your life? Make straight the way of the Lord! Other possible object lessons: Use a stuffed lamb to show the care that God shares with God's "flock" (Is. 40:11), or use visuals suggestive of John the Baptist's clothes and food (e.g., camel hair, leather belt, grasshoppers, honey)!

When it doesn't fall on a Sunday, **December 6** is the date the Church celebrates **St. Nicholas** (c. 275-343), the fourth-century Turkish bishop whose generosity made him the protagonist in numerous folktales. Often depicted as a bishop holding three bags of gold (or three golden balls), with three children in a tub at his feet, he's invoked as the patron saint of numerous groups, including brides and brewers, fishermen and pharmacists, maidens, mariners, merchants and murderers, pilgrims and prisoners, scholars and schoolchildren. In his memory, research how his day is celebrated in different countries, bake some *speculaas* (Dutch spice "Kris Kringle cookies"), share one of the many charming stories of St. Nick or *Sinterklaas*, or perform a secret act of charity. Do you have kids in your community? And do have a miter, crozier and Santa Claus beard? Share a brief lesson on the saint's generosity, then, while all sing "Jolly Old St. Nicholas," invite a congregant to enter dressed as the saint, with small gifts for the kids!

On **December 7**, the Church celebrates **St. Ambrose** (339-397), the fourth-century "honey-tongued" bishop who played a role in the conversion of St. Augustine. Often depicted with a beehive, or holding a church in his hand, he's a patron saint of bees, beekeepers, wax melters and candlemakers. In light of the Roman church's penchant for erecting barriers to the sacraments of the Church—condemned as the heresy of semi-Pelagianism—share a brief lesson on this unbaptized-catechumen-turned-bishop and/or try creating a Christ Candle for Christmas!

On **December 7**, we remember the passing of **Gabriel Biel** (c. 1420-1495), the German priest, philosopher and member of the Windesheim Community, whose writings as the "monarch of theologians" were repeatedly referenced at the Council of Trent. He won the pope's affection by siding against the archbishop of Mainz who failed to pay required annates, by advocating that all ecclesiastical jurisdiction derives from the pope, and by arguing that clergy can withhold absolution. Pray for all who similarly feel the need to curry favor with those in power!

On **December 7**, we celebrate the birth in 1941 of **Sr. Elizabeth A. Johnson**, the Roman Catholic feminist theologian whose books are widely read in theology classes. Her work, *Quest for the Living God*, which expounds new ways of thinking about God within the context of traditional Catholic beliefs, garnered criticism by the Roman church's hierarchy, fraying the already-strained relationship between Roman Catholic bishops and theologians. In her honor, find a way to support our sisters in their quest for greater participation and authority in the Body of Christ!

On **December 8,** the Roman church celebrates its "holyday of obligation" of the **Immaculate Conception**, a papal pronouncement that irreparably split the Roman church in 1854 and led to other proclamations: of the novel ideas of the Roman's bishop's universal jurisdiction and purported "infallibility" in 1870. It was exactly these new ideas that led many to refer to themselves as Old Catholics, indicating their desire to return to the beliefs and practices of the ancient Church, rather than fall prey to the novelties pushed by the Roman papacracy. Whether you celebrate the Immaculate Conception or not, this could be a tremendous teaching moment for those who celebrate with you and wish to understand the differences between Old/Independent Catholicism and the teachings of the Roman church. If you celebrate the "Patroness of the United States of America," choose Marian hymns, place white lilies near her image, and consider praying a decade (or more) of the rosary. This is also the traditional day for baking gingerbread Moravian spritz cookies: Plan a family activity of assembling a gingerbread house or of baking holiday cookies!

December 9 is the Feast of **St. Juan Diego Cuauhtlatoatzin** (1474-1548), the indigenous man to whom Our Lady of Guadalupe appeared in 1531, according to the legend written about them in 1648. A patron of Mexico, he's often pictured with roses and with an image of Our Lady of Guadalupe on his *tilma* (outer cloak). Though seemingly frightened and confused by the mandate he was given, Juan Diego obeyed and courageously sought an audience with Fray Juan de Zumárraga, the bishop of New Spain. In his honor, pray for and/or find a way to support those whose faces and courage are mirrored in this saint — including the many migrant workers who help to sustain our economy!

On **December 9**, we remember the passing of **Fulton John Sheen** (1895-1979), the American bishop known for his preaching on television and radio. For 20 years, he hosted a night-time radio program, "The Catholic Hour," before moving to television and sharing "Life is Worth Living" and "The Fulton Sheen Program." Often referred to as one of the first televangelists, Sheen was the winner of two Emmys for Most Outstanding Television Personality. In his memory, consider how you are using modern technologies to expand the reach of your preaching and teaching!

On **December 10**, the Church celebrates **St. Melchiades** (+314), the African pope who led the Church during the last persecution before Constantine granted freedom to Christians. Because Melchiades helped usher in a new era of peace, St. Augustine called him "the true child of the peace of Jesus Christ." Pause today to pray for all who are persecuted, for their persecutors, and for all who are instruments of peace in our world!

On **December 10**, we remember the passing of **Karl Barth** (1886-1968), the Swiss Reformed theologian referred to by Pope Pius XII as the greatest theologian since Thomas Aquinas. How much do you know about him? Take a moment today to increase your knowledge of Karl Barth and his works!

On **December 10**, we remember the passing of **Thomas Merton** (1915-1968), the Trappist monk, theologian, mystic and social activist who dedicated the latter years of his life to the study of comparative religions. His bestselling autobiography, *The Seven Story Mountain*, inspired countless students and veterans to enter religious life. In his memory, pull one of his works from the shelf and reacquaint yourself with his timeless wisdom!

On **December 11**, the Church celebrates **St. Damasus I** (c. 304-384), the fourth-century pope who commissioned Jerome's Vulgate translation of the scriptures. He's the patron saint of archaeologists. Share a brief lesson on the biblical canon approved at his Council of Rome (382 A.D.), and/or make a commitment to better familiarize yourself with the rich fare that we find in scripture!

On **December 11**, the Armenian Apostolic Church celebrates the anniversary of the installation in 2019 of Sahag Maşalyan as **Patriarch Sahak Mashalyan of Constantinople**. In his honor, pray for him and for the 9 million people he serves!

On **December 12**, the Church celebrates **Our Lady of Guadalupe** (1531), the Empress of the Americas, the Patroness of Latin American, and the Mother of all Mexicans!

- If you want to celebrate Our Lady of Guadalupe on December 12, remember that **the most popular celebrations of her by Mexicans occur at midnight and/or at a very early hour of the morning** (e.g., 6:00 a.m.), beginning with the singing of *"Las mañanitas."*

- If you have a Mexican community that might not gather to celebrate on December 12, consider a nod to **Our Lady of Guadalupe** during the Sunday liturgy and/or a celebration of her after your Sunday Mass.

- Invite congregants to **decorate an image of her**, perhaps with large paper flowers of the colors of the Mexican flag; congregants will also likely want to bring **roses and/or candles** in her honor as well!

- Before you begin your celebration of the eucharist, sing *"Las mañanitas"* in her honor!

- Incorporate traditional dances by *matlachines* and/or *concheros* into your liturgy and/or your gathering after Mass!

- **Share a gift** with each person present—perhaps a prayer card or pin or bookmark containing her image.

- In this Advent season of increasing light, be sure to reference the fact that she is clothed with the sun and standing on the moon. Also, note the black band around her waist—a symbol of her pregnancy: In the same way that she carried the Christ Child inside her, we are called to carry Christ within us and to share him with others!

- If you have the talent, organize a **dramatic reenactment of the appearance of Our Lady of Guadalupe to St. Juan Diego**! These *obras* are usually performed by children or teens, but consider involving adults: Juan Diego was some 57 years old at the time of the apparition—much older than most images of the saint!

- **For the intellectually-curious**, consider sharing a lesson on the *Nican mopohua*, the tale that was penned 118 years after the purported apparition, and/or on the incredible **syncretism** that we find in the image of the Aztec goddess *Tonantzín*—who is now venerated by Catholics as the mother of Christ!

- If devotion to Our Lady of Guadalupe runs especially deep in your community, invite lay leaders to host a **novena** in her honor, with the nightly praying of the rosary and singing of songs in her honor, beginning on December 3.

On **December 12**, we remember the passing of **Avery Robert Dulles** (1918-2008), the Jesuit priest, theologian and non-bishop cardinal who penned over 20 books and 700 articles, largely on ecclesiology. Raised Presbyterian, he became agnostic, then Roman Catholic, later serving as president of the Catholic Theological Society of America and of the American Theological Society. Dulles served on the International Theological Commission and worked in Lutheran/Catholic dialogue. In his memory, consider the ways in which you might more significantly contribute to theology, ecclesiology and/or to ecumenical dialogue!

Sunday, December 13, 2020

THIRD SUNDAY OF ADVENT

(rose or blue or violet)

It's *Gaudete* **Sunday**: Share a brief lesson on the joy of this day and its tie to Paul's words: "*Gaudete in Domino semper*" [Rejoice in the Lord always] (Phil 4:4)!

Do you have **rose vestments**? Today's the day to pull them out! Aim for a shade of rose that resembles the sky at dawn — and *not* a shocking pink. Be sure to coordinate the color of your vestments with any other touches of rose in your worship space, and be sure to iron or steam any wrinkles!

Light two blue or violet candles and the rose candle of the Advent wreath!

Remember: **The *Gloria* is *not* sung during the Advent season!**

The thread in today's scriptures: There's cause for rejoicing with Trito-Isaiah (Is. 61:10), Mary (Lk. 1:46-54) and Paul (1Thes. 5:16): the Lord who comes to liberate us (Is. 61:1-2) is among us — even if we don't yet recognize him (Jn. 1:26)!

Holy humor: Do you remember what happened in 2019 and how people said that the blind would rejoice this year? That's right: Some people thought that the blind would enjoy 20/20 vision this year! [Segue into the symbolism of 20/20 vision and seeing more clearly during this year that's quickly drawing to a close. As a result of this pandemic and/or other events, did we see any more clearly this year? If not, what might we do during these last 2.5 weeks of the year to "see" more clearly — and so experience a cause for rejoicing in "the reason for the season"?]

Looking for a visual aid for your homily or object lesson? Consider a blindfold! How blind are we to the Light to which John testified (Jn. 1:7)? Do we recognize the presence of the Risen Christ among us (Jn. 1:26)? If not, what "blindfolds" must we remove from the "eyes" of our hearts, so as to better recognize the presence of Christ in and around us? Other possible object lessons: a crown (Is. 61:10) or a sandal (Jn. 1:27).

Christmas is drawing near! Consider hosting a **holiday party** for clergy, lay leaders and/or volunteers! In light of this year's pandemic, host a virtual event, rather than gather them and have them bring potluck dishes. Save the holiday party games, White Elephant gift exchange, and Advent-colored Santa hats for future years when we'll gather in person again.

If your congregation is of Italian descent, invite them to bring their Christ Child figures to church for a special *Bambinelli* **Sunday** blessing, which always occurs on the Third Sunday of Advent!

This is *Gaudete* Sunday, but we also recognize that the holidays aren't necessarily a jolly time for all. **Share the joy of your community with the homebound and/or with those who might enjoy your visit at a local hospital, nursing home, or senior center!** Such activities can involve congregants of all ages: the children can create handmade holiday cards, the teens can bake cookies and sing carols, the adults can prepare to spend a little extra time listening to those whom you visit. Take with you prayer resources and news from your community!

On **December 13**, when it doesn't fall on a Sunday, the Church celebrates **St. Lucy** (c. 283-303), the third-century Greek noblewoman whose vow of virginity infuriated the young man to whom she was unwillingly wedded. The patroness of eye problems, blindness, the blind, authors, laborers, salespeople and hemorrhages, Lucy is often depicted hitched to a yoke of oxen or holding two eyes on a dish. In Croatia, Christmas wheat is planted today; plant some wheat seeds in a small pot of soil, and you'll have fresh, green wheat about eight inches tall for your manger scene by Christmas! In honor of St. Lucy's intervention in a 1582 famine, Italians abstain from grain, bread and pasta today, eating *cuccia* instead. In Lombardy, goose is eaten today, and St. Lucy brings gifts today to the children who leave hay, carrots and bowls of milk for her donkey. In Sweden, the oldest daughter of the household dons a white dress, a crimson sash and stockings, and a crown/wreath with lighted candles— don't try this at home!— to wake family members on *Luciadagen* (Lucy's Day) with hot coffee and *Lussekatter* (saffron buns). Pray Eucharistic Prayer I, which mentions her, and share a brief lesson on her life and its application to respect for women and support for all who stand with the #MeToo movement and against sexual abuse. Remember to tie her name (from the Latin root *lux, lucis*, meaning "light") to the increasing light that we see during Advent—and to pray for those who are physically and/or spiritually blind!

On **December 13**, we also remember the passing of **Pierre Martin Ngô Đình Thục** (1897-1984), the Vietnamese Roman Catholic archbishop who lived in exile after the murder of his younger brother, Ngô Đình Diệm, the president of South Vietnam. Thục was excommunicated by the Roman church for consecrating a number of bishops without the Vatican's approval during the last ten years of his life. In his memory, pray for all who continue to share his valid lines of apostolic succession with others in the Independent Catholic tradition!

On **December 14**, we remember the passing of **Guillaume Briçonnet, Sr.** (1445-1514), the French cardinal and statesman who served as secretary of Louis XI's treasury. The father of Bishop Guillaume Briçonnet, Jr., he was excommunicated by Julius II for assembling cardinals to speak of the reformation of the Church, but, after Julius' death, Leo X restored him to the College of Cardinals. In his memory, pray for all who encounter resistance in their attempts to bring reform to the Church!

On **December 14**, the Church celebrates **St. John of the Cross** (1542-1591) the 16th-century Spanish Carmelite priest who helped St. Teresa of Avila to reform the Carmelite Order. He is the patron saint of mystics, mystical theology, contemplatives and contemplative life. Share an acknowledgement that not all people are rejoicing during this holiday season. Say a prayer of blessing for those passing through the "dark valleys" of life and/or through "the dark night of the soul" during what might otherwise be a season of joy!

On **December 14**, we remember the passing of **Paul Melchers** (1813-1895), the German cardinal and archbishop of Cologne who wrote to Pius IX with 13 other bishops to express their concern that the definition of purported papal infallibility was untimely. Melchers played a prominent role at the First Vatican Council and counseled against a definition of papal infallibility. Faithful to the Roman papacracy, he later excommunicated professors who refused to accept the novel dogma, as well as two priests who joined the Old Catholic movement. In his memory, pray for all who, against their best judgment, heap burdens on others rather than risk the loss of the power and privileges they enjoy!

On **December 14**, we celebrate the birth in 1938 of **Genézio Darci "Leonardo" Boff**, the Brazilian theologian known for his support of the early Latin American liberation theology movement. A sharp critic of the "fundamentalist" Roman papacracy and of American foreign policy, he was silenced by "religious terrorist" Joseph Ratzinger. After being silenced again and barred by the Roman church from attending the Eco-92 Earth Summit, he departed his Franciscan order and abandoned his priestly ministry. In Boff's honor, reacquaint yourself with any one of his liberating works!

On **December 15**, the Church celebrates **St. Virginia Bracelli** (1587-1651), the 17th-century Italian noblewoman who, after bearing two daughters, was widowed at age 20, professed a vow of chastity, and spent the remainder of her life helping the sick, the poor, and abandoned children during times of plague and famine. Pray today for all who are bringing light and life to others during this Advent season!

In the Latino culture, **December 16** is the first day of *las posadas*, the nine-day reenactment of Mary and Joseph's search for lodging in Bethlehem. Keep these ideas in mind for future years, when we're no longer in a pandemic, and/or consider how you might celebrate *posadas* in a virtual or socially-distanced way!

- Organize a parish *posada* at your worship space, complete with candles, food and drink, a *piñata*, gifts for the kids, and maybe even a visit from Santa!
- Better yet, find nine families who are willing to open their homes for parish *posadas* — one on each night from December 16 to 24 — so that you can get out and visit them at their homes. Publish the date, time and address of each *posada*, so that parishioners can join the fun!
- Remember to incorporate a lesson on how we're all called to open the "doors" of our hearts to those around us during this holiday season — and throughout the coming year.
- If there's a *piñata*, be sure to speak to the symbolism of beating the capital sins in our lives (represented by the seven "horns" of a traditional *piñata*), so that the grace of God might spill into our lives (as symbolized by the candy)! Note: The *piñata* can be an extremely dangerous tradition. Have adults hold back eager children with a large rope circle, until a whistle is blown — which is the signal for the child with the stick to stop swinging. Take time to explain these rules and obtain understanding from children *before* the excitement begins!

December 17 is the first day for the seven daily **O Antiphons**, which are based on fourth-century titles for the Messiah. Found in the hymn "O Come, O Come Emmanuel," they are: *O Sapientia* (Wisdom), *O Adonai* (Lord and Ruler), *O Radix Jesse* (Root of Jesse), *O Clavis David* (Key of David), *O Oriens* (Dayspring), *O Rex Gentium* (King of the Gentiles), *and O Emmanuel* (God With Us). When ordered in reverse (*Emmanuel, Rex, Oriens, Clavis, Radix, Adonai*, and *Sapientia*), they form the Latin acrostic *ero cras*, which means, "I will come tomorrow." Pray today's O Antiphon and invite the Lord to come!

On **December 17**, the Church celebrates **St. Joseph Manyanet y Vives** (1833-1901), the 19th-century "Apostle of the Holy Family" who founded the Congregation of the Sons of the Holy Family and of the Missionary Daughters of the Holy Family of Nazareth, two congregations dedicated to parish ministry, teaching children, and serving families. Joseph encouraged devotion to the Holy Family, and he published the magazine, *La Sagrada Familia*. Pause today to consider how you might better serve your family and the families you encounter each week!

On **December 17**, the old *Roman Martyrology* celebrated **St. Lazarus of Bethany**, the brother of Ss. Martha and Mary of Bethany, whom the Johannine Jesus raised from the dead (Jn. 11:1-44). According to one tradition, he went on to become a missionary to Gaul (modern-day France), the first bishop of Marseilles, and a martyr during the persecutions of Domitian. Incorporate into your prayer today a meditation on John's story of Lazarus' rising from the dead!

On **December 17**, the Roman Catholic Church celebrates the birth in 1936 of **Jorge Mario Bergoglio**, who would become Pope Francis. In a spirit of ecumenism, pray for him and for the 1.3 billion Roman Catholics he serves!

On **December 18**, we remember the passing of **Michael Wadding** (1591-1644), the Irish Jesuit known as Miguel Godínez. He spent over 20 years of his life as a missionary in present-day Mexico. In his memory, pray for the missionaries of the Church—especially for those who continue to minister to the needs of Spanish-speaking persons in the U.S. and abroad!

On **December 19**, we remember the passing of **Johann Friedrich von Schulte** (1827-1914), the German canonist and historian who opposed the First Vatican Council and was the architect for the canon law of the German Old Catholic Church. He served as President of the Old Catholic Congress from 1871 to 1890. In his memory, pray for all who follow in his footsteps, leading and guiding the Old and Independent Catholic movements at the national and international levels!

On **December 19**, we remember the passing of **Arnold Harris Mathew** (1852-1919), the founder of Old Catholicism in England. Born Arnoldo Girolamo Povoleri, he served as a Roman Catholic priest until he lost faith in scripture and the divinity of Christ. Later consecrated by the Archbishop of Utrecht, who believed Mathew's assertions on the number of Old Catholics in England, Mathew shared apostolic succession with other men in the hope of cementing his legacy. Ironically, he died a lonely man. In his memory, pray for all in our movement who struggle to lead and nourish others—particularly those who feel a need to consecrate others who may be ill-equipped to fulfill the *triplex munus* of the episcopacy.

Sunday, December 20, 2020
FOURTH SUNDAY OF ADVENT
(blue or violet)

Light all four candles of the Advent wreath!

Remember: **The *Gloria* is *not* sung during the Advent season!**

The thread in today's scriptures: The second verse of today's responsorial psalm (Ps. 89:4-5) speaks of God's promise that King David's house and kingdom would endure forever (2Sam. 7:16). With the archangel Gabriel's message to Mary, betrothed to a purported descendant of King David (Lk. 1:27), we see "the revelation of the mystery kept secret for long ages" (Rom. 16:25): "The Lord God will give [Mary's son] the throne of David, his father" (Lk. 1:32)!

Holy humor: Do you speak Latin? We've used Latin terms to refer to some big events in Luke's gospel, including the *Magnificat*, Mary's song of praise upon sharing the news of her pregnancy with Elizabeth, and, in today's gospel, we have Mary's *Fiat*, her "yes" to the archangel Gabriel's news of her pregnancy. You heard that right: Mary's *Fiat* was her "yes" and *not* a car—so get that image out of your head of Mary and Joseph racing down to Bethlehem in Marys' *Fiat*! [Segue into the story of Mary's willingness to say, "Thy will be done," and our challenge to do likewise!

Looking for a visual aid for your homily or object lesson? Consider a crown! We recently celebrated Christ the King, a celebration that calls to mind his reign, a reign that is rooted in the reigns of the great King David and his son, Solomon. With today's gospel, we now see the crown passed to Mary's son, born of the house of David!

When **December 20** doesn't fall on a Sunday, the Church celebrates **St. Dominic of Silos** (1000-1073), the 11th-century Spanish Benedictine abbot who was exiled for not surrendering his monastery's land to the king. A beloved saint in Spain, he rescued Christian slaves from the Moors, and his shrine was the site where St. Dominic de Guzmán's mother prayed for a child. He's a patron saint of prisoners and pregnant women and is invoked against insects, rabies, and rabid dogs. Find a way today to show your solidarity and support for those praying for a child during this Advent season!

On **December 20**, we remember the passing of **Henry of Kalkar** (1328-1408), who inspired his friend and classmate, Geert Groote, to found the Brothers of the Common Life. An organizer of the Catholic Renaissance that found its expression in the Council of Trent, Henry's spiritual writings were distributed by Groote's Windesheim communities. Consider how you are following in Henry's footsteps and inspiring others to do great things!

On **December 20**, we remember the passing of "*die Lutherin*," Martin Luther's wife, **Katharina von Bora** (1499-1552), who was an important part of the Reformation due to her role in helping to define Protestant family life and in setting the tone for married clergy. A former nun dissatisfied with monastic life and interested in the growing reform movement, Katharina married Martin, who concluded that "his marriage would please his father, rile the pope, cause the angels to laugh and the devils to weep." She managed their brewery and cattle business to support their family, the students and visitors who boarded with them, and the hospital she operated on site in times of widespread illness. In her memory, pray for the spouses who so generously support the ministries of our clergy!

On **December 21**, the Church celebrates **St. Peter Canisius** (1521-1597), the 16th-century Dutch Jesuit priest who defended the Church by preaching, writing, founding colleges and seminaries, and contributing to the Council of Trent. Peter authored several catechisms that were translated into twelve languages during his lifetime, and he penned 1,400 letters in support of Church reform. As we celebrate this patron saint of catechism writers, consider how you're helping others to grow in their knowledge of our faith!

On **December 21**, we remember the passing of **John Newton** (1725-1807), the English Anglican abolitionist known for composing "Amazing Grace." A sailor in the Royal Navy and a captain of slave ships, he worked in the slave trade for several years until a storm at sea caused the conversion experience that propelled him to become an Anglican priest. He renounced the slave trade, became a prominent supporter of abolitionism, and he saw Britain's abolition of the African slave trade only days before his death. In his memory, pray for those who are enslaved — and for the "lost" and "blind" whose words and actions impinge on the freedom of others!

On **December 21**, we remember the passing of **F. Scott Fitzgerald** (1896-1940), the Catholic author regarded as one of the greatest American writers of the 20th century. He was raised Roman Catholic and attended Catholic schools, but, for 25 years, the Roman church denied his family's request that he be buried in the family's plot at St. Mary's Cemetery in Rockville, Maryland. In his memory, pray for all who have been marginalized in life and/or in death by misguided "representatives" of God and/or the Church!

On **December 21**, we celebrate the birth in 1940 of **Matthew Fox**, the American Episcopal priest and theologian who was an early exponent of creation spirituality. The author of 35 books that have been read by millions, Fox has sought to align contemporary ecological and environmental movements with various spiritual traditions. In his honor, consider how you employ scripture and tradition to honor God's creation!

On **December 21**, we celebrate the birth in 1951 of **Jan Michael Joncas**, the priest, liturgical theologian and composer of contemporary Catholic music, known for such songs as "On Eagle's Wings," "I Have Loved You," and "Take and Eat." In his honor, incorporate a tune or two of his into your prayer today!

On **December 22**, we remember the passing of **Giles of Rome** (c. 1243-1316), the French archbishop and prior general of the Augustinian order, who wrote a guide for princes as well as the major text on 14ᵗʰ-century papism. The "Best-grounded Doctor" took an active part in ending the controversy concerning the validity of Boniface VIII's election to the papacy. In his memory, pray for all who dedicate their lives to the defense of the Church!

On **December 22**, the Autocephalous Turkish Orthodox Church celebrates the anniversary of the installation in 2002 of Paşa Ümit Erenerol as **Turkish Orthodox Patriarch Papa Efrim IV**. In a spirit of ecumenism, pray for him and for the people he serves!

On **December 23**, we remember the passing of **St. Ivo of Chartres** (c. 1040-1115), the bishop of Chartres involved in the investiture crisis, who opposed simony and was imprisoned for opposing King Philip's decision to dismiss his wife and marry another woman. He authored three extensive canonical works that influenced Hugh of St. Victor, Peter Abelard and Gratian. In his memory, pause today to reach out and thank some of the influences in your life!

On **December 23**, we celebrate the birth in 1926 of **Robert Bly**, the American poet, essayist and activist whose bestselling work, *Iron John*, made him the leader of the mythopoetic men's movement. He pointed to the predicament of children, particularly boys, who lack models and rites of passage to guide them through life's stages. In his memory, pray for and/or reach out to those trapped between childhood and maturity, and who continue to struggle from having grown up without the love and leadership of a father and/or mother!

On **December 23**, we remember the passing of **Maurice de Wulf** (1867-1947), the Belgian Thomist philosopher at Louvain who distinguished medieval philosophy from Scholasticism, highlighting the "anti-Scholastic" thought of Scotus Erigena, the Cathars, the Albigenses, and the Pantheistic schools. In his memory, explore some of the counter movements that have enriched our world, our faith and our theology!

On **December 23**, we remember the passing of **Abraham Joshua Heschel** (1907-1972), the Polish-born American rabbi who was one of the leading Jewish philosophers and theologians of the 20th century. He was active in the civil rights movement and authored a number of widely-read books on Jewish philosophy and mysticism. In his memory, seek out a spiritual friend with whom you might share an insight or two from his works!

On **December 23**, we also remember the passing of **Edward Cornelis Florentius Alfonsus Schillebeeckx** (1914-2009), the Belgian Dominican theologian whose contributions to the Second Vatican Council made him known throughout the world. Schillebeeckx's innovative thought (including his attempt to overcome the Aristotelian categories of transubstantiation with a fresher thought of "transignification") were sometimes viewed with suspect, though never condemned by the Vatican. In his memory, consider the space that you allow the Spirit in your own theology and thought!

On **December 24**, we remember the passing of **Joseph Augustine Fitzmyer** (1920-2016), the Jesuit priest and professor *emeritus* at The Catholic University of America, who specialized in the study of the New Testament but who also made contributions to the study of the Dead Sea Scrolls and early Jewish literature. In his memory, thumb through one of his commentaries and see what new insights you might gain!

Friday, December 25, 2020
THE NATIVITY OF OUR LORD
(white)

Christmas is here: Let's decorate!

- Break out the **Christmas décor** — or, even better, smoothly transition from your Advent décor to Christmas décor by replacing the touches of Advent color with Christmas color!
- Remember: Red, white and green may be the traditional colors of Christmas in the secular world, but **white is the liturgical color for the Church's Christmas season**, often with touches of gold that bring to mind the newborn King!
- Be sure to steam or iron your **Christmas vestments** — and to coordinate the color of your vestments with other decorative details in your worship space!
- This is a high solemnity: Be sure to cover the altar with your loveliest white and/or gold altar cloth!
- Consider appropriate places for **evergreen** decorations — perhaps with wreaths on the end of pews and/or with garland that accents the architecture of your worship space. Try making your garland extraordinary with touches of boxwood, seeded eucalyptus, wax flowers, white hypernicum, pine cones, and/or other ideas you find online or at your local florist.
- Try making your **creche** extraordinary: Instead of simply placing it on a table or on the floor, nestle it in a fitting devotional space where congregants can pray and where parents and grandparents can explain the figures to their children and grandchildren. Be sure that adequate light shines on the figures — but not in the eyes of those gazing on it. Unless the placement of the Christ Child in the manger is part of your liturgy, **be sure to place the Christ Child in the manger before the Mass begins**! Remember: The magi will not arrive at the nativity scene until January 6; **find a place for the magi that suggests that they are** *en route* but still a distance away.
- Be cautious *not* to impede liturgical movement with a forest of trees in the sanctuary.
- Be prepared to leave the Christmas décor up through the end of the Christmas season (which concludes with the Baptism of the Lord) — or, if you lead a *Latino* community, consider leaving

touches of Christmas in the worship space for the entire 40 days of Christmas in the *Latino* culture, which concludes February 2.

- **Continue the decoration** into the entrance to your worship space, outdoors, and into other spaces on the grounds, including your Blessed Sacrament chapel, parish hall and classrooms! Be especially sure to **communicate "the reason for the season" outside your worship space** to passersby, perhaps with outdoor banners, wreaths, an outdoor nativity set, *luminarias* (candles in paper bags), and/or tasteful inflatables.

Christmas Eve Masses are famous for their **reenactments by children of the birth of Jesus**; this is an especially dear memory for parents and grandparents! If you have a liturgy with a child-friendly focus, be sure children leave knowing the key figures in the Christmas story!

For the intellectually-curious, find time outside the Mass to share a brief lesson on the **differences between the two nativity stories** in the gospels of Matthew and Luke—and the **lack of nativity stories in Mark and John!** Take two cans of spray paint to an old nativity set, so that adult learners can easily distinguish the elements highlighted in Matthew (Joseph, magi, camels, star) from the elements highlighted in Luke (Mary, stable, manger, ox, donkey, sheep, shepherds, the angel of the Lord). Also consider sharing the story of **the origin of the Christmas creche** and its attribution to St. Francis of Assisi! Other possible lessons might include the reason for the date for Christmas, the theology of the incarnation, the two natures of Christ, etc.

The most common question for Catholic parishes on Christmas Eve Day is, "What time is your midnight Mass?" Consider hosting a Mass *at midnight*, complete with a **candlelight service**!

- Ring a bell at midnight, begin your service in the dark with soft music in the background, and share a brief lesson on Christ's coming as the Light of the world!
- Be sure to test the environment you've created before the Mass: Some church electrical outlets might be tied to light switches!
- Before the liturgy, be sure all liturgical ministers understand the importance of the dark, quiet environment you're attempting to create; they need to know not to talk loudly and/or open doors that will allow light to flood the space.

Be sure that **hospitality ministers** are aware that holiday visitors may be joining you for this Mass; visitors should be welcomed with joy. Christmas is no time for impatience, judgment, or criticism. It's Christmas; don't be a scrooge or a grinch!

After four Sundays of "fasting" from it, **bring the *Gloria* back with gusto!** Consider asking someone to ring the church bell and/or other bells in the church to highlight the solemnity of this song!

Also, consider the use of hypoallergenic **incense** — presuming you and your thurifer have practiced how you'll handle the thurible and boat. Be sure to remind your altar server(s) when incense will be used and that the *lavabo* (handwashing) will occur *after* the incensation of the altar and gifts! If you're swinging the thurible, remember that the closer you place your fingers to the thurible, the more control you'll have. Finally, if you have a skilled thurifer, work with him/her in advance to perfect a 360-degree vertical swing of the thurible with a simple flick of his/her wrist (forward, back, circle, forward, back, circle, etc.) as s/he leads the procession down the aisle!

Homily Help: Remember that there are four sets of scriptures for today, based on when you celebrate Mass. Your worship environment is likely very special today; for the sake of the 65% of your listeners who are visual, tie your message to the visuals in your space!

Looking for a visual aid for your homily or object lesson? Look around your now-decorated worship environment for symbols to incorporate into your message: The **lights** on the trees and the **candles** remind us of Christ's coming as the Light of the world. The **evergreens** remind us of God's enduring love for us. The shape of the **poinsettias** remind us of the star leading people to Christ, and the story of the poinsettia's purported origin links to a drummer-boy-like story of a poor girl with nothing to offer the newborn King. The **creche** reminds us of the ordinary circumstances of the Lucan Jesus' birth and God's choice to come to the poor and marginalized, rather than to the rich and powerful of that time. We display these symbols at Christmas; how will we continue to proclaim the message of these symbols in our daily lives throughout the year ahead?

If you have a Latino community, consider incorporating **the last *posada*,** the traditional ***arrullo*,** the traditional **veneration of an image of the Child Jesus**, and/or a ***pastorela*!**

- Before Mass, the antiphonal singing of the traditional song for *las posadas* might be sung by congregants inside and outside your worship space, with those outside being welcomed in for Mass.
- In the Mexican culture, the image of the Child Jesus is taken from its upright position on the home altar, "rocked to sleep" with a lullaby (the *arrullo*), and placed in the manger; consider incorporating this rite into the liturgy.

- When Mexican families celebrate *las posadas*, they often place an image of the Christ Child in a basket or on a tray or platter filled with candies; individuals then come forward to venerate the image of the Christ Child with a kiss and to take a piece of candy from the basket or tray. Looking to involve young people? Invite two teens to hold the basket or platter as people come to venerate the image and take a piece of candy!
- *Pastorelas* are traditional Christmas plays portraying the journey of the shepherds to the place where the Christ Child lay; *pastorelas* involve more planning and work, but can be an extremely memorable experience for all involved!

Send congregants home with a copy of a **prayer of blessing for their creche and/or Christmas tree**!

If you begin Mass with a candlelight service (reminiscent of the Easter vigil and common in non-Catholic congregations), have hospitality ministers prepared to distribute the taper candles before Mass — and prepared to collect the taper candles after Mass.

On **December 25**, we celebrate the birth in 1968 of Bishop **John Plummer**, author of *The Many Paths of the Independent Sacramental Movement*. Reacquaint yourself with his work, and pray for our many sisters and brothers who tread the many paths of the ISM!

On **December 25**, the Georgian Orthodox Church (recognized by the Ecumenical Patriarch of Constantinople) celebrates the anniversary of the installation in 1977 of Irakli Ghudushauri-Shiolashvili as **Catholicos-Patriarch Ilia II of Georgia**. In a spirit of ecumenism, pray for him and for the 3.5 million Georgian Orthodox Catholics he serves!

On **December 26**, the Church celebrates **St. Stephen** (c. 5 – c. 33-36): Be sure to recognize and bless your deacon(s) as we celebrate the patron saint of deacons! Consider sharing with your deacon(s) a seasonal gift, perhaps a Christmas ornament with a personalized message of gratitude for their ministry to the Church. Also, don't forget to recognize those who are preparing for diaconal ministry!

On **December 26**, we remember the passing of **Bernhard Word Anderson** (1916-2007), the American United Methodist pastor and Old Testament scholar. His *Understanding the Old Testament* is a classic textbook. In his memory, thumb through one of his works and expand your knowledge of the Old Testament world!

Sunday, December 27, 2020

HOLY FAMILY OF JESUS, MARY AND JOSEPH

(white)

Like most people, Jesus of Nazareth was born into a family! Point to the **model of holiness** of the Holy Family of Jesus, Mary and Joseph; draw the connection between your community's families and the Holy Family; but also, in a spirit of inclusivity, acknowledge that **families come in different shapes and forms**!

We're still in the Christmas Octave: **Sing the *Gloria* with gusto!**

Choose the first reading you'll proclaim: Sirach's admonition to honor and care for parents, or God's promise in Genesis that the aged Abram and Sara would have descendants numbering like the stars in the sky. If you choose the former, beware of the exclusive language that can easily be remedied by changing the reading to the second person: "When you honor your parents, you atone for sins and preserve yourself from them. When you pray, you are heard....My children take care of your parents."

Select the psalm you'll sing: Psalm 128 (a traditional wedding psalm) or Psalm 105's reflection on God's covenant. If you choose the former, beware the traditional references to "man" and "wife." The latter is riddled with problematic, exclusive language: Consider changing the response to the second person, "You, Lord, remember your covenant forever," and include the names of the wives of Abraham and Isaac: Sarah and Rebecca.

Choose the second reading as well: Colossians' extended discourse with its outdated admonition of wives submitting to their husbands, the shorter version without those controversial lines, or Hebrews' recounting of the inheritance received by Abraham and Sarah.

Finally, **choose which gospel you'll proclaim**: the long version of the account of Simeon and Anna, or whether you'll spare your listeners that, proclaim the short version, and summarize the longer story as part of your homily.

The thread in today's scriptures: Bridges can be built today between the aged Abraham and Sarah (second option for the first reading) and the aged Simeon and Anna (in the long form of today's gospel), between the firm planting of our kind actions against the debt of our sins (first option for the first reading), and the psalm's image of children being olive plants. Regardless of the readings you choose, focus on the "family values" contained therein!

Holy humor: The father of a teenage daughter was washing the family car, when his neighbor hollered over the fence: "What kind of mileage do you get with that car?" He replied, "I get about five miles per gallon — and my daughter gets the other 20!" [Segue into the family values — like sharing — found in today's scriptures.]

Looking for a visual aid for your homily or object lesson? Consider a family photo! Most people have a few family photos, and, when we think of the Holy Family, we often compare the family of Jesus, Mary and Joseph to our own. How do our own families measure up? Even better, knowing that we're all human — and that we idealize and idolize the Holy Family — how can we as individuals be better family members, so as to help our family and friends grow in their relationships with God and with one another?

On **December 27**, when it doesn't fall on a Sunday, the Church celebrates **St. John the Evangelist** (c. 6 – c. 100): Share a brief lesson on his high Christology (his emphasis on the divine nature of Christ), why his gospel is symbolized by an eagle, his poetry and symbolic language, and/or some of the many differences between this gospel and the synoptic gospels!

On **December 27**, we celebrate the birth in 1938 of **Jon Sobrino**, the Spanish Jesuit theologian and co-founder of the University of Central America, known for his contributions to liberation theology. Sobrino narrowly escaped the targeted assassinations that occurred at his rectory during the El Salvador civil war, and he continues to be an outspoken advocate for peace and against the U.S. training of Latin American military officers in torture techniques at the School of the Americas. The Vatican has criticized his works for their emphasis on Jesus' human nature and purported downplaying of Jesus' divinity. In his honor, consider how you are esteeming and serving "the Church of the poor"!

On **December 27**, we remember the passing of **Sir Michael Anthony Eardley Dummett** (1925-2011), the English philosopher who has been described as "among the most significant British philosophers of the last century and a leading campaigner for racial tolerance and equality." He wrote that opposition to immigration is largely based on racism, and his work, *On Immigration and Refugees*, detailed the demands of justice for nations with respect to the movement of people between them. A convert to the Roman church, he sparked controversy in 1987 by writing that "from the earliest times, the Catholic Church, claiming to have a mission from God to safeguard divinely-revealed truth, has taught and insisted on the acceptance of falsehoods." In his memory, reflect on how you are bringing greater credibility to the Independent Catholic movement, so that it might not become, in Dummett's characterization of the Roman church, "a laughing-stock in the eyes of the world"!

On **December 28**, the Church celebrates the Memorial of the **Holy Innocents**, a purported event mentioned by Matthew (Mt. 2:16-18) but not supported by historical evidence. Pray for those who, like the fabled Herod, try to stamp out the Word of God. If you have a Mexican community, and if you have a parish gathering on December 28, prepare a prank in honor of *el día de los santos inocentes* — the equivalent of April Fool's Day in Mexico! Looking for an idea? Ask your local baker to frost a cardboard box, to look like a holiday cake. When congregants cut into it, shout the traditional April Fool's line: "*¡Inocente palomita!*"

On **December 28**, we celebrate the anniversary of the ordination in 1970 of **Ludmila Javorová** (1932-), the Czech Roman Catholic woman who helped organize the underground church of Czechoslovakia during communist rule. She and some five other women were ordained by their Roman Catholic bishop to serve women who were imprisoned and tortured but who had no access to male priests. In her honor, lift up all the women who have bravely shared of their lives and ordained ministries with our Catholic Church!

On **December 28**, we remember the passing of **Jacques Dupuis** (1923-2004), the Belgian Jesuit theologian who spent several decades in India before teaching non-Christian religions at the Gregorian University in Rome. The Roman Curia censured his book, *Toward a Christian Theology of Religious Pluralism*, due to its suggestion that non-Christian religions might possess "the seeds of truth and goodness." Regardless, Dupuis' work was praised as a pioneering effort to esteem "God's plan of salvation" in other religions. In his memory, pause to consider how God's plan of salvation might be unfolding in religions quite unlike your own!

On **December 29**, the Church celebrates **St. Thomas Becket** (1118-1170): In a special way, we pray for those who, like Henry VIII, wish to rid the world — or at least our communities — of the "meddlesome priest[s]" of the Old and Independent Catholic movements!

On **December 29**, we remember the passing of **Rainer Maria Rilke** (1875-1926), the German poet and novelist whose mystical works focus on the difficulty of communion with the Ineffable in an age of disbelief, solitude and profound anxiety. As we wind down this year, dust off his *Notebooks of Malte Laurids Brigge* and ponder his reflections on the quest for individuality, the significance of death, and the experience of time as death approaches!

On **December 29**, we celebrate the birth in 1960 of **James J. Martin**, the American Jesuit priest and writer who has written or edited over 10 books, many of which are largely about his own experiences as a Catholic, and he is a frequent commentator on national news outlets. When Glenn Beck suggested that Catholics run away from priests who preach social justice, Martin noted that "Christ asked us to work with the poor...He says that the way that we're going to be judged at the end of our lives is not what church we prayed in, or how we prayed, but really...how we treated the poor." His recent work on welcoming LGBTQ Catholics has drawn the ire of conservatives in the Roman church. In his honor, pause to share with him a few words of encouragement!

On **December 30**, we remember the passing of **Alfred North Whitehead** (1861-1947), the English mathematician and philosopher who was a defining figure of process philosophy and an inspiration for process theology. Critiquing traditional monotheistic notions of God as a divine king who imposes his will and power on the world, Whitehead envisioned a God created by our world and not necessarily tied to religion, "the unlimited conceptual realization of the absolute wealth of potentiality." In his memory, reacquaint yourself with Whitehead's views of God and religion!

On **December 30**, we remember the passing of **Huston Cummings Smith** (1919-2016), the American scholar regarded as one of the world's most influential figures in religious studies. Cumming's work, *The World's Religions*, remains a popular text on comparative religion. In his memory, spend a few minutes today broadening your perspective on other world religions!

On **December 31**, we remember the passing of **John Wycliffe** (c. 1320s-1384), the English priest, philosopher, theologian and reformer who became an important dissident within Roman Catholicism. Wycliffe translated the gospels and questioned the privileged status of clergy, monasticism, transubstantiation, *requiem* masses, veneration of the saints, and caesaropapism. In his memory, pray for all who respectfully and courageously question the traditions of our Catholic tradition, causing us to think more deeply on our beliefs and practices!

Friday, January 1, 2021
MARY THE MOTHER OF GOD
(white)

How's your devotion to Mary? This is a day for you to share your love for your Mother with others! Think how you might be able to **make this celebration special** for the people with whom you celebrate. Remember: Mass attendance on New Year's Day can be extremely challenging, particularly for those who rang in the New Year at midnight!

For the intellectually-curious, provide a brief lesson on the history of Mary's designation as the *theotokos* (the God-bearer), and the very recent renaming of this eighth-day feast from the **Feast of the Circumcision**, to the **Solemnity of Mary the Mother of God**!

The Christmas Octave concludes today: **Sing the *Gloria* with gusto!**

Be mindful of the **exclusive language** in the second reading: If you begin "Brothers and sisters," as you should, you'll need to rephrase the two instances of "son" to "son or daughter" and the two instances of "sons" to "sons and daughters."

The thread in today's scriptures: In this new year, we pray for God's blessing (Num. 6:22-27 & Ps 67:2), calling upon God as father/mother (Gal 4:6) and upon Mary as mother. Her son was born "under the law" (Gal 4:4), and she showed her devotion to God and to God's law by submitting her son to circumcision (Lk 2:21). How are we manifesting our devotion? Are we striking an active/contemplative balance in our lives this holiday season, as captured by the active response of the shepherds (Lk 2:16-17) and the contemplative response of Mary (Lk 2:19) — both of which are good!

Holy humor: We made it through Christmas! Did you hear the story of what happened at one church's Christmas pageant? All the little kids were dressed up for their roles as shepherds, magi and angels in the Nativity story, and the older kids, the eight-year-olds, simply had to memorize one line each, so that they could tell the Nativity story together. One boy had his line memorized: All he had to say was, "And the Virgin Mary was with Child." What did he have to say? "And the Virgin Mary was with Child!" How could that go wrong, right? At every rehearsal, he perfectly delivered his one line: "And the Virgin Mary was with Child!" But on Christmas Eve, stage fright got the best of him, and, while all the other children flawlessly recited their lines, when it came time for him to share his line, "And the Virgin Mary was with Child," what came out of his mouth was—are you ready for this?—"And the Viking Mary was with Child"! Imagine that for a moment: "the Viking Mary," as if Mary were some Norse personality, with a horned helmet and Thor at her side! [Segue into an even more incredible image: of a young woman chosen to be the mother of...God!]

Looking for a visual aid for your homily or object lesson? Point to Mary and the shepherds in your Christmas creche, and/or draw an invisible triangle connecting you and your listeners through the common divine father/mother figures (i.e., God & Mary) that we share! We are not strangers, but sisters and brothers (Gal 4:7), daughters and sons of Mary our Mother!

As we honor the Mother of God, consider having a **blessing for mothers of all types** (birth mothers, step mothers, mothers-in-law, mother figures, etc.)!

No plans for ringing in the New Year? Invite others to join you at midnight, to ring in the New Year with prayer and a **midnight Mass**!

- Ring a bell at midnight, then begin the service. Or, time your Mass to conclude just before midnight.

- In addition to anything that you say about Mary, speak of the important liminal moment of this celebration—even referencing **New Year's resolutions** and the two-faced, forward/backward-facing Roman god, **Janus**, after whom January is named.

- If you find yourself ministering within the context of the *Latino* culture, invite someone to bring along enough **grapes**, so that each person in attendance can enjoy the tradition of eating 12 grapes, one for each of 12 wishes s/he makes for the new year.

- End with a sampling of traditional New Year foods and/or a **toast** to the New Year with sparkling juice in plastic flute glasses!

- Conclude the night with firecrackers, traditionally used in Asia to scare away demons. You will have created a memory!

It's the New Year, and many people are making resolutions. Suggest a few **spiritual resolutions** for the new year!

January 1 is also the **World Day of Prayer for Peace**: Consider incorporating themes of peace into the intercessions, and pray for peace in the world and in all families!

On **January 1**, the Greek Orthodox Church of Antioch (recognized by the Ecumenical Patriarch of Constantinople) celebrates the birth in 1955 of **John Yazigi**, who would become Patriarch John X of Antioch. In a spirit of ecumenism, pray for him and for the 1.8 million Greek Orthodox Catholics he serves!

On **January 2,** the Church celebrates **Ss. Basil the Great** (329-379) **and Gregory Nazianzen** (329-390), two Cappadocian Fathers who defended the divinity of Christ (against the Arian heresy). If your community has a bent toward social justice, share Basil's famous words: "When someone steals another's clothes, we call him/her a thief. Should we not give the same name to one who could clothe the naked and does not? The bread in your cupboard belongs to the hungry; the coat unused in your closet belongs to the one who needs it; the shoes rotting in your closet belong to the one who has no shoes; the money which you hoard up belongs to the poor." Challenging words, indeed!

Sunday, January 3, 2021

THE EPIPHANY OF OUR LORD

(white)

Do you have a creche in your worship space? Be sure to **set out the figures of the** *magi* **(and any accompanying animals)** before Mass!

Note: **The introductory line of today's second reading is misleading.** The Letter to the Ephesians is a pseudonymous letter, written in Paul's name and spirit, but not written by Paul. Rather than confuse your listeners, begin with, "A reading from the Letter to the Ephesians"!

The thread in today's scriptures: Today's scriptures feature rich fare for inclusive Catholic communities! The mystery of God is made known to *all* people (Eph. 3:3), and people from distant lands (Is 60:6 & Ps 72:10-11) recognize the Light (Is 60:1). Now, "every nation on earth will adore [God]" (Ps 72:17) — and even the Gentiles will inherit God's kingdom (Col 3:6)! The *magi* — Gentiles from distant lands — recognize the presence of Emmanuel (Mt 2:10-11); do we?

Holy humor: There are all sorts of cartoons about the people in today's gospel: of the magi's visit to the Christ Child. You've likely seen the cartoon where the magi arrive on the scene, not with gold, frankincense and myrrh, but with gold, myrrh and...Frankenstein! My favorites, though, are those that imagine what it would have been like if the magi were women. If they *were* women, would the magi have given such impractical gifts as frankincense and myrrh? No, they would have come with talc, bottles, diapers and lots of motherly advice! [Segue into the nature of epiphanies causing us to open our eyes and see things differently—in the same way that the magi opened their eyes and recognize the presence of Emmanuel!]

Looking for a visual aid for your homily or object lesson? Point to the magi in your creche, and/or consider buying or making a king cake (then sharing it after Mass): In the same way that the figurine of the Christ child is hidden inside the bread or cake, the magi recognized the divine in the Christ child. Are we able to recognize the presence of Christ hidden in the "dough" of others' lives?

Are you able to chant a few psalm tones? Today is the traditional day for the **proclamation of the dates of the moveable feasts for the coming year**. Have a deacon or cantor sing the traditional text. Remember: Traditionally, this proclamation is *not* made by a priest, and it is omitted if not chanted!

For the intellectually-curious, there are various possible lessons today.

- Share a brief lesson on the three manifestations of Christ: the epiphany, the baptism of Jesus, and Jesus' first miracle at the wedding in Cana.

- Explain the spiritual significance of the three gifts listed in scripture: gold, frankincense and myrrh.

- Help congregants to separate fact from fiction (e.g., scripture says neither that they were "three" nor that they were "kings"; traditional names were later appended to the *magi*; in some cultures, we even assign a different animal (e.g., a horse, elephant and camel) to each *magus* to show the universality of the magi who respectively came from Europe, Africa and Asia!

- Speak of various traditions of this day, including extractions, house blessings, and the *rosca de reyes*!

If you minister in a Latino context, you'll definitely want to purchase enough *rosca de reyes* (a ring-shaped king cake) to go around. Use the *rosca* as a visual in your homily, and explain how Christ is often hidden in the "dough" of others' lives in such a way that, even though we can't see him, he's there! While at the bakery, buy extra plastic figurines of the Christ child, to be inserted into the bottom of the bread. Those who find these figurines in their piece of the *rosca* are tasked with providing the *tamales* and *atole* (a hot chocolate drink) for the traditional celebration of *el día de la candelaria* (the Presentation of the Lord) on February 2!

Remember: This is the **traditional gift-giving day** (more so than Christmas) in some parts of the world, including parts of Latin America, where the magi visit children in the night and bring them gifts! If you minister to congregants from such contexts, **have three persons dress as the traditional** *magi* **and come bearing gifts for the children and/or for all!**

Epiphany is a traditional day of **house blessing** in some cultures. At the end of Mass, share small pieces of chalk and slips of paper with the traditional "20+C+B+M+21" inscription for the year and the names of the traditional names of the magi (viz., Caspar, Melchior and Balthasar). Lead all present in blessing your worship space, then invite up to nine people to chalk the lintel with those characters!

Some religious orders have the tradition of **"extractions"** on this day: Sing a prayer to the Holy Spirit (e.g., "Come, Holy Ghost"), then have all present pull a piece of paper from a basket containing patron saints for the year, bible verses for the year, and/or words of wisdom for the year. Encourage each person present to research his/her patron saint for the year, to learn about the saint's life, and to discern why the Spirit might have "assigned" him/her that saint for the year. Encourage congregants to keep these slips of paper in a place (e.g., inside the front cover of their bible, on a bathroom mirror, or inside their nightstand) where they can be reminded of them throughout the coming year!

Everyone knows **"The Twelve Days of Christmas"**! This is the 12th day of Christmas: Consider singing the song during your post-Mass activity, perhaps with as many as 12 groups of people acting out the gift of each day, or with the alternate lyrics you've created (perhaps even with visuals), or with earlier versions of the song's lyrics (11 badgers baiting and eight hares a-running, in England, or 10 cocks a-crowing, nine bears a-beating, eight hounds a-running, etc., in early America). Or, find your favorite video version of it (perhaps the Muppets), or have a contest to see who can remember the gift of each day! Or, explain that the song was originally a memory game for kids, and have your own memory game using the names of all present!

January 3, when it doesn't fall on a Sunday, is the Optional Memorial of the **Holy Name of Jesus**: Do your congregants know that our Savior's name was *not* "Jesus" and that he *didn't* speak English? [Try telling that to those who say, "If English was good enough for Jesus, it's good enough for me"!] Catechize others on the history and meaning of the name *Yehoshua* and what the scriptures say about that name (e.g., Mt. 1:21, Jn. 14:13, Phil. 2:9-11)!

On **January 3**, we remember the passing of **Mary Daly** (1928-2010), the feminist philosopher and theologian who taught at Boston College for 33 years until refusing to allow male students into her advanced Women's Studies classes. Her book, *Beyond God the Father*, is considered a foundational work in feminist theology for its attempt to overcome androcentrism in Western religion. She focused her scholarship on ways in which men have attempted to suppress women through the "religion" of patriarchy. In her memory, consider the ways in which your own words and actions might reinforce patriarchy and/or androcentrism!

On **January 4**, the Church celebrates **St. Elizabeth Ann Seton** (1774-1821), the first native-born American saint: If the Sisters of Charity have a ministry in your area, be sure to include a brief lesson on Seton's contribution to the schools and hospital systems that bear her name!

On **January 4**, we remember the passing of **Joseph Hubert Reinkens** (1821-1896), the first German Old Catholic bishop. A professor of theology, Reinkens was known for his writings on the early Church Fathers, including his renowned *Cyprian and the Unity of the Church*. As a Roman Catholic priest, he wrote various pamphlets against purported papal infallibility and on the proceedings of the First Vatican Council. When Old Catholics separated from the Roman Church in 1873, they chose Reinkens as their bishop. It was due to his efforts that the Old Catholic movement crystallized into an organized church, with status in various German states. He consecrated Eduard Herzog as Old Catholic bishop of Switzerland, and he advocated for the validity of Anglican orders to the Old Catholic Church of the Netherlands. In his memory, pray for the pioneers and founders of the various Old Catholic churches throughout the world — and for all who continue their great work!

On **January 4**, the Georgian Orthodox Church (recognized by the Ecumenical Patriarch of Constantinople) celebrates the birth in 1933 of **Irakli Ghudushauri-Shiolashvili**, who would become Catholicos-Patriarch Ilia II of Georgia. In a spirit of ecumenism, pray for him and for the 3.5 million Georgian Orthodox Catholics he serves!

On **January 4**, we remember the passing of **Thomas Stearns "T.S." Eliot** (1888-1965), the epic essayist and poet whose post-conversion Christian poems discomfited the secular *literati* of his day. In his memory, savor a few hope-filled lines from his conversion poem "Ash-Wednesday"!

On **January 5**, the Church celebrates **St. John Neumann** (1811-1860), an early missionary who was named bishop of the largest diocese in the U.S. at that time. If your community has a place in its heart for our immigrant sisters and brothers, illuminate Neumann's love for those he served!

On **January 6**, the Church remembers **St. André Bessette** (1845-1937), the charismatic brother of the Congregation of Holy Cross to whom many miracles were attributed during his life at the St. Joseph Oratory in Montreal. Consider your own charism and your ability to attract others to God and the Church, and take a small step today to grow in this respect!

On **January 6**, we celebrate the birth in 1939 of **David Tracy**, the theologian and priest who was teaching at The Catholic University of America in 1968 when he joined other professors there in rejecting Paul VI's encyclical *Humanae vitae*. He and others were tried by the faculty senate and fired. He subsequently taught at the University of Chicago Divinity School until his retirement and is best known for his works of systematic theology. In his honor, choose to enjoy one of his works!

On **January 6**, the Church of England celebrates the birth in 1956 of **Archbishop Justin Portal Welby of Canterbury**, the Primate of England and *primus inter pares* of the worldwide Anglican Communion. In a spirit of ecumenism, pray for him and for the 85 million Anglicans he serves!

On **January 6**, the Polish National Catholic Church celebrates the birth in 1966 of **Prime Bishop Anthony Mikovsky**. In a spirit of ecumenism, pray for him and for the 26,000 people he serves!

On **January 7**, the Church celebrates **St. Raymond of Peñafort** (1185-1275), the patron saint of lawyers, known for his leadership of the Dominican Order, his collection of Church law, and his manual for confessors. Consider how you're growing in your own pastoral skills, particularly with respect to those who come to you for the sacrament of Reconciliation!

On **January 7**, we remember the passing of **Hugo von Hohenlandenberg** (c. 1457-1532), the German bishop who unsuccessfully tried to reform the Roman church. He spoke against Lenten fasting and the sale of indulgences, but, despite his romantic relationship with the mayor's daughter, he opposed the abolition of clerical celibacy. In his memory, prayerfully consider how your actions might not match your words!

On **January 8**, we remember the passing of **Richard John Neuhaus** (1936-2009), an advisor to President George W. Bush on bioethical issues and a leading advocate for denying communion to Roman Catholic politicians who voted against the Roman church's positions on women's reproductive health. He brought the conservative views of his Missouri Synod Lutheran upbringing to his ministry as a "Bushism-made-Catholic" priest, and he was named one of the 25 Most Influential Evangelicals in America at that time. In his memory, pray for all who continue to take hardline stances on issues of conscience and who seek to exclude God's holy people from the sacraments of the Church!

On **January 9**, we remember the passing of **Michel de Certeau** (1925-1986), the French Jesuit priest who worked to synthesize history, philosophy, psychoanalysis and the social sciences. His most renowned work, *The Practice of Everyday Life*, studied the way in which we unconsciously navigate the repetitive tasks of daily life. In his memory, reflect on some of the repetitive tasks that fill your "everyday life"!

On **January 9**, we remember the passing of **Anscar Chupungco** (1939-2013), the Filipino Benedictine monk and liturgical theologian known for his work on the inculturation of local customs and traditions into the Catholic Mass. He wrote against "the reform of the reform," which he saw as having "an agenda that can have a regrettable impact on the liturgical gains of the [Second Vatican] council." In his memory, consider your own views toward the liturgical reforms of the Church and the ways in which you push the liturgy forward and/or pull it backward!

Sunday, January 10, 2021
THE BAPTISM OF OUR LORD
(white)

If you have any baptisms, this is an appropriate day to **celebrate the sacrament of Baptism** during Sunday Mass! We are baptized into Christ! If you have no baptisms today, use a **sprinkling rite** as part of the introductory rite, or consider having a **renewal of baptismal vows** in place of the creed, complete with the sprinkling of holy water (as we do at the Easter Vigil)! If you want to more closely tie this action to the Easter Vigil, share **taper candles** (with bobaches) with all, and have congregants light them before the renewal of baptismal vows, and/or, even better, **invite congregants to bring their own baptismal candles** from home, to be lit on this special day as a reminder of their own baptism in Christ!

If you have a sprinkling rite and/or baptism during the Mass, be sure to prominently feature the **paschal candle** and a **large glass bowl of water** (perhaps on a stand covered with a white cloth) as part of your worship environment!

For the intellectually-curious, include a lesson on why the Jesus of the synoptic gospels underwent John's "baptism of repentance," the manifestation of the Trinity in the story, and/or the differences between the various gospel tellings of the story!

Choose the first reading you'll proclaim: Deutero-Isaiah's ode to a liberating Lord of light, or his/her lengthy invitation for the thirsty to come to the water.

Select the responsorial psalm you'll sing: Psalm 29's image of God enthroned over the waters, or Proto-Isaiah's song on joyfully drawing water from the springs of salvation.

Choose the second reading you'll proclaim: Peter's proclamation in Acts of how our inclusive God acted through the baptism of John the Baptist, or John's image of Spirit, water and blood testifying to Christ.

The thread in today's scriptures: The Marcan Baptist proclaims Christ's coming, baptizing Jesus in the Jordan. Other possible scriptures for today contain references to Spirit and water, two important symbols in Jesus' baptism—and in ours. We are baptized in water and sealed by the Spirit!

Holy humor: Many years ago, a drunk man named Marvin stumbled into a church, hoping to change his life. He met a priest there, who, after a good chat, asked, "Are you baptized?" The priest explained that she would baptize him, and that he would become a new person. So, she baptized him, pouring water on him in the name of the Trinity, then proclaiming, "You are a new creation!" This was some years ago, when people received a new name at baptism, so she said, "You are a new creation, and your name will no longer be Marvin. From now on, you will be…John!" John—his new name—enjoyed the experience and felt truly changed. Arriving home, he went directly to the fridge, took out a bottle of beer, poured water over it three times, held the bottle in the air and proclaimed, "You are a new creation! From now on, you will no longer be beer. From now on, you will be…water!" [Segue into transformation that should characterize the new creations we become through baptism.]

Looking for a visual aid for your homily or object lesson? Consider a crystal bowl of water—particularly if you're celebrating baptisms on this very appropriate day. Water is a symbol of life, death, cleansing—perfect for various catechetical lessons!

Now that a new calendar year has begun and kids are back in school, these weeks of January might be an ideal time for the **formation of your liturgical ministers**. Consider providing them a time of formation and/or retreat, where you can lead them in reflecting on their ministry during the past year and help them envision where the Lord might be leading them and their ministries in this new calendar year!

After Mass today, there's likely a lot of **Christmas décor that needs to come down**: Don't be bashful about asking for volunteers! Take leadership. Assign tasks and responsibilities. Then show your gratitude with hot chocolate and holiday cookies, or some other appropriate food and drink!

On **January 11**, we remember the passing of **Carmel Henry Carfora** (1878-1958), the Italian Roman Catholic priest who immigrated to New York, then founded St. Rocco's Independent National Catholic Church in Youngstown, Ohio to serve a large group of former Roman Catholics. Known for forming mission congregations to serve ethnic groups not well served by the Roman church, Carfora was consecrated by Bishop Rudolph de Landas Berghes and headed the North American Old Roman Catholic Church, which focused on a non-papal, pre-Vatican I Roman Catholic theology and practice. In his memory, consider how you might better contribute to the upbuilding of Independent Catholicism in our world!

On **January 12**, we remember the passing of **Theodor Hubert Weber** (1836-1906), the German theologian and professor of philosopher who served as vicar general of the first bishop of the German Old Catholic Church and was later named his successor. He was an important follower and defender of Anton Günther and his philosophy. In his Weber's, pray for our sisters and brothers of the German Old Catholic Church!

On **January 12**, we celebrate the birth in 1929 of **Alasdair Chalmers MacIntyre**, the Scottish philosopher known for his virtue ethics, as well as for his work in the history of philosophy and theology. He writes that good judgment emanates from good character, such that being a good person is not about following rules or fulfilling obligations. He explains his conversion to Catholicism by suggesting that people don't choose their religious traditions; their religious traditions choose them! In his memory, reflect on your own virtue and/or how and why you were *chosen* by the Independent Catholic tradition!

On **January 13**, the Church celebrates **St. Hilary of Poitiers** (c. 315 – c. 367), who, exiled from his bishopric, dedicated his time to study and writing. He "chanced upon" and was drawn to the Christian religion as a result of reading about the God of Exodus ("I AM Who I AM"). Reflect today on the scriptural verses that best describe God for you!

On **January 13**, we remember the passing of **James Joyce** (1882-1941), the Irish novelist, short story writer and poet who is regarded as one of the most influential authors of the 20th century. Having lapsed from the Roman church, he wrote, "Now I make open war upon it by what I write and say and do." His later works, *Ulysses* and *Finnegans Wake*, are nonetheless essentially Catholic, suggesting a reconciliation within himself with the Catholic traditions he loved, despite resisting the oppressive power of those who led the church. When he died, a Roman Catholic priest offered to celebrate Joyce's funeral, but his wife declined, saying, "I couldn't do that to him." In his memory, pray for all who have a complex relationship with—and conflicting emotions for—the church they once loved!

On **January 14**, we remember the passing of **Johann Joseph Ignaz von Döllinger** (1799-1890), the German priest, church historian and theologian whose reverence for tradition annoyed liberals and whose criticism of the papacy and its power antagonized Ultramontanes. Considered an important contributor to the doctrine, growth and development of the Old Catholic Church, Döllinger derided the dogma of purported papal infallibility as intellectually indefensible. After its proclamation, he convened 44 professors in Munich to issue a declaration to resist the Council's resolutions—and he was excommunicated by the Roman church. In his memory, recommit yourself to positively contributing to the doctrine, growth and development of Independent Catholicism!

On **January 14**, the Church of Jesus Christ of Latter-day Saints celebrates the anniversary of the installation in 2018 of President **Russell Marion Nelson**. In a spirit of ecumenism, pray for him and for the 16 million Mormons he serves!

On **January 15**, we remember the passing of **St. Maurus** (c. 512-584), the Roman and first disciple of St. Benedict often depicted as the ideal Benedictine monk. The Blessing of Saint Mauer for the restoration of health was traditionally made with relics of the "true cross," which have been replaced by the St. Benedict medal. In his honor, share a special prayer for all who are ill!

On **January 15**, the Church celebrates **St. Francis Fernández de Capillas** (1607-1648), the Spanish Dominican friar beheaded in China for disseminating "false doctrines" and inciting people against the Chinese emperor. Pray for all who find themselves surrounded by less-than-friendly people!

Sunday, January 17, 2021
SECOND SUNDAY IN ORDINARY TIME
(green)

Winter Ordinary Time is here: Invite congregants to **wear green today**!

We're jumping into Ordinary Time for seven weeks: This is an ideal time to **try out a new musical setting of a few acclamations**!

Looking for **a new touch for your worship environment**: Instead of storing the Book of the Gospels on a shelf, display it opened, on a lectern, in the entrance to your worship space, and with the ribbon across the page opposite where the gospel of the coming Sunday is located (thus drawing attention to the evangelist's words), so that anyone who passes by can glance at it!

Think through **the décor for this season**.

- Try a **darker shade of green** for Winter Ordinary Time.
- Be sure that the colors of all fabrics in the worship space are coordinated — including the color of vestments. Be sure to steam or iron your **Ordinary Time vestments**!
- Fill the space with **green plants**, to which you can add accents of white (and/or other colors) for such celebrations as the Presentation of the Lord.
- Sprinkle the décor with **objects you find outdoors** at this time of year (e.g., pine cones and/or dried, seemingly-dead branches).
- **Continue the decoration** into the entrance to your worship space, outdoors, and into other spaces on the grounds, including your Blessed Sacrament chapel, parish hall and classrooms!

For the intellectually-curious, there is an abundance of possible lessons!

- Share a refresher on the **Year of Mark**, and let them know that, after a brief hiatus, we'll return to the first gospel beginning next Sunday and for the next several Sundays. Encourage them to find time this year to read and familiarize themselves with the entire gospel — and to incorporate Mark's gospel into their personal prayer!
- Share a lesson on **how the dates of Ordinary Time are determined** (viz., beginning on the first Monday after the first Sunday after January 6, and concluding on the Tuesday before Ash Wednesday).

- Explain why **the "first" Sunday in Ordinary Time is actually the Second Sunday in Ordinary Time** (because it kicks off the second full week of the season).

- Note that **the word "ordinary" in Ordinary Time refers to the ordering of weeks with ordinal numbers** (and in no ways suggests that these weeks are not extra-ordinary).

- Let community members know that **Winter Ordinary Time consists this year of the Second through Sixth Sundays in Ordinary Time**. After that, the next Sunday of Ordinary Time, after the Lent/Easter season, will fall on June 13, with our celebration of the Eleventh Sunday in Ordinary Time. Explain what will happen to the Seventh week in Ordinary Time (viz., the Church always omits one week that would otherwise precede the resumption of Ordinary Time following Pentecost Sunday, so as to always have a total of 33 or 34 weeks [rather than 32 or 33 weeks] of Ordinary Time). Explain, too, why we won't celebrate the Eighth, Ninth, and Tenth Sundays of Ordinary Time (which is when we'll celebrate the Solemnity of Pentecost, the Solemnity of the Most Holy Trinity, and the Solemnity of the Body and Blood of Christ).

- During all of Winter Ordinary Time, the second reading will come from **Paul's First Letter to the Corinthians**. Take a moment to share of the dating, audience and context for this letter, as well as its structure and themes!

The thread in today's scriptures: Samuel readily responded to God's call (1Sam. 3:3-10), and the Johannine Andrew acted similarly, bringing his brother, Peter, to Jesus (Jn. 1:40-42). With Samuel and the psalmist, we respond, "Here I am; I come to do your will" (Ps . 40:8-9), expressing our desire to be "joined to the Lord" and become "one Spirit with him" (1Cor. 6:17).

Holy humor: A seasoned priest moved back to the farm town where he was raised and gathered together a faith community there. After Mass one Sunday, his congregants gathered for a potluck, sharing nametags for an icebreaker of imagined occupations. As a joke, on the priest's nametag, they listed his pretend occupation as..."Hog caller." The priest snickered. "Most people say that I'm the shepherd of the sheep," he said, "but...a hog caller? I guess you know one another better than I do!" [Segue into our challenge to hear and follow the call of the Good Shepherd, or, if you prefer, the Heavenly Hog Caller!]

Looking for a visual aid for your homily or object lesson? Consider a posterboard with large letters spelling "VOCATION." Speak to the etymology and meaning of the word, noting that, like Samuel, Paul, Andrew and Peter, God calls us to different vocations in life — if only we, like them, might listen and respond! Ask, "What is *your* calling? What is God calling *you* to be and do in this world?"

This weekend, the U.S. celebrates a prominent voice for civil rights, **Martin Luther King, Jr.,** who is considered a saint in some Independent Catholic churches. Intertwine his message and the Christian message of a "discipleship of equals," and share with all a bookmark or image of him!

With the holidays now fading from memory, these **dark, winter months can be a lonely and/or depressing time for some**: Encourage families to "adopt a grandparent." Create homemade cards and promote visits to the homebound and those in nursing homes. Host a canned food drive for the hungry and homeless. Find a way to enflesh the corporal works of mercy that distinguish the "sheep" from the "goats" (Mt. 25:31-46)!

On **January 17**, when it doesn't fall on a Sunday, the Church celebrates **St. Anthony the Abbot** (251-356): Challenge listeners often caught up in the busyness of the world to focus on a better active/contemplative balance and to strive for a bit of silence, solitude, and contemplative prayer today!

On **January 17**, we remember the passing of **Juan Luis Segundo** (1925-1996), the Uruguayan Jesuit theologian who played a leading role in the Latin American liberation theology movement. A physician by training, he penned numerous works on theology, ideology, faith, hermeneutics and social justice. He was also an outspoken critic of the Roman church's deafness with respect to the oppression and suffering of the poor. In his memory, pause to consider how deaf you might be to the plight and cries of the poor — and commit yourself to at least one concrete way in which you might better be the hands and heart of Christ to them!

On **January 17**, we remember the passing of **Joseph M. Champlin** (1930-2008), the American Roman Catholic priest and author of numerous paperbacks on the Roman Catholic faith, including the popular *Together for Life* marriage preparation guide. In his memory, consider how you help to prepare couples for the covenantal life of marriage!

It's the beginning of the **Week of Prayer for Christian Unity** (January 18-25)! Historical divisions have rent the Body of Christ: Reflect on the Johannine Jesus' prayer for unity (Jn. 17:22-23), and pray for those — particularly those church leaders and people of faith — who continue to divide people, rather than create the inclusive community that Jesus imagined. Participate in a local ecumenical gathering and/or prayer service—or invite a pastor or two from another faith tradition to breakfast, coffee, lunch or dinner. Use social media to raise awareness of this important week!

On **January 18**, we remember the passing of **Guillaume de Champeaux** (c. 1070-1121), the French philosopher, theologian and bishop of Châlons-en-Champagne, whose renowned viticultural chart gave rise to the modern-day Champagne wine region. The theology teacher of the arrogant, young Peter Abelard (who replaced him), Guillaume is known for nursing his friend, Bernard of Clairvaux, back to health, and for having Bernard's *Apologia* dedicated to him. In his memory, enjoy a glass of bubbly and consider how you are caring for your friends!

On **January 18**, the Coptic Catholic Church (in union with Rome) celebrates the anniversary of the installation in 2013 of **Ibrahim Isaac Sidrak** as Patriarch of Alexandria. In a spirit of ecumenism, pray for him and for the 175,000 Coptic Catholics he serves!

On **January 19**, we remember the passing of **George Errington** (1804-1886), the English Roman Catholic coadjutor bishop of Westminster whose estrangement from the provost of Westminster led to his being deprived of his coadjutorship by Pius IX in favor of the provost. Errington then declined the Vatican's invitation to travel to Scotland and restore the Roman church's hierarchy there. At the First Vatican Council, Errington opposed the neo-Ultramontanism of his rival, the new bishop of Westminster. In his memory, pray for all who suffer the personal and political attacks of their rivals!

On **January 20**, the Roman Catholic Church celebrates the birth in 1953 of **Filipe Neri António Sebastião do Rosário Ferrão**, the Latin Patriarch of the East Indies. In a spirit of ecumenism, pray for him and for the Roman Catholics he serves!

On **January 20**, the Church celebrates **St. Fabian** (+250), the farmer who was proclaimed pope when a dove landed on his head! Reflect today on your own incredible stories of the presence and activity of God's Spirit in your life and in the lives of those around you!

On **January 20**, we celebrate the birth in 1965 of **John L. Allen, Jr.**, the CNN, NPR and National Catholic Reporter journalist who, as "America's leading Vaticanist," writes on "All Things Catholic." He has authored several books, including the inside story of how Joseph Ratzinger became Pope Benedict XVI, and a work on the controversial *Opus Dei*. *Newsweek* once remarked, "Outside of the North Korean government in

Pyongyang, no bureaucracy is harder for a journalist to crack than the Vatican's. And no one does it better than John L. Allen, Jr." In his honor, indulge yourself with a quick internet search of his latest writings!

On **January 20**, we remember the passing of **Milan "Emilio" Komar** (1921-2006), the Slovene Argentinian philosopher, essayist and polyglot who spoke eight languages and whose works were more influential in Latin America, Spain and Italy, than in his homeland, where his writings were banned by the Communist regime of Slovenia. As a young man, he was involved in Slovenian Catholic Action, and he established journals, publishing houses and schools in Slovenia before emigrating to Argentina, where he taught philosophy and pedagogy to the "Komar School" that developed around him. In his memory, consider your own willingness to be a prophet in places other than your homeland!

On **January 21**, the Church celebrates **St. Agnes** (c. 291 – c. 304), who was martyred at age 12 for refusing to marry a prefect's son. 650 million women in our world today were married as children, largely as a result of tradition, poverty and/or insecurity: Learn more at girlsnotbrides.org, and use this day to advocate for all affected by the issue of child marriage!

On **January 21**, the Church of God in Christ celebrates the anniversary of the installation in 2008 of **Presiding Bishop Charles Edward Blake, Sr**. In a spirit of ecumenism, pray for him and for the 6.5 Christians he serves!

For the Roman church, **January 22** is the **Day of Prayer for the Legal Protection of Unborn Children**. Explain the pastoral challenge of such a commemoration: While we esteem a "womb-to-tomb" ethic of life, we also recognize that women and men have found themselves in extremely difficult situations where they made what they, inspired by the Spirit, believed to be the best choice at that time and in those circumstances. Rather than judge and condemn them, we want to be the loving, healing and forgiving face of Christ: Widen your prayer today to include those who've suffered such circumstances, those who are considering abortion, and those who call themselves "pro-life" but are unable to take strong pro-life stands against the death penalty and/or on such life issues as homelessness, hunger, incarceration, care for immigrants/refugees, and support for public education!

On **January 22**, we remember the passing of **Jan van Schoonhoven** (c. 1356-1432), the Flemish theologian and writer who, as a member of the Windesheim Community, defended his friend, Jan van Ruysbroeck, against critics. He played an important role in the spiritual evolution from van Ruysbroeck and Geert Groote, to Desiderius Erasmus. Consider how you come to the defense of others and your own role in the spiritual evolution of your community!

On **January 23**, we remember the passing of **Otfrid of Weissenburg** (c. 800 – after 870), the German monk and first-named German poet known for his *Evangelienbuch*, a gospel written in 7,104 couplets — the first use of rhyme in German literature. In his memory, engage in a "right-brain" activity today — perhaps even writing your own rhyme or poem!

On **January 23**, the Church celebrates **St. Vincent of Saragosa** (+304), who inspired others with his heroic witness of faith. We also celebrate **St. Marianne Cope** (1838-1918), who cared for the sick and continued St. Damien of Moloka'i's ministry to Hawaiian patients infected with leprosy. Lift them up as models and mirrors of holiness!

On **January 23**, the Serbian Orthodox Church (recognized by the Ecumenical Patriarch of Constantinople) celebrates the anniversary of the installation in 2010 of Miroslav Gavrilović as **Patriarch Irinej of Serbia**. In a spirit of ecumenism, pray for him and for the 12 million Serbian Orthodox Catholics he serves!

Sunday, January 24, 2021

THIRD SUNDAY IN ORDINARY TIME

(green)

The thread in today's scriptures: Like Jonah (Jon. 3:1-5 & 3:10), Paul believed the world was passing away (1Cor. 7:31) and John the Baptist called the people to repentance (Mk. 1:15), showing sinners the way (Ps. 25:8). We are challenged to respond like the people of Nineveh, who repented, and like Peter and Andrew, who dropped what they were doing to follow Christ!

For the **intellectually-curious**, note how today's gospel presents a very different story of the call of Andrew and Peter than last week's gospel!

Holy humor: The fourth-grade science teacher told her class that it was physically impossible for a whale to swallow a human. "Whales," she explained, " are very large mammals, but they have very small throats." Startled, and obviously interpreting the Bible very literally, one girl raised her hand and insisted that Jonah was swallowed by a whale. The teacher reiterated that it is physically impossible for a whale to swallow a human. The girl retorted, "When I get to heaven, I'm going to ask Jonah!" Calmly, her teacher asked, "And what if Jonah isn't in heaven?" The girl replied, "Then *you* ask him!" [Segue into the age-old dichotomy preached by Jonah, of salvation vs. destruction, which caused the city of Nineveh to repent and turn toward God—and which has motivated countless people throughout the centuries to strive for a place in God's kingdom!]

Looking for a visual aid for your homily or object lesson? Consider a sandwich board or cardboard sign with a message like "The end is near!" or "Prepare for the end of the world!" People holding such signs have been satirized in cartoons. This was, in essence, the message that Jonah preached! [Other possible object lessons: an old fishing net, symbolizing the things we might need to leave behind, to follow Christ.]

We're nearing the end of the **Week of Prayer for Christian Unity** (January 18-25). Mark the occasion with a prayer for unity!

On **January 24**, we remember the passing of **Guillaume Briçonnet, Jr.** (1472-1534), the French bishop who worked to reform his diocese in Meaux, improving clergy training and monastic discipline, and advocating for a return to the theology and practices of the early Church. In his memory, consider your own role in reclaiming the riches of the ancient Church!

On **January 24**, when it doesn't fall on a Sunday, the Church celebrates **St. Francis de Sales** (1567-1622), the Swiss bishop who inspired the development of lay spirituality with his first-of-its-kind book written for laity (and not for clerics), *An Introduction to the Devout Life*. In his honor, lift up the holiness of the laity—who are the backbone of the Church and who share in the universal priesthood of Christ—and, in your own time of prayer and contemplation, meditate on de Sales' words: "The measure of love is to love without measure"!

On **January 24**, we remember the passing of **William Griffith "Bill" Wilson** (1895-1971), the co-founder of Alcoholics Anonymous, the twelve-step spiritual program that helps two million people in some 10,000 groups to achieve and maintain sobriety. AA focuses on belief in a higher power, incorporates prayer into its gatherings, and assists members with the task of reconciliation. In Bill's memory, perform some small act that might benefit those suffering from any number of addictions!

On **January 25**, the Church celebrates the **Conversion of Paul** (c. 31-36)—proof that no one is outside of God's grace, that even the hardest of hearts can melt, and that "with God all things are possible" (Mt. 19:26)!

On **January 25**, we remember the passing of **Bl. Henry Suso** (1296-1366), the German Dominican friar considered the most popular German writer of the fourteenth century. A popular preacher and spiritual director, Henry famously defended Meister Eckhart, who was posthumously condemned as a heretic. In his memory, consider how you might hone your own gifts for writing, preaching and/or spiritual direction!

On **January 25**, we celebrate the birth in 1958 of **James C. "Jim" Collins**, the American author, lecturer and executive coach known for his study of organizations. His bestselling work, *Good to Great*, chronicles the lessons of organizations that went from good to great — and many of which are now gone. In his honor, consider the lessons from his works that might help to ensure that your ministry is "built to last"!

On **January 25**, we remember the passing of **Richard Peter McBrien** (1936-2015), the Catholic priest and Notre Dame professor who authored 25 books, including his popular *Catholicism*, which was criticized by the U.S. Conference of Catholic Bishops. He garnered the ire of conservatives for singling out "single-issue, anti-abortion Catholics," criticizing church policy on obligatory celibacy and the ordination of women, and for suggesting in 1991 that "ecclesiastical hardliners" were engaged in a "prolonged, slow-motion coup…attempting to reverse the new, progressive course set by Pope John XXIII." In his memory, consider concrete ways in which you might further the "new, progressive course" of the Church!

On **January 26**, the Church celebrates **Ss. Timothy** (+97) **and Titus** (+c. 96-107), Paul's associates who are a study in contrasts with the Apostle: Paul circumcised Timothy, so that Timothy would be accepted by Jewish Christians, but he refused to circumcise Titus after coming to believe that the gospel freed Gentiles from the Jewish Law. Are you the Paul of Timothy, hoping to fit in, or the Paul of Titus, taking a stand? Both Timothy and Titus were considered important enough by early Christian communities that pseudonymous letters were penned in their names and in their spirit; be sure to clarify that these Pastoral Letters were *not* penned by the persons whose names they bear!

On **January 26**, we remember the passing of **Dietrich Richard Alfred von Hildebrand** (1889-1977), the German Catholic philosopher and theologian deemed "the 20th-century Doctor of the Church" by Pius XII. A vocal critic of Vatican II reforms, he especially resented the Council's liturgical reforms, stating: "Truly, if one of the devils in C.S. Lewis' *The Screwtape Letters* had been entrusted with the ruin of the liturgy, he could not have done it better." In his memory, pray for all who block the full and active participation of God's holy people in the Church and/or who resist attempts to make the Body of Christ more loving, inclusive, accessible, and true to the traditions of the ancient Church!

On **January 27**, the Church celebrates **St. Angela Merici** (1474-1540), who was moved by the plight of uneducated girls and laid the foundation for the Order of the Ursulines. Share her story and inspire those for whom she is a matron saint: the ill, the disabled, the physically-challenged, and those grieving the loss of a parent!

On **January 27**, we remember the passing of **Scipione de' Ricci** (1741-1810), the Italian bishop of Pistoia with Jansenist sympathies whose diocesan reforms were opposed by the pope. He championed improvised liturgies, founded a Jansenist press, discouraged the veneration of relics and images, and condemned devotion to the Sacred Heart. His posthumous memoirs were immediately placed on the Index of Forbidden Books. Pray for all whose zeal for reform is dampened by the reactions of others!

On **January 28**, we remember the passing in 814 of **Charlemagne** (748-814), the king of the Franks and Lombards who was crowned on Christmas Day 800 as Holy Roman Emperor by the assaulted Leo III. Charlemagne alienated Eastern Christians not only through his acceptance of the *filioque*, but also through the symbol of the new empire's unwillingness to recognize the legitimacy of Empress Irene of Constantinople. Considered the "Father of Europe," he was the first to rule the empire from Western Europe since the fall of Rome three centuries earlier, and his rule spurred the Carolingian Renaissance, a period of great intellectual activity in the Western Church. In his memory, pause to consider the politics that are part of any religious institution!

On **January 28**, the Church celebrates **St. Thomas Aquinas** (1225-1274), whose thought was used to bring uniformity to the nascent seminary system of a fortress church: In honor of his day, take a break from his "straw" and indulge in some good post-scholastic philosophy and/or theology!

On **January 29**, we remember the passing of **Angélique de Saint Jean Arnauld d'Andilly** (1624-1684), the French Jansenist nun of Port-Royal-des-Champs who opposed the *Formulary of Submission for the Jansenists*. Arrested and imprisoned at the Annonciades convent, she wrote an account of her captivity, reflections and conferences, and a necrology of the nuns of Port-Royal-des-Champs. In her honor, consider how you are recording and sharing your own experiences and reflections!

On **January 29**, we celebrate the birth in 1954 of **Oprah Gail Winfrey**, the American media executive, actress, talk show host and philanthropist sometimes ranked as the most influential woman in the world. The longtime host of *The Oprah Winfrey Show*, she broke taboos and allowed LGBTQ people to enter the mainstream of television appearances, and she would later reinvent her show with a focus on literature, self-improvement, mindfulness and spirituality. In her honor, consider how you might reinvent your ministry to reach more minds, hearts and souls!

On **January 29**, we remember the passing of **Ralph Matthew McInerny** (1929-2010), the Notre Dame professor known for his Father Dowling mystery series, which was the basis for the 1980's television series. After nearly 20 works of philosophy and theology, he wrote more than 60 works of fiction using five pseudonyms. In his memory, consider the creative ways in which you might interest others in our Catholic faith!

On **January 30**, we remember the passing of **Mohandas Karamchand "Mahatma" Gandhi** (1869-1948), the Indian activist who inspired nonviolent movements for freedom and civil rights throughout the world. His vision of religious pluralism was especially important in a nation torn by Hindu, Sikh and Muslim factions. In his memory, reflect on how you are championing the Catholic values of social justice and peace in our world!

On **January 31**, the Church celebrates **St. John Bosco** (1815-1888), the patron saint of schoolchildren, magicians, disadvantaged youths, and juvenile delinquents. If you have congregants with a Salesian bent, consider hosting a children's celebration in his honor. Stop by a local magic store and learn a gospel trick or two. Provide simple, kid-friendly food and drink. Invite a clown, balloon artist and/or magician!

Sunday, January 31, 2020
FOURTH SUNDAY IN ORDINARY TIME
(green)

The thread in today's scriptures: Moses shared a prophecy that God would raise a prophet from among the people, to serve as God's mouthpiece (Dt. 18:18). As if to fulfill that prophecy, Jesus appeared on the scene, astonishing people with his teaching (Mk. 1:22). May we be mindful of the distractions of this world (1Cor. 7:35), which keep us from hearing God's voice (Ps. 95:8) in our lives — thus keeping us from being the prophets we were baptized to be!

Holy humor: There's an old joke that says, "When you speak to God, we call it prayer — but when God speaks to you, we call it...schizophrenia!" [Segue into the stigma attached to mental health issues (e.g., roughly 1 in 1,000 people globally suffers from schizophrenia, and 6 in 1,000 suffer from bipolar disorder), acknowledging that the hearing of voices is part of the symptomology of various mental health conditions. Speak to some of the ways in which we might "hear" God's voice — in healthy ways — in a world filled with noise and distraction!]

Looking for a visual aid for your homily or object lesson? Consider a mask! To introduce the etymology of the English word "prophet," share that the ancient Greeks invented theater and various theatrical genres, including comedy, tragedy and satire. They created a Greek word, *prophenein*, for the act of "speaking through a mask." Invite an altar server to put on the mask and to speak through it. Who's talking: the mask or the altar server? In the same way, a prophet is a "mask" through which God speaks to our world! We are all baptized prophets: Are you allowing God to speak through you to those around you? Are you "hearing" how it is that God might be speaking to you through others?

On **January 31**, the Chaldean Catholic Church (in union with Rome) celebrates the anniversary of the installation in 2013 of **Louis Raphaël Sako** as Catholicos-Patriarch of Babylon. In a spirit of ecumenism, pray for him and for the 640,000 Chaldean Catholics he serves!

On **February 1**, we remember the passing of **Henri van Caelen** (1583-1653), the Dutch archpriest and diocesan censor who approved and glowingly recommended Jansen's *Augustinus*. Henri was named bishop of Roermond, but the pope refused to confirm his appointment. In his memory, reach out to those who have experienced a recent disappointment — and be the hands and heart of Christ to them!

On **February 1**, we remember the passing of **Ernst Melzer** (1835-1899), the German philosopher and educator who was a prominent supporter of Güntherianism, became part of the German Old Catholic Church, and wrote a biography of theologian Johann Baptista Baltzer. In his memory, consider your own stance toward those with novel ideas—even with respect to theology and religion!

On **February 1**, the Russian Orthodox Church (recognized by the Ecumenical Patriarch of Constantinople) celebrates the anniversary of the installation in 2009 of Vladimir Mikhailovich Gundyayev as **Patriarch Kirill of Moscow**. In a spirit of ecumenism, pray for him and for the Russian Orthodox Catholics he serves!

On **February 2**, the Church celebrates the **Presentation of the Lord** (or "Candlemass")!

- It's the 40th day of Christmas, the day on which Mary and Joseph appeared in the temple for Mary's "purification." **Pull touches of white into your décor** (perhaps with white flowers among your Ordinary Time greenery).

- In honor of the traditional celebration of Candlemass on this day, consider **blessing all the candles you'll use during the next year**, and invite congregants to bring candles to be blessed as well, for use in their prayer at home. Share **taper candles** (with bobaches) before the hymn of gathering, bless all candles and sprinkle them with holy water, then light the candles for a **procession** into your worship space—to symbolize entering the temple with Jesus, Mary and Joseph. Have your thurifer (with incense and boat), crucifer (cross bearer) and lucifers (candle bearers) lead the procession. Place a large container of sand in the sanctuary, where congregants can leave their candles burning during the liturgy.

- **For the intellectually-curious**, note that, for farmers in an age before Groundhog Day, the weather on this day purportedly forecasted whether spring was on its way. The ancients believed that if it was sunny on Candlemass (similar to the groundhog seeing its shadow!), winter would return, and farmers would say: "When the wind's in the East on Candlemass Day, there it will stick 'til the second of May!"

- This is a big day in the *Latino* culture! For *Latinos*, it's *el día de la candelaria*, the traditional day for taking down the Christmas creche and bringing the image of the Child Jesus (along with candles) to church, to be blessed. Upon returning home from

Mass, rather than pack the image of the Child Jesus in a box for the year, *Latino* families sit their images of the Christ Child upright on their home altars. If you have a *Latino* community, **invite congregants to bring their images of the Child Jesus to church for a special blessing**, then share with them a copy of the prayer for the traditional *levantar el Niño Dios*, the rite of placing the image upright on their home altar.

- If you're celebrating at night, illuminate the path to your worship space with *luminarias* (candles inside paper bags).

- Looking for a great community-building activity? **Invite those who found the image of the Child Jesus in their *rosca de reyes* on Epiphany, to bring the *tamales* and *atole* for a post-Mass gathering!**

- Do you have a relationship with a religious order and/or congregation? The Feast of the Presentation is also **World Day for Consecrated Life!** Honor those who have given their lives to religious life, invite them to renew their vows on this day, and challenge congregants of all ages to reflect on whether God might be calling them to such a life!

On **February 3**, the Church celebrates **St. Blaise** (+c. 316): Consider having the traditional **blessing of throats** after Mass! Before Mass, be sure to find two long wax candles that can be tied with ribbon, in the form of a cross. Forego the tradition of lighting the candles: you won't distract people with dripping wax, and you'll avoid both a fire hazard and a seemingly-shamanistic expression!

On **February 3**, we remember the passing of **Cornelius Loos** (1546-1595), the first Roman Catholic priest and theologian to write against the witch trials that raged in Europe during the 1580's and 1590's. He was imprisoned and forced to recant, and his work was confiscated and suppressed by his church, only to be discovered 300 years later. In his memory, pray for all whose words, works and contributions are not appreciated during their lifetimes!

On **February 3**, we remember the passing of **Frederick Charles Copleston** (1907-1994), the Jesuit priest, philosopher and historian of philosophy most known for his eleven-volume work, *A History of Philosophy*. He achieved popularity by debating atheist Bertrand Russell on the BBC in 1948. In his memory, wrestle with a paragraph or two of his history of philosophy!

On **February 5**, we remember the passing of **Rabanus Maurus** (c. 780-856), the Frankish Benedictine monk, theologian, poet, encyclopedist and military writer known as "the teacher of Germany." The archbishop of Mainz, he authored several works, many of which are only now being translated to English. In his memory, consider how you help to make the works of others available to those thirsting to learn more about their faith!

On **February 5**, the Church celebrates **St. Agatha** (c. 231 – c. 251), who was tortured and killed for spurning a senator's wish to marry her. Pray Eucharistic Prayer I, which mentions her. If you missed the celebration of St. Agnes on January 21, you might steal ideas from that day. Otherwise, Agatha is the matron saint of breast cancer patients: Consider hosting a health fair and/or bringing in a survivor or some other guest speaker to speak on preventative measures for breast cancer. Other forms of cancer — including testicular cancer — are also very real: If you're going to have a moment of raising awareness to cancer, consider the various cancers that might affect your congregants!

On **February 5**, we celebrate the birth in 1928 of **Martin Emil Marty**, the American Lutheran religious scholar who has written extensively on religion in the U.S. He has written more than 5,000 articles and encyclopedia entries — in addition to the two books that he authored and edited each year of his professorship. In his honor, consider what you're writing — or not — about our faith!

On **February 6**, the Church celebrates **St. Paul Miki** (c. 1562-1597) **and his 25 companions**, missionaries to Japan who were forced to march 600 miles to their crucifixion in Nagasaki. Share prayers for modern-day martyrs who are persecuted for their faith!

On **February 6**, we remember the passing of **Franjo Petriš** or Franciscus Patricius (1529-1597), the Venetian philosopher and scientist of Croatian descent, who undertook a comprehensive study of contemporary science and defended Platonism against followers of Aristotle. He advanced that, whereas Plato foreshadowed Christian revelation, Aristotle's teaching was in direct opposition to Christianity. In his memory, consider the Aristotelian notions — like transubstantiation — of your own theology and spirituality!

On **February 6**, we remember the passing of **Auguste Joseph Alphonse Gratry** (1805-1872), the French priest and gifted academic who held the seat formerly occupied by Voltaire and who advocated for modern scientific exploration in tandem with theology. He helped to reconstitute the French Oratory, a society of priests dedicated to education. Most notably, he was one of the principal opponents of the dogma of purported papal infallibility at the First Vatican Council. In his memory, pray for all who have the courage to question the thoughts and beliefs that are imposed on them by others!

Sunday, February 7, 2021
FIFTH SUNDAY IN ORDINARY TIME
(green)

February is here! **For the intellectually-curious,** incorporate the etymology of this month's name into your words at some point during this month! "February" comes from the Latin root, *februa*, "to cleanse." *Februalia* was the month during which the ancient Romans celebrated their annual festival of purification and atonement. This year, appropriately, Lent begins before the conclusion of *Februalia*!

On this first Sunday of February—which is Black History Month—U.S. Roman Catholic bishops invite their faithful to mark the **National Day of Prayer for the African American Family**. Consider your own honoring of **Black History Month**, perhaps even inviting a pastor from a local African-American congregation to preach to your community!

The thread in today's scriptures: Covered with painful sores from the soles of his feet to the crown of his head (Job 2:7), Job was in need of healing and recognized the finite nature of life (Job 7:6-7). Like God, who binds the wounds of the brokenhearted (Ps. 147:3), Jesus "cured many who were sick" (Mk. 1:34), including Peter's mother-in-law (Mk. 1:30-31). Like Job, we sometimes share in suffering (1Cor. 9:22), but, like Paul and Jesus, we recognize that we have been "entrusted with a stewardship" (1Cor. 9:17)—with gifts to share in the service of others (1Cor. 9:19)!

Holy humor: What would you do if you only had four weeks left to live? One woman was asked that question—what she would do if she only had four weeks to live—and she instantly replied, "I'd go to my mother-in-law's home for four weeks!" When asked why, she replied, "Those would be the four longest weeks of my life!" Now, far be it from me to tell mother-in-law jokes—but we all know why Peter denied Jesus three times, right? Because Jesus healed Peter's mother-in-law! [Segue into Peter's unnamed wife (1Cor. 9:5), suspected by some of dying before Peter followed Jesus) and mother-in-law (Mk. 1:30-31, Mt. 8:14-15, Lk. 4:38-39). In a patriarchal society, within an androcentric world, women occupied the "basement" of societal life, depending on the importance of their husband, son or—in Peter's case—son-in-law. Reaching out to the poor and most vulnerable, Jesus showed that the joke was on those who believed that God only blessed the healthy, wealthy and most powerful!]

Looking for a visual aid for your homily or object lesson? Consider inviting listeners to blow on their hand and see how quickly the evidence of their breath disappears. That's the image that Job gives us of how quickly our lives come to an end (Job 7:7), faster than a weaver can get the fast-moving shuttle of weft (i.e., of yarn, wool or fabric scraps) from one side of the loom to the other (Job 7:6). It's also how quickly Jesus acted to heal and make whole those who suffered around him. And you? How quickly do you respond in the service of others? How quickly are you weaving a "tapestry" of service to those around you?

On **February 7**, we remember the passing of **Daniel J. Harrington** (1940-2014), the Jesuit New Testament professor who edited the 18-volume *Sacra Pagina* series of New Testament commentaries. His writing interests included biblical interpretation, Second Temple Judaism, the Dead Sea Scrolls, biblical language and theology, the synoptic gospels, and Pauline theology. In his memory, choose a volume of *Sacra Pagina*, and see what you can learn from a quick read of a paragraph or two!

On **February 8**, the Church celebrates **St. Jerome Emiliani** (1486-1537) and **St. Josephine Bakhita** (c. 1869-1947). Jerome was dedicated to the poor and disadvantaged; encourage visits to hospitals and orphanages in his honor. Josephine was enslaved for more than 15 years; bring a spotlight to the various slave trades that persist in our world!

On **February 8**, we remember the passing of **Matthias Tanner** (1630-1693), the Bohemian Jesuit who served as rector of the imperial university and as superior of his province. He fostered devotion to the Mass and dedicated his leisure time to sharing the heroic deeds of prominent Jesuits. In his memory, consider how you're sharing your leisure time!

On **February 9**, the Old Catholic Church remembers the passing of **Gerard Gul** (1847-1920), the seventeenth archbishop of Utrecht, known for assisting the establishment of the Polish National Catholic Church in the United States. Gul also consecrated Arnold Mathew Harris, the founder of the Old Catholic Church in Great Britain. Pray today for all who so courageously act to establish new communities and ministries to serve the people of God in new and diverse ways!

On **February 9**, we celebrate the birth in 1925 of **John Boswell Cobb, Jr.**, the American theologian, philosopher and environmentalist often referred to as the preeminent scholar in the fields of process philosophy and process theology. The author of more than 50 books, he has written on religious pluralism, interfaith dialogue, the need to reconcile religion and science, and our need to preserve the world on which we depend. In his honor, consider your own stances toward these important issues!

On **February 9**, we remember the passing of **John Harwood Hick** (1922-2012), the English theologian and philosopher of religion who contributed to theodicy, eschatology, Christology and religious pluralism. He is known for comparing the "Ptolemaic view of religion" — that Christianity is the only way to true salvation and knowledge of God — with "Copernican" views of religious pluralism. In his memory, reflect on how your view of religion might be like the parable of the blind men and the elephant — and consider your stance toward the many spiritual and religious paths that lead up the mountain of the Most High!

On **February 10**, the Church celebrates **St. Scholastica** (c. 480-543), the twin sister of St. Benedict, who invoked a storm to keep him from leaving her deathbed. Consider ways to spend a bit more time with those you love!

On **February 10**, the Old Catholic Church remembers the passing of **Francis Kenninck** (+1937), the 18th archbishop of Utrecht, who abolished compulsory clerical celibacy in the Old Catholic Church and cleared the path to restored communion between the Old Catholic Church and the Anglican Church. Perform a small act today that might lead to greater unity in the beautifully-diverse body that is the Church!

On **February 10**, the Greek Orthodox Church of Antioch (recognized by the Ecumenical Patriarch of Constantinople) celebrates the anniversary of the installation in 2013 of John Yazigi as **Patriarch John X of Antioch**. In a spirit of ecumenism, pray for him and for the 1.8 million Greek Orthodox Catholics he serves!

On **February 11**, we remember the passing of **Hugh of Saint Victor** (c. 1096-1141), the Saxon canon and mystical theologian who wrote several significant philosophical and theological works that influenced St. Bonaventure and the "School of St. Victor." He expounded on a theology of love, embraced science and philosophy as tools for approaching God, and viewed the sacraments as God's divine gifts for our redemption. Take a moment today to reacquaint yourself with one of his works!

On **February 11**, the Roman church celebrates the optional memorial of **Our Lady of Lourdes**, the 1858 apparition in which Mary self-identified under the recently-proclaimed (1854) title of the Immaculate Conception and to whom many miracles of healing have been attributed. John Paul II declared February 11 the **World Day of the Sick** and encouraged prayers for those in need of healing. Encourage congregants to call and/or visit family members and friends who might be ill. Host a celebration of the sacrament of Anointing of the Sick. Have congregants reach out to the homebound who might be able to join you, if provided a ride. Consider blessing all who work in healing professions as well!

On **February 11**, we remember the passing of **René Descartes** (1596-1650), the French philosopher, mathematician and scientist who laid the foundation for 17th-century rationalism and is considered one of the most notable intellectual figures of the Dutch Golden Age and of the Scientific Revolution. Known for his *cogito ergo sum* ("I think, therefore I am"), he rejected the splitting of corporeal substance into the Aristotelian categories of matter and form, and he insisted on the absolute freedom of God's act of creation. In his memory, consider other possible eucharistic theologies than the outdated Aristotelian categories contained in "transubstantiation"!

On **February 12**, we remember the passing of **Friedrich Daniel Ernst Schleiermacher** (1768-1834), the German theologian, philosopher, and biblical scholar known for his attempt to reconcile the criticisms of the Enlightenment with traditional Christianity. Known as the "Father of Modern Liberal Theology," he played an important role in modern biblical hermeneutics. Karl Barth's neo-orthodoxy was largely an attempt to challenge Schleiermacher's "liberal Christianity." In his memory, take a moment today to reacquaint yourself with his life and works!

On **February 12**, we remember the passing of **Richard A. McCormick** (1922-2000), the Jesuit theologian who helped reshape Catholic thought in the U.S. by his writings on moral theory and social teachings. An expert in Catholic medical ethics, he was one of five moral theologians who crafted in 1964 a political position that would permit abortion in U.S. law. He wrote that the prohibition of discussion of *Humanae vitae* led to "a debilitating malaise that has undermined the credibility of the [Roman Catholic] magisterium in other areas." In his memory, familiarize yourself with his works and/or send up a prayer for the brave moral theologians who continue to explore positions that may not be accepted by more conservative voices!

On **February 13**, we celebrate the birth in 1943 of **Elaine Pagels**, the American religious historian and Princeton professor who wrote widely on early Christianity and the Gnostic gospels. Her works highlight the way in which women have been viewed throughout Jewish and Christian history. In her honor, perform your own brief study of a Gnostic gospel that didn't "make the cut" in the scriptural canon, so that you can enrich your preaching and storytelling!

Sunday, February 14, 2021
SIXTH SUNDAY IN ORDINARY TIME
(green)

The thread in today's scriptures: Once "unclean" due to leprosy and marginalized from society (Lev. 13:46), a man with leprosy encounters healing through Jesus (Mk. 1:40-45) and experience "the joy of salvation" (Ps. 32:7)! We should imitate Paul and Jesus (1Cor. 11:1), who worked for the good of others: that others might be saved (1Cor. 10:33)!

Holy humor: There are several very tasteless leper jokes on the internet. Perhaps the least tasteless are: "What should you do after shaking a leper's hand? Give it back!" Or, "I don't know how to feel about my friend who has leprosy. On the one hand, he gave me leprosy. On the other hand...oh, wait!" [Segue into the serious nature of Hansen's disease (which still affects some 200,000 people globally) and its physically- and socially-debilitating effects in the ancient world. Help your listeners imagine how wonderful it would have been to be cured of leprosy and reintegrated into society!]

Looking for a visual aid for your homily or object lesson? Consider torn clothes and/or disheveled hair (Lev. 13:45) or a bell—all signs that one had leprosy and was to be avoided! If you preach with a digital presentation, find a less-repulsive image of a person suffering the debilitating effects of Hansen's disease.

In the U.S., we celebrate **President's Day** tomorrow: Be sure to pray in a special way today for our President and for all world leaders!

Today is **World Marriage Day**! Consider floral arrangements in your worship space to honor and celebrate married couples. Invite couples to stand and renew their vows to one another. Cue couples to stand, invite each person standing to take the hands of his/her spouse, and decide who will recite the vows first. You'll also need to cue them to insert appropriate names after the words "I" and "you." Be conscious of the fact that some couples may be same-sex couples: To be inclusive, consider using the words: "I, ___, take you, ___, to be my spouse" or "...as my beloved." Immediately after the renewal, invite all who are seated to extend their hands for a prayer of blessing, then lead all in a round of applause for all who renewed their vows!

Valentine's Day is here! Secure a volunteer to set up a Valentine's Day photo booth or photo wall, so that couples can get their photos after Mass. Avoid schmaltzy cupids, and be sure the photographer is thinking about how the photos will look when cropped. Looking to score a few points? Print copies of the photos and share them next Sunday with those in the photos!

It's the **last Sunday before Lent**:

- **Invite congregants to bring their palms from past years**, and have a ritual burning of palms in a large brazier at the end of the celebration. Grind the remains, or run them through an old flour sifter, and you have your ashes for Ash Wednesday!

- Host an intergenerational *Mardi Gras* celebration after Mass, with projects and activities to enhance Lenten prayer and reflection at home. Play *Mardi Gras* music in the background. Host a *Mardi Gras* parade with hats and masks (and possibly beads, depending on the symbolism of these in your community), with congregants singing songs like "We Are Marching in the Light of God."

- Lent is almost here! Is your **Lenten calendar** finalized? Consider opportunities of prayer, like the weekly Stations of the Cross, the praying of the Sorrowful Mysteries of the rosary, and/or a parish mission/retreat. Think about community-building opportunities, like fish fries or soup dinners. Consider "fasting" from a parish meeting or two, as a way of honoring this season and allowing people more time to focus on the reason for the upcoming season. Schedule times for individual confession and a communal rite of reconciliation and a celebration of the rite of anointing. Are your palms and paschal candle ordered? Will you have a live enactment of the Way of the Cross? Do you have catechumens who will receive sacraments at the Easter Vigil? Remember that the Church's sacraments of initiation are *not* celebrated during Mass on the Sundays of Lent.

- To prepare for the Lenten season of reconciliation, consider how your environment might be made more hospitable and welcoming; host a **"wheelchair challenge,"** where clergy and lay leaders tour all parts of your property and facilities in wheelchairs and/or walkers, to see what aspects of the property and facilities might be made more accommodating for persons with more limited mobility. Those who participate will grow in empathy and have several ideas for improvements!

On **February 14**, when it doesn't fall on a Sunday, the Church celebrates the brother-saints **Cyril** (c. 826-869) **and Methodius** (815-885), the "Apostles to the Slavs"! They were a "bridge" between the West and the East: In their honor, learn about Eastern cultures and/or reach out to persons of other language groups!

On **February 15**, the Syriac Catholic Church (in union with Rome) celebrates the anniversary of the installation in 2009 of **Ignatius Ephrem Joseph III Yonan** as Patriarch of Antioch. In a spirit of ecumenism, pray for him and for the 205,000 Syriac Catholics he serves!

On **February 16**, we celebrate the birth in 1948 of **Ulrich Leonard "Eckhart" Tölle**, the German-Canadian spiritual teacher and bestselling author referred to as "the most spiritually influential person in the world." After struggling with depression for the first 29 years of his life, he experienced a transformation and went on to pen *The Power of Now* and *A New Earth*. In his honor, be inspired by his works and/or reach out to a loved one who might be suffering from depression!

Wednesday, February 17, 2021
ASH WEDNESDAY
(purple)

Catholics are famous for wanting their ashes and their palms: Be sure to **schedule your Ash Wednesday Mass(es) and/or service(s) at times that are convenient** for those who have families and/or other responsibilities, like work or school!

Be sure that **your worship environment** expresses the starkness of Lent.
- **Strip the altar and ambo**.
- **Remove all flowers, green plants, and unnecessary furnishings**.
- Find a way to draw attention to the **crucifix** (e.g., drape purple cloth behind the head and over the arms of the cross), and to the **Stations of the Cross** (if they adorn your space).
- **Use fabric sparingly**, remembering that purple is used to mark the season, not to decorate it.
- Consider incorporating **decorative accents**, like, burlap, ashes, rocks, sand, broken pottery and cacti.
- **Decorate the entrance to your worship space** with wood or metal crosses and/or wreaths of dried grapevines.

- Be sure to steam or iron your **Lenten vestments** — and to coordinate the color of your vestments with any other touches of purple in your worship space!

Think through **the details of this day**:

- Do you have ashes?
- How, when and by whom will they be blessed? [Remember: Ashes are only blessed once.]
- Will you share them after the homily, or outside the Mass?
- Will you need other ministers (clergy and/or laity) to assist with the distribution? When/how will you train them? Which formula will they use for the imposition of ashes? Do they know how they will clean the sacramental of ashes from their fingers, perhaps with premoistened towelettes that are later burned?
- Do you have a song or instrumental music to accompany the distribution of ashes?
- Try something different: Because the Church's rite doesn't mandate pushing ashes into the pores of a person's forehead, designate (and announce) a minister who will be happy to assist with the more ancient symbol of sprinkling ashes on the heads of those who, in line with the gospel mandate (Mt. 6:16-18), would like a different experience of Ash Wednesday!

Remember: The Penitential Rite is *not* used due to the distribution of ashes, the Creed is omitted, and the *Gloria* and Alleluia are *not* sung today; lead the congregation in another, easy-to-sing gospel acclamation!

Holy humor: The story is told of the youth minister who was a bit of a prankster. He was invited to be an ash minister on Ash Wednesday, and to share ashes with some of the young people who were known to pull pranks on him from time to time.(You know where this story is going, right?) So when the young man who often instigated the most pranks stepped up to him for ashes, the youth minister traced a cross of ashes on the young man's forehead [trace a cross in the air with your right thumb, as if sharing ashes with an invisible person], reverently saying, "Repent and believe the good news." And then he quickly swiped his ash-filled thumb over the young man's upper lip [make a small arc with your thumb, as though marking the person with a big ash moustache]. The youth minister flashed a wry smile, thinking revenge is so sweet, and you know what he said, right? "Happy 'Stache Wednesday!" [Segue into a lesson on the symbolism of the ashes and why we don't wear the ashes like a moustache, but instead have them sprinkled on our heads or marked on our foreheads in the shape of a cross.]

Looking for a visual aid for your homily or object lesson? Consider the ashes! Congregants will leave with ashes: Tie a strong message to that visual! As your "hook" (to pique interest), invite congregants to sing with you "Ring around the rosie," then draw attention to the imagery of "ashes, ashes" and note how "we all fall down" in death—hence, the symbolism of the ashes, which come from a plant that has died and been burned! Speak to the ancient connection of ashes with repentance.

Congregants will likely default to the thinking with which they were programmed: that they should "give up something" for Lent (e.g., candy, desserts, soda, coffee, smoking, Facebook). Explain that these are forms of fasting. Encourage them to consider instead **a Lent of service** as a sacrifice that might help others: assisting an elderly neighbor, serving a meal at a soup kitchen, visiting the homebound, etc.

Encourage congregants to go deeper in their exploration of all three traditional Lenten practices. For those on social media, suggest a **"virtual" Lenten journey**:

- Pray by sharing scripture, prayers and reflections on social media;

- Fast from mean comments, mean-spirited memes, and rigid views on religion and/or politics;

- Fast by spending less time on social media and/or by abstaining from sites that may detract from holiness; and

- Engage in almsgiving by raising awareness of and contributing to worthy online campaigns for persons and organizations in need!

Ash Wednesday is a traditional day to **abstain from meat**: consider sharing the connection between going meatless and protecting the environment. Search the internet for resources (e.g., https://www.downtoearth.org/go-veggie/top-10-reasons).

For the intellectually-curious, share a history of Lent, how the first day of Lent is determined, how the 40 days are counted, and how Sundays are not numbered among the 40 days of Lent!

If you're thinking ahead to Easter, this may be an opportunity to share giving envelopes with those wishing to help buy **Easter lilies**, to decorate your worship space for the Triduum! Tell them what the suggested donation is for each lily, and tell them that they'll be able to take their lily/lilies home with them at the conclusion of the Easter Mass they attend. These lilies can be shared with loved ones on Easter and/or planted outside!

On **February 17**, when it does not fall on Ash Wednesday, the Church celebrates the **Seven Founders of the Servite Order** (died over nearly 50 years, 1266-1310), seven prominent men of Florence who withdrew to monastic life while finding ways to support their wives and widows. Pause today to consider the active/contemplative balance in your life!

On **February 17**, we remember the passing of **Juan de Mariana** (1536-1624), the Spanish Jesuit scholastic and historian who, due to ill health, retired to Toledo and wrote a 30-volume history of the Iberian peninsula. A Monarchomach, he opposed monarchy and helped paved the way to social contract theories of "popular sovereignty." In his memory, consider the ways in which you are (or are not) helping to capture history!

On **February 17**, we remember the execution in 1872 of **GomBurZa**, the three Filipino priests—Mariano Gómez, José Burgos, and Jacinto Zamora—accused of mutiny against Spain, which claimed sovereignty over the Philippines. Their controversial deaths, for their role in the purported Cavite Mutiny, contributed to the birth of Filipino nationalism, which resulted in the overthrow of the Spanish government in 1898. In their memory, pray for all who suffer the scapegoating of others!

On **February 17**, we celebrate the birth in 1934 of **John Dominic Crossan**, the Irish-American New Testament scholar and historian of early Christianity known for both his scholarly and popular works. A former Catholic priest, he has focused his research on the historical Jesus and the cultural anthropology of the New Testament world. Crossan's work has garnered controversy due to his suggestions that Jesus' divinity is metaphorical and that the second coming of Christ is a late corruption of Jesus' message. In his honor, enjoy some time reading up on the historical Jesus and his message!

On **February 18**, we remember the passing of **Martin Luther** (1483-1546), the German Roman Catholic priest who dared to question the teachings and practices of his church, including indulgences and salvation through works. He translated the Bible to the vernacular, esteemed scripture as the only source of divinely-revealed knowledge, and brought attention to the priesthood of all the baptized. A composer and professor of theology, Martin refused to renounce his views and was excommunicated by Leo X and condemned as an outlaw by Emperor

Charles V. In his memory, pray for all who are ostracized by those whom they love!

On **February 19**, we remember the passing of **Jeanne-Catherine-Agnès Arnauld** (1593-1671), the Cistercian abbess known as "Mother Agnes," who led Port-Royal-des-Champs at the height of the anti-Jansenist movement. The sister of Antoine Arnauld, she was confronted by the Archbishop of Paris for organizing resistance to the *Formulary of Submission for the Jansenists*. In her honor, consider your own courage in standing for your beliefs and convictions!

On **February 20**, we celebrate the birth in 1947 of **John Calvin Maxwell**, the American pastor, speaker and author whose many books primarily focus on leadership. Considered by many to be the #1 author on leadership, he often shares stories of the struggles he faced as a young pastor attempting to build congregations. In his honor, prayerfully consider how you are developing the leader within you — and the leaders around you!

On **February 20**, the Ancient Church of the East celebrates the anniversary of the installation in 1972 of Shlemun Giwargis as **Catholicos Patriarch Addai II of Baghdad and Basra**. In a spirit of ecumenism, pray for him and for the people he serves!

Sunday, February 21, 2021
FIRST SUNDAY OF LENT
(green)

Remember: The *Gloria* and Alleluia are *not* sung today. Lead the congregation in another, easy-to-sing gospel acclamation!

Note: **The introductory line of today's second reading is misleading**. The Letters of Peter are pseudonymous letters, written in Peter's name and spirit, but not written by Peter. You might find a way to clarify this confusion.

The thread in today's scriptures: Impelled by the Spirit (Mk. 1:12), the Marcan Jesus was "tempted by Satan" (Mk. 1:13) and, according to other accounts (Mt. 4:1-13, Lk. 4:1-13), remained faithful to God's covenant and walked in the Lord's ways of love and truth (Ps. 25:10). As a result of their covenant, Noah and his family were faithful to God, just as God was faithful to them (Gen. 9:8-15). Like Noah and his family, we are "saved by water" (1Pet. 3:20-21), and, like Jesus, we are tempted. May we keep God's covenant and walk in the Lord's ways of love and truth!

Holy humor: Have you heard any good Noah jokes? Share a few, then segue to todays' scriptures with a line like, "Seriously, though, as we see in today's scriptures, Noah, Jesus and Paul took their relationship with God very seriously…"

- Does anyone need an ark? I Noah guy!
- Do you know how the guy who built the ark got his name? When he was born, his mother asked his father if he had a name in mind, and his father replied, "No, uh…"!
- I think the whole story of Noah and the ark is crazy. Hearing from God, building a boat, gathering animals: The whole thing sounds…delugional!
- What animal did Noah regret taking on the ark? The woodpeckers!
- Why couldn't Noah see the animals that he led aboard his big boat? Because it was d'ark!
- What type of lights did Noah have on the ark? Flood lights!

Looking for a visual aid for your homily or object lesson? Consider a rainbow flag or some other image of a rainbow—a symbol of God's faithfulness and of the faithfulness to which we're called!

If you have **catechumens** who will receive sacraments at the Easter Vigil, consider hosting the **Rite of Election** as part of your Mass today, with your catechumens' bishop in attendance! Prepare lovely copies of the Creed and Lord's Prayer, to be shared with them. Provide catechesis on the elements of the rite, including the *ephphetha*.

If you haven't already given a nod to **Black History Month**, this might be an ideal Sunday for hosting an African-American preacher with all the energy and enthusiasm s/he might bring!

On **February 21**, when it doesn't fall on a Sunday, the Church celebrates **St. Peter Damian** (1007-1072), the gifted scholar and Doctor of the Church who spoke out against clerical abuses and challenged bishops to recommit themselves to their vocation. When is the last time that you spoke out against clerical abuse(s)? If you are a bishop, recommit yourself today to your vocation of leading, teaching and sanctifying God's people—with a special focus on leading, since you can't teach and sanctify others if you're walking alone!

On **February 21**, we remember the passing of **William Franklin "Billy" Graham, Jr.** (1918-2018), the prominent Southern Baptist evangelist and advisor to U.S. presidents whose annual "crusades" and sermons helped some 2.2 billion people during his lifetime to explore the Bible and its connection to daily life. He encouraged new converts to become members of the Protestant and Catholic churches near them. In his memory, consider what you're doing to expand and multiply your efforts to evangelize!

On **February 22**, the Roman church celebrates the **Chair of St. Peter**, the foundational teaching *cathedra* presumed to have been passed by Peter to his purported successors. The feast traces to the fourth-century celebration of *Parentalia*, a winter commemoration of deceased family members and friends when a chair (*cathedra*) was left empty in memory of the deceased. Pray in a special way today for the bishops and church leaders who influenced you. If you celebrate Mass, draw attention to an empty chair as a symbol of their abiding presence with us!

On **February 22**, we remember the passing of **Hendrik Herp** (c. 1400-1477), the Dutch mystical writer who founded and led a community of the Brothers of the Common Life before becoming a Capuchin Franciscan. His writings, including the *Mirror of Perfection*, were widely translated and distributed, influencing future mystics throughout Europe. His work, *On Mystical Theology*, dedicated to Ignatius of Loyola, however, was assigned to the Index of Forbidden Books. Pause to consider how you are gazing into the Mirror of Perfection and encouraging others to do likewise!

On **February 22**, we remember the elevation in 1940 of **Tenzin Gyatso** as the Dalai Lama, the foremost spiritual leader of the Buddhist people of Tibet. An ecumenical figure holding together disparate religious and regional groups, the Dalai Lama actively models and promotes Buddhist values and traditions to the world. In his honor, consider your own stance toward our sisters and brothers of diverse religious traditions!

On **February 23**, the Church celebrates **St. Polycarp** (c. 65-155), the presumed friend of various eyewitnesses of Jesus' ministry. The Romans tried to burn him at the stake — and failed. Pray today for those members of the Roman church whose fixations and lack of psychological and/or emotional health continue to affect our ministries in the Independent Catholic tradition!

On **February 24**, we remember the passing of **Franz Jacob Clemens** (1815-1862), the German philosopher and Catholic layman who defended the theological stances of the Church. He was so popular that

70 students followed him when he was transferred from the University of Bonn to the University of Münster. In his memory, consider your own defense of our liberating faith!

On **February 24**, we remember the passing of **Anton Günther** (1783-1863), the Czech-Austrian priest whose "liberal Catholic" Hegelian ideas of the Trinity, of the person of Christ, and of creation as the "non-ego" of God were condemned by scholastic theologians of his day. After the First Vatican Council, many adherents of Güntherianism joined the Old Catholic Church. In his memory, pray for all who attempt to enrich theology with ideas and perspectives from other disciplines!

On **February 24**, the Bulgarian Orthodox Church (recognized by the Ecumenical Patriarch of Constantinople) celebrates the anniversary of the installation in 2013 of Simeon Nikolov Dimitrov as **Patriarch Neophyte of Bulgaria**. In a spirit of ecumenism, pray for him and for the 11 million Bulgarian Orthodox Catholics he serves!

On **February 25**, we celebrate the birth in 1939 of **Paul Francis Knitter**, the theology professor known for his writings on religious pluralism. Criticized by Joseph Ratzinger, he was one of 97 Catholic theologians and leaders in 1984 who signed a statement calling for pluralism in the Roman church's conversations on its myopic position on abortion. In his honor, consider the place of pluralism in your own views and theology!

On **February 25**, the Maronite Catholic Church (in union with Rome) celebrates the birth in 1940 of **Cardinal Patriarch Bechara Boutros al-Rahi**. In a spirit of ecumenism, pray for him and for the 3.5 million Maronite Catholics he serves!

On **February 27**, we remember the passing of **Hugues Félicité Robert de Lamennais** (1782-1854), the French priest, philosopher and political theorist who is considered a forerunner of liberal and social Catholicism. In response to Rome's reactionary absolutism, he renounced his priesthood and published a polemic against the Roman church and its conspiring with kings against the people. Gregory XVI condemned the work, calling it "small in size, but immense in perversity" — an act largely seen as squelching open expression of modernist ideas in Catholic circles. Lamennais' views on religion and government softened, giving way to staunch Ultramontane views. In his memory, pause to consider how your own views and beliefs have changed over time!

On **February 27**, we remember the passing of **Fred McFeely Rogers** (1928-2003), the Presbyterian minister, musician and writer who became the beloved American television personality in "Mr. Rogers' Neighborhood." Known as a kind, neighborly educator of kids, he was famous for saying, "You've made this day a special day, by just your being you. There's no person in the whole world like you, and I like you just the way you are." In his memory, take a moment today to let as many people as possible know that…you love them just the way they are!

On **February 27**, the Old Catholic Church celebrates the birth in 1971 of **Bernd Wallet**, who was installed as Archbishop of Utrecht in 2020, thus becoming the 84th successor to St. Willibrord as Old Catholic Archbishop of Utrecht. Pray today for Archbishop Wallet and his flock in the Old Catholic tradition!

Sunday, February 28, 2021

SECOND SUNDAY OF LENT

(purple)

Remember: The *Gloria* and Alleluia are *not* sung today. Lead the congregation in another, easy-to-sing gospel acclamation!

The thread in today's scriptures: Like God, who handed over God's only son (Rom. 8:32), Abraham was willing to sacrifice his son, Isaac. Abraham listened to God (Gen. 22:1-18), and we, too, are called to be faithful servants (Ps. 116:15-16), recognizing and listening (Mk. 9:7) to the transfigured Christ in our world!

Holy humor: Every day, a man walked into the same bar and ordered three beers, which he quietly drank at his own table. One day, the bartender asked him why he always ordered three beers. The man explained that he had two brothers and that they promised that they would always order two extra beers in remembrance of one another. Some time later, the man walked into the bar and only ordered two beers. "My condolences," the bartender said. "Am I correct in thinking that one of your brothers passed?" "No," the man said. "My brothers are alive and well, but I decided to give up drinking for Lent—so these two beers are for my brothers!" [Segue into the nature of faithfulness and covenants, then to the story of Abraham.]

Looking for a visual aid for your homily or object lesson? Consider pouring sand from one clear glass to another. Ask listeners to guess how many grains of sand are in the glass. Just imagine the promise made to Abraham and Sarah: that their descendants would be as numerous as "the sands of the seashore" (Gen. 22:17)!

Will you be sharing any **Easter cards** this year with those who support the ministries of your community? If so, you might begin thinking now about the design and printing of Easter cards!

On **February 28**, we remember the passing of **Martin Bucer** (1491-1551), the German Dominican friar who renounced his vows to champion Church reform. Excommunicated by the Roman church, he attempted to reconcile Martin Luther and Ulrich Zwingli, who differed on Eucharistic theology. An early pioneer of ecumenism, he later brought reformers together to agree to the Tetrapolitan Confession and the Wittenberg Concord, and he attempted to unite Roman Catholics and Protestants into a national German church separate from Rome. In his memory, pray for all who use their gifts to build bridges and bring together people of differing perspectives!

On **February 28**, we remember the passing of **Hugh George de Willmott Newman** (1905-1979), the Independent Catholic bishop known as Mar Georgius I, whose conditional "cross-consecration" with bishops from 1945 to 1955 resulted in the consolidation of several lines of apostolic succession that were subsequently shared with hundreds of bishops around the world. In his memory, share a prayer of thanksgiving for all who have allowed Independent Catholics throughout the world to enjoy the Church's sacraments!

On **February 28**, the Ethiopian Orthodox Tewahedo Church celebrates the anniversary of the appointment in 2013 of Teklemariam Asrat as **Catholicos and Co-Patriarch Abune Mathias I**. In a spirit of ecumenism, pray for him and for the people he serves!

On **February 29**, the Church celebrates **St. Auguste Chapdelaine** (1814-1856), the French missionary whose beating, hanging and beheading in China sparked the Second Opium War, which concluded with a treaty allowing Christian missionaries to spread their faith and own property in China. Pray for all whose suffering paved the path for others to enjoy the lives they live!

On **February 29**, the Eastern Orthodox Church celebrates the birth in 1940 of **Dimitrios Arhondonis**, who became Ecumenical Patriarch Bartholomew I of Constantinople. In a spirit of ecumenism, pray for him and for the 260 million Eastern Orthodox Catholics he serves!

In **March**, we remember the passing of **Jacques Lefèvre d'Étaples** (c. 1455-1536), the French theologian and biblical translator who attempted to reform the Roman church from within. Though he enjoyed the friendship and protection of King Francis I of France, many of his ideas were condemned as heretical—including his suggestion that Mary

Magdalene, Mary the sister of Lazarus, and the woman who anointed Jesus' feet were different women. In his memory, expand your knowledge of contemporary insights into our Christian scriptures!

On **March 1**, the World Evangelical Alliance celebrates the anniversary of the installation in 2015 of **Secretary-General Efraim Tendero**. In a spirit of ecumenism, pray for him and for the 600 million Evangelicals he serves!

On **March 3**, the Church celebrates **St. Katharine Drexel** (1858-1955), the American heiress-turned-educator who dedicated her life to Native Americans west of the Mississippi. Consider how you are working for racial justice, and inspire philanthropists with stories of their matron saint!

On **March 3**, we remember the passing of **Franz Heinrich Reusch** (1823-1900), the Roman Catholic priest excommunicated for his stance against purported papal infallibility. He went on to exercise his priestly ministry in the Old Catholic Church, serving as Vicar General for Old Catholic Bishop Joseph Reinkens—a position he resigned when the German Old Catholic Church allowed clergy to marry. A prolific writer, he served on the Old Catholic theological faculty at the University of Bonn and was the official reporter of the Reunion Conferences held in Bonn during those years. In his memory, pray for all who struggle to find a home in the various manifestations of the Catholic Church!

On **March 3**, the Russian Old Orthodox Church celebrates the anniversary of the installation in 2003 of Alexander Kalinin as **Patriarch Alexander of Moscow and all Russia**. In a spirit of ecumenism, pray for him and for the people he serves!

On **March 4**, we remember the passing of **Rupert of Deutz** (c. 1075-1129), the Benedictine exegete who wrote widely on liturgy and music. He was criticized for his support of impanation, the belief that the bread and wine are united to Christ's divine person. Consider how you encourage the musical gifts of others and alternate expressions of the great mystery that is the Eucharist!

On **March 4**, the Church celebrates **St. Casimir** (1458-1484), the Polish prince renowned for his piety and devotion. He was made weak from fasting, and he died of a lung disease. Pray and/or reach out today to those who might be growing weak under the burdens of life!

On **March 4**, we remember the passing of **Peter Richard Kenrick** (1806-1896), the Roman Catholic archbishop of St. Louis, Missouri, who courageously stood against American Ultramontane bishops and opposed the definition of purported papal infallibility at the First Vatican Council. He wrote, "We think it most inopportune to define as a dogma of faith an opinion which seems to us a novelty in the Church, destitute of solid foundation in Scripture and Tradition, and contradicted by indisputable evidence." Subsequent harassment caused him to turn over his archdiocese to his coadjutor. In his memory, pray for all who take courageous stands on issues, knowing that such strong stands may result in unexpected consequences!

On **March 5**, we celebrate the birth in 1933 of **Walter Kasper**, the German Roman Catholic cardinal and theologian who built bridges between various denominations as President of the Pontifical Council for Promoting Christian Unity. For 10 years, he met with like-minded cardinals to discuss reforms of the Roman church with respect to such issues as collegiality, the appointment of bishops, the primacy of the papacy, and the Church's approach to sexual morality. He is known for his proposal to admit divorced and remarried couples to communion — but also for his criticism of the Anglican Church, for its allowance of female clergy and same-sex marriage. In his honor, pray for all who esteem and work to strengthen ecumenical relations!

On **March 5**, we celebrate the birth in 1963 of **Joel Scott Osteen**, the American televangelist and author whose sermons are viewed by seven million viewers each week. He has written ten books that have been ranked #1 on *The New York Times* bestseller list. In his honor, listen to one of his sermons and/or read a chapter from one of his books, to see what you might learn and apply to your own style of preaching, teaching and community building!

On **March 5**, the Syro-Malankara Catholic Church (in union with Rome) celebrates the anniversary of the installation in 2007 of Isaac Thottumkal as **Moran Mor Baselios Cleemis, Major Archbishop-Catholicos of Trivandrum**. In a spirit of ecumenism, pray for him and for the 500,000 Syro-Malankara Catholics he serves!

Sunday, March 7, 2021
THIRD SUNDAY OF LENT
(purple)

Remember: The *Gloria* and Alleluia are *not* sung today. Lead the congregation in another, easy-to-sing gospel acclamation!

Choose the first reading you'll proclaim: the longer version of the Ten Commandments, which includes two very long sentences on the bad theology of intergenerational punishment by God (plus three long sentences on the sabbath), or the more sensible, shorter version.

The thread in today's scriptures: Jesus, "the wisdom of God...wiser than human wisdom" (1Cor. 1:24-25), interpreted the actions of the moneychangers in the temple as an affront to God (Jn. 2:13-16). Placing money above God is forbidden by the Ten Commandments (Ex. 20:1-17) — memorized by children as "wisdom to the simple" (Ps. 19:8) — guidance on how to avoid sinning against God and others!

Holy humor: Think about this: The next time someone asks you, "What would Jesus do?" remind them that freaking out and flipping over tables is something Jesus did! [Segue into Jesus' actions in today's gospel, a sign of his faithfulness to God and to God's commands!]

Looking for a visual aid for your homily or object lesson? Consider using the physical space in which you find yourself! What did it take to build that church or home in which you find yourselves? How long do you imagine it took? How would you have responded if you heard Jesus say that he'd rebuild the temple in three days — and what was Jesus really talking about? [The last answer is in Jn. 2:21!]

If you have Elect (a.k.a., catechumens who have celebrated the Rite of Election and are preparing to receive sacraments at the Easter Vigil), celebrate the **First Scrutiny** during Mass today!

Daylight Saving Time begins next Sunday: Be sure to remind people to "spring forward" — or they'll arrive an hour late for Mass!

March is here! **For the intellectually-curious**, share a lesson on the etymology of this month! Named after Mars, the Roman god of war, March was the month to resume military campaigns interrupted by the winter. As the outside world thaws, reflect on those "frozen" aspects of your life that might benefit from a bit of thawing!

On **March 7**, when it doesn't fall on a Sunday, the Church celebrates **Ss. Perpetua and Felicity** (+c. 203), the wealthy noblewoman and slave girl who were united through their martyrdom. Both were mothers of very young children. Pray Eucharistic Prayer I, which mentions them, and find a way to acknowledge the many sacrifices parents make as they "lay down their lives" for their children!

On **March 7**, we celebrate the birth in 1946 of **Daniel Goleman**, the journalist and author best known for his longtime bestseller, *Emotional Intelligence*. He has written on a wide variety of topics, including self-deception, creativity, transparency, meditation, and the ecological crisis. In his honor, consider how you might enhance your own EQ—and that of those around you!

On **March 8**, the Church celebrates **St. John of God** (1495-1550), who suffered temporary insanity, was sobered by life inside the mental institutions of his day, and dedicated the rest of his life to ministering to those living in such places. Take advantage of this day to raise awareness of the mental illnesses that afflict one in every four to five American adults!

On **March 8**, the Armenian Apostolic Church celebrates the birth in 1947 of **Pedros Keshishian**, who would become Catholicos Aram I of Cilicia. In his honor, pray for him and for the 9 million people he serves!

On **March 9**, the Church celebrates **St. Frances of Rome** (1384-1440), who inspired the wealthy of her day to visit the poor and to care for the sick. In a spirit of Lenten almsgiving, share of your time, talent and/or treasure with the poor and the sick in your community!

On **March 9**, we remember the passing of **Josef Fuchs** (1912-2005), the German Jesuit theologian credited with achieving in moral theology what Karl Rahner had accomplished in systematic theology. He chaired the Pontifical Commission on Population, Family and Birth, whose report on artificial birth control within marriage was rejected by Paul VI. In his memory, pray for all who struggle with the very real conundrum of differing with those who hold power over them!

On **March 10**, we remember the passing of **Richard of Saint Victor** (+1173), the Scottish philosopher and mystical theologian known for his dogmatic theology on the Trinity and his psychological analysis of the contemplative experience. Pause today to reacquaint yourself with his works!

On **March 11**, we celebrate the birth in 1933 of **Walter Brueggemann**, the American Protestant theologian widely considered one of the most influential Old Testament scholars of the 20th century. His research has focused on the Hebrew prophetic tradition and the sociopolitical imagination of the Church. In his honor, consider how prophetic your stances really are toward consumerism, militarism and nationalism!

On **March 12**, we remember the passing of **Denis the Carthusian**, the Limburgish theologian, mystic and "Ecstatic Doctor" who divided each day between prayer and his study and writing. He detailed the purgative, illuminative and unitive stages of the path to supernatural wisdom, and was consulted as an oracle by bishops and princes. In his memory, consider where you are on the path to wisdom — and possible actions for taking a step in the direction of union with God!

On **March 12**, we celebrate the birth in 1936 of **Michał Kazimierz Heller**, the Polish priest and professor of philosophy and science who has authored more than 50 books and who received the Templeton Prize for his attempts to reconcile the "known scientific world with the unknowable dimensions of God." His current research provides new perspectives on quantum entanglement and the EPR paradox. In his honor, consider your own attempts to simultaneously honor what science tells us about our world, and "the root of all possible causes" that forms the foundation of our faith tradition!

On **March 13**, we remember the passing of **Johann Gropper** (1503-1559), the Westphalian cardinal whose "most detailed and most important pre-Tridentine dogmatic of the Reformation period" was placed on the Index of Forbidden Books. A student of Erasmus, he rooted his writings in scripture and the Church Fathers. Gropper was denounced to the Inquisition and died in poverty. In his memory, pray for all who faithfully serve institutions that later disappoint them!

On **March 13**, the Roman Catholic Church celebrates the anniversary of the installation in 2013 of Jorge Mario Bergoglio as **Pope Francis**. In a spirit of ecumenism, pray for him and for the 1.3 billion Roman Catholics he serves!

Sunday, March 14, 2021
FOURTH SUNDAY OF LENT
(rose or purple)

It's *Laetare* **Sunday**:

- Pull out the **rose vestments**, if you have them; make sure they're ironed or steamed!
- Incorporate **small touches of rose** into your otherwise-stark worship environment!

Remember: The *Gloria* and Alleluia are *not* sung today. Lead the congregation in another, easy-to-sing gospel acclamation!

Note: **The introductory line of today's second reading is misleading**. The Letter to the Ephesians is a pseudonymous letter, written in Paul's name and spirit, but not written by Paul. Rather than confuse your listeners, begin with, "A reading from the Letter to the Ephesians"!

Choose the gospel you'll proclaim: the excruciatingly-long first version, which always fails to hold the attention of listeners, or the more sensible, shorter version, which will be supplemented by your preaching.

The thread in today's scriptures: What irony that the man born blind could see—while the Pharisees were "blind" (Jn. 9:1-41)! Similarly, Jesse failed to recognize the anointed one in his family (1Sam. 16). Anointed (Ps. 23:5), filled with the Light of Christ, and trusting that God will shepherd us through the dark valleys of life (Ps. 23:1 & 4), we strive to be "light in the Lord, [living] as children of light" (Eph. 5:8)!

Holy humor: There are a plethora of blind jokes. My favorite blind joke is about the nun who was told by her mother superior to paint a certain room in the convent without getting a drop of paint on her habit. The nun found herself in a quandary: How would she paint the room without getting a drop of paint on her habit? She decided to lock the door, take off her habit, and paint the room…in her underclothes! All was well until there was a knock at the door. She froze, then asked, "Who is it?" "Blind man," said the voice on the other side of the door. A blind man? What harm would come from her opening the door in her underclothes to a blind man, right? She opened the door. Surprised, the man said, "Nice underclothes, Sister. Where would you like me to put these window blinds?" [Segue from the "blind man" who saw, to the blind man who saw in today's gospel—and the blindness of the Pharisees who had sight.]

Looking for a visual aid for your homily or object lesson? Consider a blindfold — a symbol of those things that keep us from seeing and of how it is that, even possessing the gift of sight (like the Pharisees in today's gospel), we can sometimes be "blind"!

If you have Elect (a.k.a., catechumens who have celebrated the Rite of Election and are preparing to receive sacraments at the Easter Vigil), celebrate the **Second Scrutiny** during Mass today!

On **March 14**, we remember the passing of **Virgilio P. Elizondo** (1935-2016), the Mexican-American Roman Catholic priest and activist who was a leading scholar of Hispanic theology and Latin American liberation theology. Widely regarded as "the father of U.S. Latino religious thought," he examined the similarities between Jesus' Galilean background and the *mestizo* experience. He viewed Our Lady of Guadalupe as the ultimate symbol and product of *mestizaje*, the mixing of people of different backgrounds. In his memory, reacquaint yourself with any one of his many works!

On **March 16**, we remember the passing of **Christoph von Utenheim** (1450-1527), the Swiss bishop who unsuccessfully advocated for reform of the Roman church. His attempts to reform abuses in his diocese were resisted by his cathedral chapter. Pray for all who whose innovative spirits are opposed by others!

On **March 16**, we celebrate the birth in 1955 of **Tina Beattie**, the English professor of Catholic Studies who has raised awareness of social justice, non-violence, women's rights, same-sex marriage and women's ordination. Beattie has challenged the Roman church's teachings on contraception and has advocated for a more-nuanced ethical approach to the question of early abortion. In her honor, consider how you are raising awareness of the key social justice issues that intersect with theology!

On **March 17**, the Church celebrates **St. Patrick** (c. 415-493), the Romano/British missionary and "Apostle of Ireland." Reflect on his analogy of the shamrock for the mystery of the Trinity and/or note that the color originally associated with St. Patrick was…blue!

On **March 17**, we celebrate the birth in 1948 of **George Augustus Stalling, Jr.**, the Roman Catholic priest excommunicated after announcing on the Phil Donahue Show his renouncement of papal authority and the Roman church's teachings on contraception, abortion, homosexuality and divorce. Known as the first Independent Catholic in the U.S. to gather together a vibrant Black community, he founded the Imani Temple African American Catholic Congregation in Washington,

D.C. In his honor, consider how you might better esteem and lift up our Black sisters and brothers!

On **March 17**, the Armenian Apostolic Church celebrates the birth in 1962 of **Sahag Maşalyan**, who would become Patriarch Sahag II Mashalian of Constantinople. Pray for him and for the 9 million people he serves!

On **March 18**, the Church celebrates **St. Cyril of Jerusalem** (c. 315 - c. 386), the early Church theologian thrice-exiled for teaching that Jesus was fully divine. He sold his gifts from the emperor, to raise money for the poor. If you're hosting a parish auction in place of the St. Joseph Table (see March 19), connect what you're doing to the actions of this saint. If not, consider your own support for those in need!

On **March 19**, the Church celebrates the **Solemnity of St. Joseph**, Jesus' stepfather and the patron saint of workers and of the Universal Church!

- Wear white — and the *Gloria* may be sung today.

- Pray the **Litany of St. Joseph** and consider **cultural celebrations**, like the St. Joseph Blessing of Bread, the blessing of the St. Joseph Table (a Sicilian tradition of blessing food principally intended for the poor) and/or the sharing of ravioli (another Italian tradition) on this day! If you're in New Orleans, build your three-tiered St. Joseph altar and bake your *pupa cu l'ova*!

- **For the intellectually-curious**, share a lesson on what the scriptures say (and don't say) about today's saint. Note that he was a *tekton* (literally, a handyman, and *not* a carpenter, as mistranslation and popular imagination suggest), that he protected Jesus from the slaughter of the Innocents, and that there is no mention of him after Luke's story of the child Jesus in the temple. Explain that we infer that he died prior to Jesus' public ministry, and certainly before Jesus' death (or else he would have claimed Jesus' body from the cross). Share the tradition of him dying in the arms of Jesus and Mary, and thus being known today as the patron of a happy death. Also, speak to the superstitions and shamanistic rituals related to this saint (e.g., burying a statue of St. Joseph upside-down to sell your home, stealing a lemon from the St. Joseph altar to find a spouse, the carrying of blessed fava beans as a talisman, and freezing bread to ward off hurricanes).

- As an alternative to the St. Joseph Table, consider hosting a **Lenten auction** of donated breads and homemade pastas, with the income designated for a Lenten alms project.

On **March 19**, we remember the passing of **Péter Pázmány** (1570-1637), the Hungarian Jesuit who was a noted statesman, philosopher, theologian and cardinal. An important figure in the Counter-Reformation of Hungary, he created the Hungarian literary language. In his memory, pray for the people of Hungary who continue to benefit from his legacy!

On **March 19**, we celebrate the birth in 1928 of **Hans Küng**, the Swiss Catholic priest, theologian and author known for his rejection of purported papal infallibility. Despite not being officially allowed to share Roman Catholic theology, Küng continues to teach ecumenical theology at the University of Tübingen. In his honor, pray for all who are persecuted for following their Spirit-enlightened consciences!

On **March 20**, we remember the passing of **Johann Nepomuk Huber** (1830-1879), the German philosopher and theologian who opposed purported papal infallibility and was an early leader in the Old Catholic Church. He attracted attention by pseudonymously co-authoring *The Pope and the Council*, which challenged Ultramontane promoters of the First Vatican Council. He also pseudonymously published *Roman Letters*, a redaction of secret reports leaked from Rome during the Council. In his memory, pray for all who lack the freedoms we take for granted — including freedom of the press!

On **March 20**, we remember the passing of **Christopher Wordsworth** (1807-1885), the English Anglican bishop who wrote several books and hymns, including "Songs of Thankfulness and Praise." He represented the Anglican Church at the Reunion Conferences of 1874 and 1875, where Old Catholic, Anglican and Orthodox clergy convened to discuss possible paths to unification. In his memory, pray for all who continue to open their hearts to and build relationships with persons of different backgrounds!

On **March 20**, we celebrate the birthday in 1943 of **Richard Rohr**, the prolific Franciscan spiritual writer who founded the New Jerusalem Community in Cincinnati and the Center for Action and Contemplation in Albuquerque. Emphasizing an "alternative orthodoxy" that allows for advocacy against such issues as religious-based oppression of LGBTQ persons, Father Richard has inspired millions of readers and listeners. In his honor, ruminate on a few paragraphs of his wisdom!

Sunday, March 21, 2021

FIFTH SUNDAY OF LENT

(purple)

Remember: The *Gloria* and Alleluia are *not* sung today. Lead the congregation in another, easy-to-sing gospel acclamation!

Note: **The introductory line of today's second reading is misleading**. The Letter to the Hebrews is a pseudonymous letter, written in Paul's name and spirit, but not written by Paul. To avoid this confusion, you might proclaim, "A reading from the Letter to the Hebrews."

The thread in today's scriptures: On this last Sunday before Palm Sunday, we see Jesus reflecting on his impending death, from which God could save him (Heb. 5:7), though he would not pray for this (Jn. 12:27). Lent is an appropriate time for spiritual "spring cleaning" — for praying that God might "create a clean heart in [us]" (Ps. 51:12) and place God's law of love within our hearts (Jer. 31:33)!

Holy humor: There once was a man who knew the year he was going to die. In fact, he also knew the month he was going to die. Even more specifically, he knew the very day he was going to die. And, as if that weren't enough, he even knew the hour that he was going to die. How did he know? The judge told him! [Segue into Jesus knowing of his death (in today's gospel) and not shying away from it. Not knowing the year, month, day or hour of our deaths, are we living with a clean heart? Is it clear to others that we're living with God's law of love within our hearts?]

Looking for a visual aid for your homily or object lesson? Consider a feather duster and/or a rag and a cleaning agent. As part of spring cleaning and Easter preparations, many of us are cleaning our homes. As we approach Holy Week, are we also focused on the "cleanliness" of our hearts?

If you have Elect (a.k.a., catechumens who have celebrated the Rite of Election and are preparing to receive sacraments at the Easter Vigil), celebrate the **Third (and final) Scrutiny** during Mass today!

Have you hosted a **Lenten reconciliation service** already? If not, consider a communal celebration of the sacrament today!

On **March 21**, we remember the passing of **Jean Guitton** (1901-1999), the French philosopher and theologian who was the first lay person to be invited to be an observer of the Second Vatican Council. During the course of 60 years, he authored some 50 books on a wide range of philosophical and theological topics. In his memory, pause to consider the great gifts of the lay persons who enrich the Church!

On **March 21**, the Roman Catholic Church celebrates the anniversary of the installation in 2003 of **Filipe Neri António Sebastião do Rosário Ferrão** as Latin Patriarch of the East Indies. In a spirit of ecumenism, pray for him and for the Roman Catholics he serves!

On **March 21**, we remember the passing of **Vekoslav Grmič** (1923-2005), the Slovenian bishop and theologian known as "the red bishop" for his strong Socialist leanings. A supporter of liberation theology, of the political-religious thought of Swiss reformer Hans Küng, and of the collaboration of the Catholic Church with Marxism in Yugoslavia, Grmič was removed from his bishopric by John Paul II. He was the author of more than 40 books and several translations. In his memory, pray for all who champion the apostolic ideals of shared ownership of resources and the equitable distribution of goods and services in our world!

On **March 21**, the Church of England celebrates the anniversary of the installation in 2013 of **Archbishop Justin Portal Welby of Canterbury**. In a spirit of ecumenism, pray for him and for the 85 million Anglicans he serves!

On **March 22**, we celebrate the birth in 1930 of **Joseph Bracken**, the American Jesuit philosopher and theologian who has attempted to synthesize Christian trinitarian doctrine with the process theology of Alfred North Whitehead and Charles Hartshorne. In his honor, reacquaint yourself with Bracken's works and/or with the works of process theology!

On **March 22**, we remember the passing of **Clemente Domínguez y Gómez** (1946-2005), one of the more bizarre stories in the Independent Sacramental Movement! Domínguez y Gómez was a blind Palmarian bishop (consecrated by Roman Catholic archbishop Pierre Martin Ngô Đình Thục) who claimed to enjoy apparitions and the stigmata, and who proclaimed himself the successor of Pope Paul VI, took the name Pope Gregory XVII, and reigned for only 11 days less than his "rival," Pope John Paul II. He admitted sexual improprieties with several of his priests and nuns, and was satirized in the Spanish film "*Manuel y Clemente*." In his memory, pray for all whose eccentricities and questionable words and actions cast long shadows over the Independent Sacramental Movement!

On **March 23**, the Church celebrates **St. Turibius of Mogrovejo** (1538-1606), the Spanish nobleman who traveled all of Peru as bishop there. He is most known for baptizing St. Rose of Lima (the first saint of the

Americas) and St. Martin de Porres, and for his defense of the native peoples against the injustices of the Spanish government. In his honor, commit to doing a better job of visiting those entrusted to your spiritual care, and consider how you might better advocate for those who suffer injustice in our world!

On **March 23**, we remember the passing of **Henry Nutcombe Oxenham** (1829-1888), the English Anglican priest who converted to the Roman church, traveled to Germany, and began a friendship with Döllinger, whose work he translated to English. He also translated Hefele's *History of the Councils of the Church*, and he published several pamphlets on the reunion of Christian churches. In his memory, pray in a special way for all who support us in our ministry and in our efforts to bring unity to the Body of Christ!

On **March 24**, the Church celebrates **St. Óscar Arnulfo Romero y Galdámez** (1917-1980), the archbishop of San Salvador who spoke out against poverty and violence during the civil war in El Salvador. Hailed as a hero by social activists and liberation theologians, Romero actively denounced violations of human rights, particularly against the most vulnerable. As a result, the United Nations has proclaimed March 24 as International Day for the Right to the Truth Concerning Gross Human Rights Violations and for the Dignity of Victims. In Romero's memory, pause to consider how you are defending human rights and promoting the dignity of those who suffer violence!

On **March 25**, the Church celebrates the **Annunciation**—the archangel Gabriel's appearance to Mary of Nazareth with the incredible news that she would conceive and bear God's Son!

- If you want to place **an image of the Annunciation** in your worship space, search for one that portrays Mary as something other than a literate, Italian noblewoman. Decorate the image with **candles and lilies** or other white flowers.
- Invite an art historian to talk about the **iconography of Mary**.
- Find time to pray the Joyful Mysteries of the Rosary—or at least **the first Joyful Mystery**.
- Wear white, and the *Gloria* can be sung today.
- **For the intellectually-curious**, explain the timing of this solemnity (exactly nine months before the celebration of Jesus' birth), and the different annunciation stories in Matthew and Luke.
- Many **women's religious communities** celebrate this day with great festivity: Take a moment to pray a rosary for the religious

sisters who have touched your life, and consider gathering together those who might be open to discerning their own vocation to religious life and/or ordained ministry in the Church!

On **March 25**, we remember the passing of **Marcel François Marie Joseph Lefebvre** (1905-1991), the French Roman Catholic bishop who was a leading conservative voice at Vatican II. Lefebvre founded the Society of Saint Pius X for seminarians, then consecrated four bishops in 1988 against the expressed prohibition of Pope John Paul II, who excommunicated him and the four bishops he had consecrated. In his memory, pray for persons of all theological stripes who seek to live their Catholic faith outside the structures and strictures of Rome!

On **March 25**, the Maronite Catholic Church (in union with Rome) celebrates the anniversary of the installation in 2011 of **Bechara Boutros al-Rahi** as Cardinal Patriarch of Antioch. In a spirit of ecumenism, pray for him and for the 3.5 million Maronite Catholics he serves!

On **March 25**, the Roman Catholic Church celebrates the anniversary of the installation in 2012 of **Francesco Moraglia** as Latin Patriarch of Venice. In a spirit of ecumenism, pray for him and for the Roman Catholics he serves!

On **March 26**, we remember the passing of **Eduard Herzog** (1841-1924), the Swiss priest and theologian who became the first Old Catholic bishop in Switzerland. After the First Vatican Council, he expressed his opposition to purported papal infallibility at the Old Catholic Congress of 1872 and began serving as an Old Catholic priest and professor. He was consecrated by Joseph Reinkens of the German Old Catholic Church and was subsequently excommunicated by Pius IX. In his memory, pray for all who have the courage to step outside the institutions they love, in order to faithfully follow the promptings of the Spirit!

On **March 26**, we remember the passing on Palm Sunday in 1961 of **Carlos Duarte Costa** (1888-1961), the Roman Catholic bishop who shared valid lines of apostolic succession without the permission of the Roman papacracy. Known by many as St. Carlos of Brazil, the patron saint of Independent Catholicism, he was a vocal critic of papal encyclicals, of clergy and popes with loyalties to Nazi and Fascist regimes, and of the Brazilian government's mistreatment of the poor. Honor his memory by considering how courageous you are in denouncing mistruths and mistreatment!

On **March 27**, we remember the passing of **Friedrich zu Schwarzenberg** (1809-1885), the Austrian prince who became archbishop of Salzburg at age 26 and a cardinal at age 33. He was sympathetic to the adversities suffered by Reformers and their families as a result of being expelled from the empire. He zealously defended his teacher, Anton Günther, repeatedly appealing to Rome to prevent the condemnation of Günther's writings. In his memory, pray for all our friends and advocates in other churches—including the Roman church—who courageously speak up for and defend us!

On **March 27**, the Ukrainian Greek Catholic Church (in union with Rome) celebrates the anniversary of the installation in 2011 of **Sviatoslav Shevchuk** as Patriarch of Kyiv-Galicia. In a spirit of ecumenism, pray for him and for the 4.5 million Ukrainian Greek Catholics he serves!

Sunday, March 28, 2021
PALM SUNDAY
(red)

"Get your palms!" **Let people know when your Palm Sunday Masses are**—and they'll show up!

Decorate your worship space!
- Decorate with **plentiful palm plants and fronds**, using them to draw attention to the altar and ambo.
- Use **red ribbon** to attach large fronds to the processional cross.
- Consider a **long red runner** hanging down over the sides of an otherwise bare altar.
- Be sure all **red vestments** are ironed or steamed—and that they match any other shades of red used in the worship space. If there is a procession, be sure to steam the **cope** as well!
- **Continue the decoration** into the entrance to your worship space, outdoors, and into other spaces on the grounds, including your Blessed Sacrament chapel, parish hall, and classrooms. Pique the curiosity of congregants and passersby with outdoor touches of palms and red ribbon!

Be sure to familiarize yourself with the details of today's rite!
- Decide whether you'll have a **solemn or simple entrance**.
- Be sure your deacon is **prepared to proclaim both gospels** today.
- Have **a bowl of holy water and an aspergillum** on hand for the blessing of palms, and think through whether your worship

space permits a procession with the palms. Consider swapping out your metal aspergillum (which likely shares very few drops of water with every swing) for a natural broom sprinkler adorned with red ribbons.

- If you'll have a procession, **prepare a song to accompany the ritual action**, and be sure those leading the procession (viz., your thurifer, cross bearer & candle bearers) know the route you'll use.
- If you'll use **incense**, be sure the thurible, charcoals, and boat of incense are prepared.
- If processing with several people and/or a long distance, **think through how you'll sustain the singing in unison throughout the procession**. To maintain singing, place gifted vocalists at the beginning, middle and end of the procession.
- If you'll be using a **cope** during the procession, prepare your altar servers to know when to take it from you, and when to hand you your chasuble.
- Let your altar servers know that **the passion will be proclaimed without incense or candles**.
- If the passion will be proclaimed by multiple people, be sure you have sufficient copies and that all ministers are prepared.

Have hospitality ministers share palms with congregants as they arrive. Instead of skimping, order plenty of extra palms and encourage congregants to take an extra palm to share with a homebound family member, friend or neighbor. Be sure, though, to **divide your supply of palms across all your Masses**, so that the last Mass won't be left without sufficient palms!

Remember: The *Gloria* and Alleluia are *not* sung today. Lead the congregation in another, easy-to-sing gospel acclamation.

Be sure the person who proclaims (or begins) **the passion** knows that there is no greeting ("The Lord be with you") before the passion, nor is the Book of the Gospels signed before proclaiming the passion. Consider dividing the proclamation of the passion among various voices, but know that only a deacon asks for the blessing of the presider before proclaiming the gospel. Or, even better, have various cantors chant the passion this year, to highlight the solemnity of this day!

During the proclamation of the passion, remember to **kneel for a prolonged period of silence after Jesus' death**. Remember: True silence begins when all shuffling, rustling and other noises end. Find a way to say this without words (e.g., in your Mass program and/or PowerPoint), so that all will know to kneel in silence to reflect on Jesus' death.

Choose the gospel you'll proclaim at the beginning of Mass: Mark's more-extended account, which includes details of the securing of the processional colt, or John's more-succinct telling of the same story.

The thread in today's scriptures: The "roller coaster" of Holy Week has begun: Today's first gospel (Mk. 11:1-10 or Jn. 12:12-16) begins on an extremely high note, with the people of Jerusalem acclaiming Jesus as king. By the end of today's second gospel (Mk. 14:1−15:47), the same people have clamored for Jesus' crucifixion, and he has been executed. We'll again hear the story of his passion and death on Good Friday, but we know his descent to the dead is not the end of the story — and, at the Easter Vigil, we'll celebrate his rising to new life! We all pass through dark valleys, when we feel the buffets and beatings of life (Is. 50:6), perhaps when we even feel abandoned by God (Ps. 22:1). Paul's words (Phil. 2:6-11) gives us the hope that we, too, might one day be exalted with Christ!

Holy humor: We just heard the proclamation of Jesus' death on the cross, so skip any attempts at humor. Today's solemn celebration marks the beginning of Holy Week. Perhaps it's best to try another "hook" to grab listeners' attention today? It could be as simple as a show of hands: How many of us have ever ridden a roller coaster? How many of us love roller coasters? How many of us would never ride a roller coaster, even if we were paid to? Segue into the "roller coaster" of Holy Week, which has already "left the station"!

Looking for a visual aid for your homily or object lesson? Consider drawing a big counter-clockwise circle in the air (so that it appears clockwise to your listeners) and/or appealing to the palms with which we began this liturgy! Saint Bonaventure was fond of the image of the circle: Christ started in heaven (start with your hand above your head), then came down to earth (begin drawing the circle counter-clockwise, so that it's clockwise from the vantage of your listeners, until you reach the bottommost point of the circle), and was exalted to the heavens again (complete the circle)! The palms we hold today remind us of the same polarities: They were waved to proclaim victory, and they are burned to make the ashes that recall our own deaths. Christians know that death does not have the final word — and that what goes down…must come up!

Know that many families who leave after Mass today will not return until next Sunday: **Encourage them to be part of your *Triduum* celebrations!** Be sure that everyone leaves Mass today knowing your *Triduum* schedule. Consider printing special postcards for those who might be willing to help spread word of your Triduum services this week. As we enter Holy Week, encourage congregants to re-read the passion narrative later today or sometime this week.

In some places, Palm Sunday is known as **Carling Sunday**, named for carling peas. In other places, it's known as **Fig Sunday**, due to the tradition that Jesus ate figs after his entry into Jerusalem. If you're looking for appropriate dishes to share after Mass, consider split pea soup, peas porridge, and/or figs!

Holy Week is the traditional time for the annual **Chrism Mass**.

- If your bishop is joining you for the Triduum, consider when you'll celebrate the Chrism Mass as a community. Know that **Tuesday is a common day** for this celebration.

- **Spread word of the celebration**, so that all can join you in this **celebration of the priesthood** — complete with the blessing of the oils that we'll use during the next year!

- Be sure to incorporate **the burning of this year's holy oils** as part of your parish mission or a Lenten night of prayer: Simply pour the oils into a flame-resistant receptacle and add a wick!

On **March 30**, we remember the passing of **Joachim of Fiore** (c. 1135-1202), the Italian theologian considered the most important apocalyptic medieval thinker. Inspiring an entire movement of "Joachimites," he prophesied the coming Age of the Holy Spirit — a new dispensation of love that would supersede the law. Though Joachim was held in high regard, all the ideas and movements around him were condemned. In his memory, consider how you contribute to the "Age of the Holy Spirit"!

On **March 30**, we celebrate the birth in 1934 of **Charles E. Curran**, the Roman Catholic priest and moral theologian known for his dissenting views on contraception, his co-authoring of a response to *Humanae Vitae*, and his suggestion in 1971 that homosexual acts within committed relationships may not be morally evil. In 1986, he was removed from his faculty position at The Catholic University of America for his dissent of the Roman church's moral teaching. His views on divorce, artificial contraception, masturbation, pre-marital sex, and homosexual acts were later condemned by Joseph Ratzinger. In his honor, pray for all moral theologians and persons of faith who, while respecting the teaching office of the Church, find themselves led by the Spirt to disagree with the sometimes-myopic moral views of others!

On **March 30**, we remember the passing of **Karl Rahner** (1904-1984), the renowned 20th-century Jesuit philosopher and theologian. Perhaps the greatest voice on the post-conciliar understanding of the Catholic faith, Rahner was a prolific writer of voluminous—and often difficult-to-understand—works. In his memory, pull one of his works off the shelf and wrestle with a paragraph or two of his profound thought!

On **March 31**, the U.S. celebrates civil rights advocate **César Chávez** (1927-1993): Incorporate his social justice message into your preaching!

On **March 31**, we remember the passing of **Francisco de Osuna** (c. 1492 – c. 1540), the Spanish Franciscan friar who authored some of the most influential spiritual works of 16th-century Spain. His *Third Spiritual Alphabet* shared an ABCs for the spiritual life. Consider how you are making our faith more accessible to persons of all levels of education!

On **March 31**, we remember the passing of **John Norman Davidson Kelly** (1909-1997), the British Anglican priest who specialized in biblical studies, patristics, and early Christian creeds and doctrines. For years, his *Early Christian Creeds* and *Early Christian Doctrines* were standard seminary textbooks. In his memory, thumb through his works and reacquaint yourself with the beliefs of the early Church!

On **March 31**, the Syriac Orthodox Church celebrates the anniversary of the election in 2014 of Sa'id Karim as **Patriarch Ignatius Aphrem II of Antioch and All the East**. In a spirit of ecumenism, pray for him and for the people he serves!

Thursday, April 1, 2021
HOLY THURSDAY
(white)

Remember: Unless you have a Chrism Mass, **no Mass is celebrated today until the evening celebration of the Lord's Supper**. Lent officially ends when your celebration of the Lord's Supper commences, and this evening's celebration is the beginning of a **three-day liturgy**—our *Triduum*: There is no blessing and dismissal tonight or tomorrow, and there is no introductory rite for Good Friday or the Easter Vigil. We begin the Mass of the Lord's Supper with the introductory rite—and the solemn blessing and dismissal will come at the conclusion of this three-day rite, at the Easter Vigil on Saturday night!

Our Easter *Triduum* begins: Be sure to think through the details of your **worship environment** as we transition to white today, then to red for tomorrow, then back to white for the Easter Vigil.

- Use **flowers** in moderation, reserving a full flowering of your worship space for the Easter Vigil.

- Prepare easily-visible **footwashing stations** for the *mandatum*, perhaps even throughout the church. Have on hand **enough pitchers of warm water, basins, towels and a mop**. If using paper towels instead of towels, have baskets or small trash receptacles into which used paper towels can be placed. Designate persons to quietly clean up after the footwashing ritual, with minimal distraction. Have a means for the presider to wash his/her hands after the rite of footwashing, preferably with warm water and soap.

- Create an **altar of repose** conducive to prayer and meditation, perhaps bringing to mind the Synoptic Jesus' prayer in the Garden of Gethsemane. If necessary, place a kneeler for the presider before the altar of repose; otherwise, leave the altar unobstructed. Be sure to have enough seats for those who might wish to spend time in prayer with the Blessed Sacrament.

- Think of possible accents (e.g., candles or *luminarias*) that might **illuminate the journey from your worship space, to the altar of repose**. Beforehand, fill the space with green plants, illuminated by candlelight, and turn off any overhead lights.

- Be sure the **cope** and **humeral veil** are ironed or steamed.

Will you incorporate your **reception of the holy oils** into this Mass? If so, consider the following:

- Will you incorporate this into the introductory rite, or as part of the presentation of gifts?

- Prepare an ambry table in the sanctuary to receive the holy oils.

- Have texts that speak to the symbolism of the oils, and of the function of each.

- To emphasize the symbolism of each oil, consider having a catechist or student carry the Oil of Catechumens, a medical professional carry the Oil of the Sick, and a member of the clergy or someone who has recently received (or will receive) the sacraments of initiation carry the Sacred Chrism!

Be sure to familiarize yourself with the rite of this special day! **Think through how you'll do the washing of feet**:

- Will seats be reserved for this, or will chairs need to be discretely placed and removed?
- Choose an easy-to-sing musical setting for this ritual action, perhaps a Taizé-style refrain or a song that can be sung antiphonally between the cantor and congregation.
- Consider addressing a few pastoral words to those who might find footwashing countercultural and/or awkward.
- If you'll be washing a large number of feet, think through details like the refilling of pitchers (with warm water), the emptying of water basins, and what to do with soiled towels (or paper towels).
- If you'll be removing your chasuble for this rite, let altar servers know if you'll need their assistance with your vestments.
- Will you wash the feet of others, or have a more-inclusive gesture of inviting them to wash one another's feet? If you alone will be washing the feet of others, choose a representative cross-section of women and men, young and wise, healthy and less-mobile, clergy and laity, persons of different language groups, etc. Consider going to them, rather than having them come to you! Be sure your actions are highly visible, so that people are not left wondering "What's happening?"

We're celebrating a solemnity: **Consider using incense!**

- Make sure your thurifer is familiar with all his/her responsibilities and is ready with the thurible (with burning charcoals) and boat: for the hymn of gathering, gospel acclamation, preparation of gifts and the procession to the altar of repose.
- Be sure those who are leading music know that the hymn of gathering and/or preparation of the altar and presentation of gifts may be prolonged due to incensation.
- Be sure your deacon knows how to incense the Book of the Gospels prior to proclaiming the gospel. Remember: If your thurible is on a chain, the closer you hold the chain to the thurible, the more control you'll have over the swinging thurible!
- Be sure to tip off your altar server(s) to the fact that the handwashing will occur *after* the incensation of the altar and gifts!

If you have a multilingual community, **think through how you'll make a single community celebration meaningful to persons of all languages!**

- Consider music that incorporates all languages.
- Divide the scriptures between languages, and, so that all can understand them, consider printing the scriptures in the language in which they're not being proclaimed.
- Have a multilingual psalm and proclamation of the gospel.
- Be sure the presider and homilist are able to easily transition between languages for prayers and preaching, without sharing a homily that's repeated in two languages.
- Share a multilingual invitation to share the sign of peace.
- Invite people to pray the Lord's Prayer in their own languages.
- Rather than guess the language of those coming to communion, train eucharistic ministers to alternate between "The Body of Christ" (or "The Blood of Christ") and its equivalent in the other language(s).

Think through the details of your **procession to the altar of repose**.

- Will you need assistance putting on the cope?
- Will the altar be stripped while you hold the consecrated elements?
- Will incense be used?
- Does the person leading the procession know the route?
- What will you sing during the procession? Is the song easy to sing while walking in the dark? (Remember: *Pange lingua* is the traditional hymn for this in many places, but many people don't know Latin and/or don't know the lyrics well enough to sing them in the dark.) Consider a Taizé-style refrain, or, if you have a Spanish-speaking community, the refrain of "*Bendito, bendito, bendito sea Dios.*"
- To maintain the song, place gifted vocalists at the beginning, middle and end of the procession.
- Beforehand, invite people to stay as long as they wish, to pray before the altar of repose.

Be sure to prepare all ministers, so that they know their role and responsibilities for this special celebration. For the smoothest-possible liturgical experience, consider having a rehearsal!

Have the traditional **ringing of bells** during the *Gloria* — with someone ringing the church bell and/or with altar servers and congregants ringing bells. (Remember to never allow anyone to ring a bell who hasn't practiced in advance: The liturgy is never an appropriate time to practice ringing a bell!) If you have an organ, use it for the *Gloria*. Remember: After the ringing of the bells at the *Gloria* tonight, all bells will remain silent until the *Gloria* at the Easter Vigil.

Inform musicians that, after the singing of the *Gloria*, **the music becomes increasingly solemn this evening**, with musical instruments used after the *Gloria* only to support the singing.

Remember: The Alleluia is *not* sung today. Lead the congregation in another, easy-to-sing gospel acclamation!

The thread in today's scriptures: The Jewish celebration of Passover (Ex. 12:1-8 & 11-14) was an important part of Jesus' faith tradition: God led God's people to life and liberty! Indeed, how can we make a return to the Lord for all the good God has done for us (Ps. 116:12)? As Jesus prepared to celebrate the Passover with his friends, with the traditional bread and wine (1Cor. 11:23-26), he shared with them — and with us — a lesson on servant leadership (Jn. 13:1-15)!

Holy humor: A lot of work goes into planning the liturgies — the services — of Holy Week, so have you heard this one before: What's the difference between a liturgist — a person who plans Masses like this — and a terrorist? If you've been to a seminary — a place where lots of people are planning lots of Masses — you know the answer. What's the difference between a liturgist and a terrorist? You can negotiate with a…terrorist! [Segue into the Johannine Peter's firm-as-a-liturgist attitude against having his feet washed, and the Johannine Jesus' line-in-the-sand statement that servant leadership is a necessary part of discipleship. "Unless I wash your feet, you will have no part with me" (Jn. 13:8) is a clear non-negotiable!]

Looking for a visual aid for your homily or object lesson? Consider an image of the Last Supper and/or a pitcher and basin! Paul provides a snapshot for the foundation of traditional images of the Last Supper — but, interestingly, John provides us a whole different picture: of Jesus stooping down to wash the dirty feet of his friends! We call ourselves followers of Jesus: How often do we humble ourselves and find ways to figuratively "wash one another's feet" (Jn. 13:14-15)?

Will you have a **collection** during this special liturgy? Let your hospitality ministers know!

Many presiders fall into a rut of always using the same eucharistic prayer: **Use a different, perhaps-lengthier eucharistic prayer today**, to bring attention to the Lord's Supper!

If the Blessed Sacrament is brought from the tabernacle before communion, have a minister **leave the tabernacle door open and extinguish the vigil light there**, so that it will be clear that **the tabernacle will remain empty** until the Blessed Sacrament is returned there at the conclusion of the Easter Vigil.

Post-Vatican II communities share the Eucharist under the forms of bread and wine. If your community doesn't ordinarily **share communion under both forms**, consider doing so tonight!

Be prepared for **the many details of the procession to the altar of repose**:

- Have all eucharistic ministers bring any remaining bread and wine to the altar after communion.
- After communion, add incense to the thurible, kneel before the Blessed Sacrament, and incense it three times.
- Put on the humeral veil and take the Blessed Sacrament.
- Remember: Tonight's procession is led by the cross bearer and candle bearers, followed by the assembly, then followed by the thurifer and presider.
- Conduct the procession to the altar of repose with reverence and noble simplicity.
- Be sure that those who lead the procession walk slowly enough that congregants stay together!
- Place the Blessed Sacrament on the altar of repose, or, if it is placed in a tabernacle, leave the door open until after the Blessed Sacrament is incensed there.
- Be sure the thurifer is ready to assist with the incensing of the Blessed Sacrament at the altar of repose.
- Let all ministers know that all (who are able) will kneel before the Blessed Sacrament, and that ministers will *not* leave the space in procession; instead, all ministers will stand, genuflect, and depart, with no formal procession—a functional leaving of ministers, rather than a ritual departure.
- Invite congregants beforehand to remain in prayer before the Blessed Sacrament as long as they'd like.
- Be sure that those who decorate your worship space aren't immediately rushing off after this service to change the décor for

Good Friday—particularly if these actions will be seen or heard by those praying at the altar of repose!

Some churches have a traditional **distribution of loaves** on this night: Visit your local baker and ask him/her to individually package small loaves for you, to which you can add a prayer for the breaking of bread as family!

Friday, April 2, 2021

GOOD FRIDAY

(red, without chasuble/dalmatic)

Good Friday is a somber day:

- We meditate on Jesus' death and entombment. The environment and lack of instrumental music should reflect this.
- Abstain from ringing bells today.
- For those looking for ideas on how to pray on this day, suggest the Stations of the Cross and/or the Sorrowful Mysteries of the rosary.
- Noon is traditionally marked as the hour of Jesus' crucifixion, and 3:00 p.m. as the hour of his death: Know that any services at these hours may be sparsely attended by those who work during the day. Some churches have a *Tre Ore* (three hours) service and/or time of prayer during this time.

Think through **the details of today's worship environment**:

- **Today's color is red, except for the veiling of the cross, which is violet**. Remember, though, that color is used today to highlight, not to decorate.
- **Remove all images and crosses** from your worship space. **Cover with red cloth those images and crosses that can't be removed**.
- **Take away all plants and flowers and candles.**
- **Strip the altar**. (Remember: There are no crosses, candles, bookstands, images or accoutrements on post-Vatican II altars; on this day, in particular, there should be nothing—*nothing*—on the altar.)

- **Empty fonts of holy water**, and consider filling them with sand instead. In this way, people aren't left wondering, "Did someone forget to fill the holy water fonts?"

- There is no need to decorate anything today — but do **cover with a violet cloth the cross that will be used for the adoration of the cross**. Be sure the cross is without a *corpus* (Jesus' body). Let the symbol speak: Find a large cross for this rite, perhaps even inviting an artist in your community to craft this. Before the liturgy, place the cross in a spot where the person carrying it will know where to find it. Have a plan for the cross after the adoration: Ideally, find a way for it to remain upright in the sanctuary.

- No Mass is celebrated today, so **the credence table is not prepared as usual**. Know, though, whether the corporal (and/or any other items) will be brought to the stripped altar during the rite, and by whom.

This is the one day each year in which **no Mass is celebrated anywhere in the world**. Because the chasuble and dalmatic are worn only for the celebration of Mass, be sure to **vest only with alb and stole** — and perhaps with a cope for the presider.

Think through music for this commemoration of the Lord's suffering and death. **Totally abstain today from musical instruments**, and have *a capella* music; or, if necessary, soft accompaniment simply to sustain singing. Also, **prepare a song for the adoration of the cross!**

If the passion will be proclaimed by multiple people, be sure all ministers are prepared and that you have sufficient copies of the passion for them!

Good Friday (like Ash Wednesday) is one of two days of **fasting *and* abstinence** in the Western Church: Invite congregants to participate in this ancient ritual as a way of preparing for the celebration of Christ's resurrection!

If you have a multilingual community, **think through how you'll make a single community celebration meaningful to persons of all languages!**

- Consider music that incorporates all languages.

- Divide the scriptures between languages, and, so that all can understand them, and consider printing the scriptures in the language in which they're not being proclaimed.

- Have a multilingual psalm and proclamation of the gospel.

- Be sure the presider and homilist are able to easily transition between languages for prayers and preaching, without sharing a homily that's repeated in two languages.
- Share a multilingual invitation to share the sign of peace.
- Invite people to pray the Lord's Prayer in their own languages.
- Rather than guess the language of those coming to communion, train eucharistic ministers to alternate between "The Body of Christ" (or "The Blood of Christ") and its equivalent(s) in the other language(s).

Be sure to prepare all ministers, so that they know their role and responsibilities for this special celebration. For the smoothest-possible liturgical experience, consider having a rehearsal!

The liturgy begins in the silence, with the ministers coming to the sanctuary and lying prostrate before the altar.

- The cross, candles and Book of the Gospels are not part of this procession.
- Think through whether all ministers are able to lie prostrate, or whether accommodations need to be made.
- Ideally, all congregants kneel during this action; think through a way of communicating this without speaking it — perhaps with a note in your Mass program and/or PowerPoint.
- While lying prostrate, the presider should allow for a prolonged period of true silence, which begins when all shuffling, rustling, and other noises end.

Remember: The liturgy continues with the collect (opening prayer), but without the customary "Let us pray." (This is a continuation of the liturgy that began last night, so the sign of the cross and greeting are omitted.)

The Alleluia is *not* sung today. Lead the congregation in another, easy-to-sing Gospel Acclamation!

During the proclamation of the passion, remember to **kneel for a prolonged period of silence after Jesus' death**. Remember: True silence begins when all shuffling, rustling and other noises end. Find a way to communicate this without words (e.g., in your Mass program and/or PowerPoint), so that all will know to kneel in silence to reflect on Jesus' death.

Note: **The introductory line of today's second reading is misleading**. The Letter to the Hebrews is a pseudonymous letter, written in Paul's name and spirit, but not written by Paul. To avoid this confusion, you might proclaim, "A reading from the Letter to the Hebrews."

The thread in today's scriptures: Deutero-Isaiah says it well: "Who would believe what we have heard?" (Is. 53:1). Like the Lord's servant (Is. 52:13 – 53:12), Jesus suffered and was led to the slaughter (Jn. 18:1 – 19:42). We believe that "he suffered, and, when he was made perfect, he became the source of eternal salvation for all" (Heb. 5:9), and so we trust in God, saying with the Johannine Jesus: "Father, into your hands I commend my spirit" (Ps. 31:5).

Looking for a visual aid for your homily or object lesson? Consider foregoing any type of object lesson today. Today's environment is stark. Today's liturgy is somber. Keep your words brief. Let silence speak.

Today is an especially appropriate day for **periods of silence** during the liturgy. Consider a moment of prolonged silence after your homily.

Think through **how you'll bring the cross into your worship space**:

- Will the deacon retrieve it alone or be accompanied by altar servers with candles?
- Be sure the person who holds it has practiced the chant "Behold the wood."
- Instruct him/her to pause three times: inside the entrance to the church, in the middle of the church, and at the entrance to the sanctuary.

Think through **how you'll perform the adoration of the cross**:

- What will you sing, and will congregants know how to respond?
- Who will lead the adoration of the cross, and who will invite congregants to participate in this action?
- Will hospitality ministers assist the flow of people?
- Remember: We genuflect to the cross on this day! ("Genuflect" is church vocabulary; tell people more simply that we "touch the floor with our right knee.")
- Try something new this year: If you're wearing sandals, slip them off before you approach the cross and/or invite all to remove their shoes (a ritual gesture common in many world religions), to symbolize the holiness of the act and the "holy ground" now marked by the cross.

- In many places, there is a custom of wiping the cross with a purificator at the place at which a person kisses it. Will this be done? If so, by whom? If you fear the spread of contagion, consider using a disinfectant wipe instead of smearing germs with a purificator.
- After the adoration, is there a way to stand the cross upright in the sanctuary, perhaps flanked by the candles that accompanied it in procession?

Know how you'll share the **solemn intercessions** on this day.

- Will you use the traditional rite, shared between the deacon and presider, with periods of silence and alternating times of kneeling and standing — or will you avoid the up-and-down movement by inviting congregants to kneel for a prolonged time of silent prayer only once during the entire rite?
- Be sure that all assisting with this (e.g., your deacon) know how these prayers will be shared and any instructions that need to be shared with the congregation (which is part of the role of the deacon).

Will you have a **collection** during this special liturgy? Let your hospitality ministers know! It's Good Friday; you might do well to abstain from a collection today. The Roman church has the custom of taking up a collection on this day for the Holy Land; if you have a collection, consider having it for such a need, outside the operating expenses of your community.

Think through the **Rite of Communion** today:

- Plan how the Blessed Sacrament will come from the altar of repose to your worship space at the appropriate time. This might best be performed by your deacon, with a humeral veil. Ideally, have an altar server or two accompany the Blessed Sacrament with candles.
- After communion, return the Blessed Sacrament to the altar of repose without procession, then be sure to consume the consecrated bread and wine after the service, so that none is left.
- Extinguish the candle at the tabernacle, and leave the tabernacle door open, so that no one will think that the Blessed Sacrament is inside.
- Think through **the details for concluding today's rite**:
- At the conclusion of the service, all ministers genuflect to the cross, then depart in silence.

- Invite all to remain after the service to adore the cross—a parallel action to the adoration of the Blessed Sacrament last night.

- Be sure that those who decorate your worship space aren't immediately rushing after this service to change the décor for the Easter Vigil—particularly if these actions will be seen or heard by those spending time in prayer before the cross!

Designate persons—perhaps clergy, eucharistic ministers, and/or altar servers—to help **consume any of the Blessed Sacrament that remains** after today's commemoration. The altar of repose can be disassembled after this liturgy as well.

If you have a vibrant *Latino* community with plentiful lay leaders and creative talent, consider organizing the necessary talent to host a ***Viacrucis en vivo***, the live reenactment of the Way of the Cross that is popular in Latin America. Begin the Way of the Cross in one location, with the judgment of Jesus by Pontius Pilate, then recite the rosary or sing mournful songs *en route* to the place of crucifixion. Various *Latino* traditions can be appended to such a celebration, including hooded penitents, the **seven last words of Jesus**, the *pésame a la Virgen* (an expression of condolence to Jesus' mother), the **veneration of an image of the entombed Jesus**, and the popular *quema de Judas*—the burning of an effigy of Judas filled with firecrackers!

On **April 2**, when it does not fall on Good Friday, the Church celebrates **St. Francis of Paola** (1416-1507), a hermit dedicated to solitude, asceticism and the contemplative life. Lift him up as a model of Lenten prayer!

On **April 2**, we remember the passing of **Robert Harold Schuller** (1926-2015), the American Christian televangelist, motivational speaker and author who shared his weekly, televised "Hour of Power" from the Crystal Cathedral in Garden Grove, California. Schuller focused on the positive aspects of our Christian faith and deliberately avoided condemning people for sin, saying that Jesus "met needs before touting creeds." In his memory, consider how positive and non-judgmental your words, actions and ministry are!

Saturday, April 3, 2021
THE EASTER VIGIL
(white)

Research online when the sun will set at your place of worship. **Plan to begin this evening's service** *after* **sunset**. Remember: Each day of the Jewish calendar begins at sunset (hence the Church's celebration of vigils). If you light the Easter fire outside, and if the hour of your service is close to the start time, invite congregants to come and watch the sunset — and to experience the dawning of a "new day" — before you light the Easter fire!

Transform your worship space into a proclamation of the Easter message!

- Place **the stand for the paschal candle** next to the ambo, and consider decorating it with flowers and/or ribbon.
- Locate **the symbol of baptismal water** in close proximity.
- Have a **bowl and aspergillum** ready for the sprinkling after the renewal of baptismal vows. Let the symbol speak: Consider swapping out your metal aspergillum (which likely shares very few drops of water with every swing) for a natural broom sprinkler adorned with white and gold ribbons.
- Be sure **the holy water fonts of the church are empty**, ready to be filled after the sprinkling rite.
- Don't skimp on the **Easter lilies** — the traditional Easter flower that resembles the trumpets announcing Christ's resurrection! Rather than leave the lilies in plastic-wrapped pots, think how you'll cover the pots in a way that ties them to your décor.
- Consider decorating the space with **flowering plants and floral arrangements** as well.
- Cover the altar with your **finest altar cloth**.
- Be sure to **steam or iron your Easter vestments** — and coordinate the color of your vestments with other decorative details in your worship space!
- If your worship space contains the **Stations of the Cross**, consider removing them or making it clear that they culminate in the 15th Station, the resurrection of Christ from the dead!
- Jesus is off the cross: Consider removing or replacing any crucifix that has a *corpus* (Jesus' body) on it. Drape white fabric behind the

head and over the horizontal bars of every sizeable cross, to create the look of the "**Easter cross**."

- Think how you might use white cloth to **draw the eyes of congregants upwards**, perhaps with sheer, white fabric suspended over the congregation and/or between pillars.

- If you have a Latino community, have congregants create **white/gold paper flowers or** *papel picado* (cut tissue paper) that might lift eyes upward and toward the sanctuary.

- Consider **banners** with images of Easter joy and/or the Easter symbol of the empty tomb.

- **Continue the decoration** into the entrance to your worship space, outdoors, and into other spaces on the grounds, including your Blessed Sacrament chapel, parish hall and classrooms!

- If you're celebrating with an outdoor **Easter fire**, gather the necessary materials: a pit, newspaper, wood, a lighter, a wick to transfer the Easter fire to the paschal candle, and a nearby fire extinguisher. Let the symbol speak: Be sure to have a skilled camper build and tend a bonfire; don't risk an inexperienced fire-builder placing a few fire starters among loosely-wadded newspaper and green twigs. Have a "Plan B" for a smaller, indoor fire (perhaps in a small, tabletop grill), in the event of inclement weather.

- Prepare the necessary **taper candles (with bobaches)** and Mass programs.

- Ready the **paschal candle** and its **nails**. The Roman church mandates that the paschal candle "must be made of wax, never be artificial, be renewed each year, be only one in number, and be of sufficiently large size so that it may evoke the truth that Christ is the light of the world"; reflect on how this fits with your practice, particularly if your "paschal candle" is a plastic tube with an oil canister.

- If there may be any hint of wind, be sure to have a **glass topper** on hand to protect the flame — and a "Plan B" in the event that the wind extinguishes the paschal candle while the procession is in process.

- Be sure the **thurible** is ready, that you have plenty of **charcoal**, and that the **boat is filled with incense**.

- Prepare for Mass as usual, making sure to include **gluten-free hosts** in the communion bowl, if necessary.

- If it's your community's custom to bring to the altar during the Lamb of God a ciborium with the Blessed Sacrament, let the appropriate person know that **there is no Blessed Sacrament in the tabernacle this evening**, so there in nothing to be brought to the altar.
- Before the first congregant arrives, **be sure all lights in the church are turned off, no candles are lit, and that all ministers know to maintain a prayerful environment.**
- Designate someone to **share Mass programs and taper candles with congregants** as they arrive; think of this as a ministerial opportunity for children and/or for the families of those who will be receiving sacraments.

If you have a multilingual community, think through how you'll make a single community celebration meaningful to persons of all languages!

- Consider music that incorporates all languages.
- Divide the scriptures between languages, and, so that all can understand them, and consider printing the scriptures in the language in which they're not being proclaimed.
- Have a multilingual psalm and proclamation of the gospel.
- Be sure the presider and homilist are able to easily transition between languages for prayers and preaching, without sharing a homily that's repeated in two languages.
- Share a multilingual invitation to share the sign of peace.
- Invite people to pray the Lord's Prayer in their own languages.
- Rather than guess the language of those coming to communion, train eucharistic ministers to alternate between "The Body of Christ" (or "The Blood of Christ") and its equivalent(s) in the other language(s).

Be sure to prepare all ministers, so that they know their role and responsibilities for this special celebration. For the smoothest-possible liturgical experience, consider having a rehearsal!

Think through the details of **the procession from the Easter fire into the worship space**:

- Be sure your thurifer is ready for his/her responsibilities tonight—including his/her leading of the procession and assistance with the deacon's (or presider's) incensation of the paschal candle.

- Be sure your deacon (or the person carrying the paschal candle) knows how to chant "Light of Christ" and where s/he will stop to chant it. Have him/her consider chanting this from the same three spots from which the proclamation "Behold the wood" was chanted on Good Friday.

- Plan how you'll spread the Light of Christ quickly and reverently after the second singing of "Light of Christ."

- Have the person holding the paschal candle place it in its stand after the third singing of "Light of Christ."

- Let altar servers know when to light all candles in the sanctuary and when to turn on the lights of the church (e.g., before the *Exsultet* is proclaimed — as a symbol of the paschal candle completely illuminating everything — or during the singing of the *Gloria*, as a symbol of Light of Christ becoming flesh).

- Similarly, your deacon should know when to tell congregants to extinguish their taper candles.

The *Exsultet* is a complex chant: today is *not* the day to begin practicing it. Weeks in advance, select the deacon or cantor who will proclaim this, so that s/he can be preparing over the course of weeks! If it is your deacon, s/he should approach the presider for a blessing, which is the same blessing as the one given before the proclamation of the gospel at Mass, except that the words "paschal praise" are used instead of "gospel."

The singing of the *Gloria* returns the congregation to the **full instrumental use** that we haven't heard since the *Gloria* on Holy Thursday. Like Holy Thursday, consider the **ringing of bells** during the *Gloria*. For all other music before the *Gloria* (e.g., the responsorial psalms), use *a capella* singing or softer accompaniment.

The Alleluia returns for the first time since Winter Ordinary Time: Sing it with gusto! Consider using a **triple Alleluia** tonight, with three verses from Psalm 118. For the musically-proficient, sing each succeeding refrain a half-step higher. Remember: Candles are not used during the proclamation of the gospel on this day!

For all other songs after the Alleluia, **consider tunes that might be familiar** to those who may not attend Mass very often outside of Christmas and Easter. Also, consider ways in which you might **assist them in knowing the responses of the assembly**!

This is an especially appropriate night for celebrating the Church's **sacraments of initiation!**

- Know whether you'll be celebrating sacraments this evening, and, if so, for whom.
- Be sure recipients of sacraments are prepared and that they know how you'll celebrate these sacraments and what they need to do.
- Prepare the necessary oil(s).
- Have baptismal candles and white vestments on hand.
- Have a plan for dressing the newly-baptized in these white garments after they are baptized; consider giving them a space in which they can dry off and change clothes (if necessary), while the "veteran" Catholics renew their baptismal vows.
- Consider incorporating into the Litany of Saints the patron/matron saints of the newly-baptized and also of your community.
- Make the newly-baptized feel "part of the family": Be sure to include their names in the Prayers of the Faithful.

Will you have a **collection** during this special liturgy? Let your hospitality ministers know!

Because of the complexity of this service and its various rites (e.g., for the reception of sacraments by persons of different age groups, or for celebrations in which no sacraments are received), **consider assembling your own "missal" for this Mass,** inside a beautiful binder!

We celebrate the solemnity of solemnities tonight: Consider using **hypoallergenic incense** during your liturgy—but be sure that all who touch the thurible and/or boat have practiced in advance. (We've seen far too many carpets burned by inexperienced thurifers!) Be sure to tip off your altar server(s) to the fact that the handwashing will occur *after* the incensation of the altar and gifts! Because of the high nature of this solemnity, train your thurifer to swing the thurible during the song of sending forth in a vertical circle, with his/her swinging forearm parallel to the floor and his/her elbow at his/her side. It's a simple flipping of the wrist: forward, back, loop forward, back, loop forward, back, etc. Be sure s/he understands the laws of physics: Once the thurible (with flaming charcoals) is set in motion, the centrifugal force can't be stopped when the thurible is upside-down in the air!

The thread in today's scriptures: Like people gathered around a campfire, we listen tonight to highlights from the story of our salvation: The creation of the world (Gen. 1:1 – 2:2), the great faith of our ancestors

(Gen. 22:1-18), and God's great act of freeing us from slavery (Ex. 14:15 – 15:1). We hear God speaking through the prophets, telling us how God's love is everlasting (Is. 54:5-14), how God is merciful, generous and forgiving (Is. 55:1-11), and how we are called to walk in the ways of prudence, wisdom and understanding (Bar. 3:9-15 & 3:32 – 4:4), with the hope that God will replace our hearts of stone with hearts of flesh (Ez. 36:16-28). The glorified Christ was raised from the dead (Lk. 24:1-12), and Paul assures us that we, too, will "live in newness of life" (Rom. 6:4)!

Holy humor: The Sunday school teacher had prepared a lesson on Christ's resurrection on Easter Sunday. She asked her students, "What did Jesus do on Easter Sunday?" There was no response. So she gave her students a hint: "It starts with the letter R..." And one boy blurted out, "Jesus recycled?" [Segue from "resurrection," the answer the teacher expected, to the fact that Christ's resurrection from the dead broke the cycle of sin and death, bringing us full-circle from death, back to life! It's Easter: Feel free to point to other examples of life-to-death-to-life, like the Easter lilies in your worship space, which are alive today, will eventually die, but will bloom with life again next Easter!]

Looking for a visual aid for your homily or object lesson? Consider the objects in your worship environment! The paschal candle is a symbol of the Light of Christ vanquishing the darkness, and the tapers are symbolic of our sharing in the Light of Christ! The water has returned (recall that Good Friday is the one day in which our holy water fonts are empty) and is symbolic of the new life we receive in baptism, our being cleansed from sin, and the fact that we have died with Christ in baptism and will share in his resurrection! The Easter lilies recall the trumpets that heralded Christ's resurrection! Imagine for a moment what this world would be like if we took seriously our baptismal promises and, nourished by Word and Sacrament, went forth to be heralds of Christ's light in this world!

Know how you'll celebrate **the blessing of water, the renewal of baptismal promises, and the sprinkling rite**.

- Be prepared to remove the paschal candle from its stand and lower it into the water once (or three times, depending on local custom), holding it in the water for the remainder of the prayer.

- Be sure to have a taper on hand, for relighting all tapers from the paschal candle, for the renewal of baptismal promises. Have a plan for quickly relighting the taper candles of all congregants at this moment in the rite. Consider having instrumental music to accompany this action.

- If you anticipate a large number of congregants and a generous sharing of water, consider having an altar server follow you with another pitcher or bowl of holy water.

- If, at the end of the sprinkling rite, you have only a small amount of holy water left in the bowl you're carrying, let the symbol speak: Hand the aspergillum to your altar server, and conclude the rite by tightly holding the bowl and throwing the remaining water high over the heads of all congregants!

- Instruct an altar server on the moment during the rite in which s/he should use a pitcher to take the newly-blessed water, to fill all holy water fonts of the church.

After communion, **the Blessed Sacrament is returned to the tabernacle**, which has remained open since Holy Thursday. Instruct the appropriate minister to lock the tabernacle and light the vigil light there.

Be sure your deacon knows how to **chant the double Alleluia of the dismissal**.

After Mass, have hospitality ministers prepared with baskets, in which they can **collect the taper candles**.

If you serve a *Latino* community, consider having **holy water bottles** for purchase: In many places in Mexico, people are accustomed to taking holy water home at the conclusion of Easter Masses!

On **April 3**, we celebrate the birth in 1927 of **Joseph Blenkinsopp**, the Old Testament scholar who wrote widely on the Pentateuch, the prophets, and Ezra-Nehemiah. In his memory, explore more deeply the prophetic tradition of the Hebrew scriptures!

On **April 3**, we remember the passing of **Graham Greene** (1904-1991), the Nobel Prize-winning novelist who explored ambivalent moral and political issues through a Catholic perspective. He is best known for *The Power and the Glory*, which told the story of a renegade "whisky priest" during the government suppression of the Catholic faith in Mexico. In his memory, pray for the "whisky priests" of our world, who, like Greene's protagonist, teach high standards while manifesting signs of weakness!

Sunday, April 4, 2021

THE RESURRECTION OF OUR LORD

(white)

This is a high solemnity: **Keep in place all décor** from your celebration of the Easter Vigil!

Be sure your hospitality ministers are ready to **welcome the "Christmas and Easter Catholics"** who may not often come to church. Encourage ministers to make newcomers feel so welcomed that they might consider returning!

The Church shares four "great sequences" each year: Today's is the *Victimae Paschali Laudes*. Consider having a gifted cantor sing or chant a setting of this, before segueing into the gospel acclamation!

The thread in today's scriptures: Filled with Christ's Spirit, Peter (previously known for his denial of Jesus) now boldly proclaims the risen Christ (Acts 10:34a & 37-43), whose rising is told in today's gospel (Jn. 20:1-9). With the psalmist, we sing: "This is the day the Lord has made: Let us rejoice and be glad!" (Ps. 118:24).

Holy humor: Sometimes Easter can be stressful — with early-rising children eager to see what the Easter Bunny brought them, getting everyone dressed for church, preparing for family gatherings, and all the other details that fill this day. So, do you want to know how to make Easter easier? I'll tell you how to make Easter easier. How do you make Easter *easier*? Simply replace the "t" of Easter with an "i," and you've just made "Easter" "easier"! [Segue into the fact that maybe the simple change of a letter won't necessarily make Easter easier, but, through his resurrection, Christ changed an otherwise-ordinary Sunday into the reason for our hope and the source of our salvation! He changed our destiny from death, to life! From sin, to mercy and forgiveness! From darkness, to light! He is risen! Alleluia!]

Looking for a visual aid for your homily or object lesson? Consider a baseball! Easter signals that spring has arrived, and baseball season is right around the corner. Throw the baseball in the air, and note the physical laws of this world: What goes up…must come down! We know that God often sees this world from a very different perspective; indeed, from God's perspective, as evidenced in today's scriptures, what goes *down* (into the grave)…must come *up*!

Consider having a **sprinkling rite** this morning, with the holy water from the Easter Vigil: This could be at the beginning of Mass (in place of the

Penitential Rite), or after the Renewal of Baptismal Promises (which would be in place of the Creed).

For the intellectually-curious, speak to the etymology of Easter (with Eostre, the Anglo-Saxon goddess of the dawn), explain that Easter is a moveable feast (celebrated on the first Sunday after the first full moon after the spring equinox), note that the bunny was an ancient Egyptian symbol of fertility, and/or share how eggs, a symbol of new life, were forbidden during Lent by the medieval Church! Note also that, though we're in the Year of Mark, we won't hear from Mark again on a Sunday until the Eleventh Sunday in Ordinary Time; John and Luke will "fill in" until Mark's reappearance on June 13!

Happy Easter! Consider engaging kids through an **Easter egg hunt** and/or a visit from the **Easter Bunny**. Photos with the Easter bunny can be extremely popular and will likely be posted by congregants to social media! Even better, print copies of photos and make them available at no cost next Sunday; they'll hang on refrigerators and be framed in homes for years to come!

Lent is over: For those who survived without meat on the Fridays of Lent, suggest a continued practice of **"Meatless Mondays"** or **"Fruit & Veggie Fridays"** as a way to address the impact we have on our environment through our consumption of meat!

On **April 4,** when it doesn't fall on Easter Sunday, the Church celebrates **St. Isidore of Seville** (c. 560-636, not to be confused with St. Isidore the Farmer, who is celebrated on May 15). Isidore organized the church of Spain through his theology and the hosting of councils. Consider how conciliar or authoritarian you are, and allow today's saint to challenge you toward a spirit of greater conciliarity!

On **April 4**, the Greek Orthodox Church of Jerusalem (recognized by the Ecumenical Patriarch of Constantinople) celebrates the birth in 1952 of **Ilias Giannopoulos**, who would become Patriarch Theophilus III of Jerusalem. In a spirit of ecumenism, pray for him and for the 500,000 Greek Orthodox Catholics he serves!

On **April 5**, the Church celebrates **St. Vincent Ferrer** (c. 1350-1419), the Dominican friar who forced Spanish Jews to convert to Catholicism. Pray today for all who mistakenly believe that God's salvation could be limited to their church alone, and for all throughout history whose fervor for "evangelization" was responsible for erasing indigenous cultures and centuries of rich religious traditions!

On **April 6**, we remember the passing of **John Dobree Dalgairns** (1818-1876), the English Catholic convert and friend of John Henry Newman who translated Aquinas, wrote on Cistercian saints and German mystics, and included a history of Jansenism in his *Devotion to the Sacred Heart of Jesus*. In his memory, consider your own contributions to theology and/or to the sharing of the stories of the saints whom you've known!

On **April 7**, the Church celebrates **St. John Baptist de la Salle** (1651-1719), the first to emphasize classroom teaching over individual instruction. This patron saint of teachers taught in the vernacular, rather than Latin. In his honor, lift up and pray for all teachers in your community!

On **April 8**, we celebrate the birth in 1926 of **Jürgen Moltmann**, the German Reformed theologian who contributed to a number of areas of Christian theology. He shared his "theology of hope," a form of liberation theology predicated on a view that God suffers with humanity but that the hope of the resurrection promises us a better future. In his memory, consider the place that hope holds in your own theology and worldview — and how it is that you might be a better instrument of hope in this world!

On **April 8**, we remember the passing of **Antony Garrard Newton Flew** (1923-2010), the English philosopher of religion and advocate for atheism known for his criticism of concepts of God, life after death, free will, and the problem of evil. Late in life, he shocked colleagues by changing his position, choosing to believe in an intelligent creator, and clarifying his own personal concept of God. In his memory, pray for all who struggle to believe the good news we daily teach and preach!

On **April 9**, we remember the passing of **William of Ockham** (1285-1347), the English Franciscan friar and scholastic philosopher and theologian who was one of the major figures of medieval thought and stood at the center of major intellectual controversies of the 14th century. He is known for "Ockham's razor," the problem-solving principle that simpler solutions are more likely correct than complex solutions. In his memory, reflect on simple solutions to the various challenges you face!

On **April 9**, we remember the passing of **Dietrich Bonhoeffer** (1906-1945), the German pastor and theologian executed by the Nazi regime and best known for *The Cost of Discipleship* and other writings on justice, the role of faith in a "world come of age," and a "religionless Christianity" where God might be unfettered from the metaphysical constructs of the previous 1900 years. In his memory, consider ways in which you might shed a "garment" or two covering your own faith!

On **April 10**, we remember the passing of **Pierre Teilhard de Chardin** (1881-1955), the French paleontologist, idealist philosopher and Jesuit priest who popularized Vladimir Vernadsky's concept of the noosphere and conceived the vitalist idea of the Omega Point toward which the universe is evolving. In his memory, reflect on possible connections that might be made between his thought and the daily lives of your community members!

Sunday, April 11, 2021
SECOND SUNDAY OF EASTER
(white)

It's the Easter season: The **paschal candle** remains in close proximity to the ambo!

This Sunday was traditionally known as *dominica in albis* (White Sunday): Invite the newly-baptized to round out the Easter octave by wearing their white gowns, shirts or dresses again this Sunday! Even better, spread word a week or two in advance, and invite all congregants to wear a touch of white!

The thread in today's scriptures: The early community of disciples "bore witness to the resurrection of the Lord Jesus" (Acts 4:33), who, according to John, appeared to the apostles on Easter night (Jn. 20:19-31). We, too, are victors when we believe that Jesus is the Son of God (1Jn. 5:5), and we share our joyful shout of victory (Ps. 118:15) in honor of the good and loving God who raised Christ from the dead (Ps. 118:1)!

Holy humor: I couldn't make this up: Early Greek Christians referred to the Sunday after Easter as "Holy Humor Sunday"! It was a day of great joy and laughter, to celebrate the "joke" that Jesus played on Sin and Death by conquering them! So, in the spirit of the early Greek Christians, who would tell jokes on this day, I'll share with you the story of the day that Jesus and Moses…played golf in heaven! So there they were, Jesus and Moses, playing golf in heaven, and, darned the luck, they both hit their golf balls into the same water trap! So Jesus turned to Moses and said, "Didn't you do something with water once?" And Moses said, "I did," and he did his trick of parting the waters, and he fetched his golf ball from the water trap. Then Moses turned to Jesus and said, "Didn't you do something with water once?" And Jesus said, "I did," and he stepped out onto the water. But almost immediately, he sank into the water. Puzzled, he got out of the water and tried again, this time with a running start—but he ended up in water up to his waist. Jesus was now confused and embarrassed, so Moses asked him, "What are you trying to do?" And Jesus replied, "I used to be able to walk on water." Moses smiled and asked, "But the last time you tried it, did you have those holes in your feet?" [Acknowledge once more that it's Holy Humor Sunday, and segue into the holes in Jesus' feet and hands and side—the proof that he had died on the cross and was now raised from the dead!]

Looking for a visual aid for your homily or object lesson? Consider a large button! The English word "peace" comes from an ancient Greek root that literally mean "to fasten" or "to button." Just as a button fastens together two pieces of cloth, we are ideally united in the peace that the risen Christ wished his friends. Every time we wish one another peace—at every Mass—we show our desire to be "buttoned" to all those other members of the Body of Christ!

It's the final day of the Easter Octave: Be sure your deacon knows how to **chant the double Alleluia of the dismissal**.

It's **Divine Mercy Sunday**: Find a way to incorporate this into your preaching and/or catechesis! Many people are not familiar with the Chaplet of the Divine Mercy; consider the possibility of having a lay leader guide all present in this prayer!

On **April 11**, when it doesn't fall on a Sunday, the Church celebrates **St. Stanislas** (1030-1079), the patron saint of Poland, who bravely spoke out against a cruel and unjust king. In iconography, he's the bishop being cut to pieces at the foot of an altar. In his memory, listen to Franz Liszt's last and unfinished work, the *Oratorio St. Stanislaus*, and/or voice support today for the courageous prophetic women and men who, inspired by the Spirit, continue to speak out against injustices and/or unjust leaders.

On **April 12**, the Church celebrates **Julius I** (+352), the pope who defended Athanasius against Arian accusers. In his honor, pray for those who courageously stand in defense of others!

On **April 12**, we remember the passing of **Jacques-Bénigne Bossuet** (1627-1704), the French Catholic bishop who drafted Louis XIV's anti-papal declaration, declared null and void by the pope for its suggestion that the king could limit the power of the pope. At an 1882 assembly of French clergy, he drafted the Gallican Articles, asserting the king's independence from Rome in secular matters—and that the pope can never be regarded as infallible without the consent of the Church. Pause today to pray for all who blur the line between Church and State and for those who, in Bossuet's day, insisted on purported papal infallibility!

On **April 12**, we remember the passing of **Johann Adam Möhler** (1796-1838), the German priest and theologian who died at age 41 but was influential on other young minds, like Henri de Lubac and Yves Congar. A prominent exponent of liberal thought, he supported Döllinger's criticisms of the papacy and its claims of purported papal infallibility. In his memory, pray for the young people who dedicate their lives to bringing fresh thought to sometimes-stale institutions!

On **April 13**, the Church celebrates **St. Martin I** (+655), the pope imprisoned by Emperor Constans II and who died as a consequence of the mistreatment he received from fellow Christians. In iconography, he's a pope in a prison cell or a pope holding money. In his memory, read up on the Lateran Council that he convened and the Monothelitism and Monothelites condemned at that council, and/or pray today for all who are persecuted by "Christians" and by our fellow Catholics—and for those "Christians" who fail to see the error of their myopic ways!

On **April 13**, the Church also celebrates **St. Hermenegild** (+585), the Visigoth (Spanish) prince who defied his Arian father by converting to Catholicism, the religion of his devout wife (who was the daughter of the king of the Franks. Hermenegild was imprisoned and beheaded, which is why he's depicted in iconography as a prince in chains and/or holding an ax and being lifted to heaven above the king and bishops below him. His courage inspired his younger brother, Recared, to convert to Catholicism as well. In honor of the patron saint of converts, pray for all who have come to embrace our faith from other traditions!

On **April 15**, we remember the passing of **Charles Journet** (1891-1975), the Swiss theologian and cardinal who co-founded the theological journal *Nova et Vetera* with Jacques Maritain and was influential in the Second Vatican Council's writing of *Dignitatis humanae* and *Nostra aetate*. In his memory, reflect on your own concrete efforts to bring to flesh "the Church of the Word Incarnate"!

On **April 16**, the Roman church celebrates the birth in 1927 of **Joseph Aloisius Ratzinger**, who headed the Roman church for eight years as Benedict XVI. Originally a liberal theologian questioning literal interpretations of the resurrection of Jesus, he adopted conservative views after Vatican II and became John Paul II's closest advisor and "Rottweiler" as head of the Congregation for the Doctrine of the Faith. Lift a prayer heavenward today for this "pope *emeritus*"—and for the church that will long feel his legacy of attempting a "reform of the [Vatican II] reform"!

On **April 17**, we remember the passing of **Louis de Berquin** (c. 1490-1529), the French lawyer, linguist and reformer. "Providentially guided to the Bible, he was amazed to find there 'not the doctrines of Rome, but the doctrines of Luther.'" Apart from a few translations of Erasmus, all his works are lost: He was forced to watch the burning of his books, his tongue was pierced, and, refusing to recant, he was burned at the stake the next day. In his memory, pray for all who mistreat others in defense of their own fragile "truths."

On **April 17**, we celebrate the birth in 1938 of **Elisabeth Schüssler Fiorenza**, the Romanian-born, German, Roman Catholic feminist theologian who co-founded the *Journal of Feminist Studies in Religion*. Her book, *In Memory of Her*, argued for the retrieval of the overlooked contributions of women in the early Church. In her honor, find a way today to advocate for Jesus' vision of a "discipleship of equals"!

Sunday, April 18, 2021
THIRD SUNDAY OF EASTER
(white)

It's the Easter season: The **paschal candle** remains in close proximity to the ambo!

Also, Catholic worship spaces are famously decorated with explosions of lilies on Easter Sunday, only for those spaces to begin looking barren when the Easter lilies begin to die.

- Create a plan this year to **spread your Easter decorating budget over the 50 days of Easter**, so that, even after the Easter lilies wither, you'll have a way to brighten your worship space with color and natural beauty through Pentecost. Consider ivy and potted flowers, like calla lilies, azaleas, and begonias, which can thrive for weeks.

- Decide what to do with the Easter lilies that you cycle out of your worship space: Plant them outside (presuming there's someone to water and care for them), or give them away to congregants with a "green thumb"!

The thread in today's scriptures: Now filled with the Spirit, Peter (who previously denied Jesus three times) preaches the resurrection of Christ, the "expiation for our sins" (1Jn. 2:2), that we might repent and "be converted, [and] that [our] sins may be wiped away" (Acts 3:15 & 18-19). Luke had already suggested "that repentance, for the forgiveness of sins, would be preached in his name to all the nations" (Lk. 24:47). For the ancient Israelites this reconciliation was imagined as God turning again toward the people, allowing the light of God's countenance—God's face—to shine upon the people (Ps. 4:7).

Holy humor: Perhaps you've seen the meme: It's a picture of a very saintly Jesus, and the words below—as if to suggest that we *should* sin!—say, "If you don't sin, Jesus died for nothing." I'm not going to suggest that you should go out and sin, but think about the deep truth of that meme: Jesus died…for our sins! [Segue into the themes of repentance and expiation that unite today's three readings.]

Looking for a visual aid for your homily or object lesson? Consider a tissue and a handheld whiteboard with the word "SIN" written on it several times in large, legible letters. As you talk about Peter's message, slowly wipe the words from the whiteboard, highlighting the ancient yet popular belief that forgiveness is somehow like the action of wiping away! [Segue to other ways of imagining sin and salvation, including Rahner's and Fuchs' notions of fundamental option and fundamental stance, as well as to the reference to the word "repentance" in today's gospel, which literally means "turning again" of one's fundamental stance. Remember: Today's gospel comes from Luke, who also told the story of the son who, though far off, was "saved" the moment he turned toward his father (Lk. 15:17-20)!

On **April 19**, we remember the passing of **Philip Melanchton** (1497-1560), the systematic theologian who contributed to the reform of the Church through his questioning of transubstantiation, the sacrament of penance, justification through works, and the medieval Church's exaggerated cult of saints. In his memory, consider multiple perspectives on these and other theological issues!

On **April 19**, the Syro Malabar Catholic Church (in union with Rome) celebrates the birth in 1945 of **Major Archbishop George Alencherry**. In a spirit of ecumenism, pray for him and for the 5.1 million Syro Malabar Catholics he serves!

On **April 20**, we remember the passing of **Victor IV** (1095-1164), the cardinal and "antipope" supported by Emperor Frederick Barbarossa after the election of Alexander III, whom five cardinals, the priests of St. Peter's and the Roman people refused to recognize as pope. Consecrated by the dean of the College of Cardinals, Victor IV took control of Rome, causing Alexander III to flee to Sicily. A fascinating split in the Church ensued, with kings, clergy and laity forced to decide which pope they supported. After miracles were reported at Victor's tomb, Gregory VIII ordered it to be destroyed. In Victor's memory, consider the lessons learned from the instances you've witnessed of politics entering the Church!

On **April 21**, the Church celebrates **St. Anselm** (c. 1033-1109), the archbishop of Canterbury whose metaphysical works continue to shed light on the attributes of God. He resisted his king's efforts to use the Church's money in a war against the king's brother. Consider today how you are stewarding the resources entrusted to your care!

On **April 21**, we remember the passing of **Peter Abelard** (1079-1142), the medieval French scholastic philosopher and theologian now legendary for his love affair with Héloïse d'Argenteuil. His work, *Sic et Non*, brought together opposite opinions on doctrinal points from various Fathers of the Church. In his memory, consider opposing perspectives to some of your most strongly-held thoughts and beliefs, and/or re-watch the 1988 film, "Stealing Heaven," which attempted to tell the tale of these lovers!

On **April 21**, we celebrate the birth in 1939 of **Sr. Helen Prejean**, the Roman Catholic sister who authored the bestseller, *Dead Man Walking*, and who became a leading advocate for the abolition of the death penalty in the U.S. Sister Helen founded groups to help the family members of murder victims. In her honor, call to mind others who have lost a family member or friend to similar tragic circumstances — and find a small way to reach out to them today, to let them know you care!

On **April 21**, the Roman Catholic Church celebrates the birth in 1965 of **Pierbattista Pizzaballa**, the Latin Patriarch of Jerusalem. In a spirit of ecumenism, pray for him and for the Roman Catholics he serves!

On **April 21**, we remember the passing of **Catharina Joanna Maria Halkes** (1920-2011), the Dutch feminist theologian who gained notoriety when she was forbidden to address John Paul II during his visit to the Netherlands in 1985. Considered the mother of feminist theology in the Netherlands, she held the first chair of Feminism and Christianity at Radboud University. In her memory, consider your own commitment to gender equality in the Body of Christ (Gal 3:28)!

April 21 is **Administrative Professional's Day**: How will you recognize those who assist the administrative functions of your community, and/or how will you empower others to assist with such details?

April 22 is **Earth Day**: Is there anything that your community might do to mark this day? Consider planting trees, putting in place bins for recyclables (as well as a system for ensuring that objects placed there are recycled), and/or inviting a high school environmental sciences class to do an audit of the trash/recyclables/composting efforts of your community!

On **April 22**, we remember the passing of **Mircea Eliade** (1907-1986), the Romanian philosopher and religious historian who established paradigms for religious study that continue to be used today. He suggested that myths and rituals allow us to actually participate in hierophanies. In his memory, reflect on how our Catholic stories and rituals connect us with the larger spiritual motifs shared by peoples throughout our world!

On **April 23**, the Church celebrates **St. George** (+c. 303) and **St. Adalbert** (956-997). George was a soldier in the imperial guard, tortured and martyred for refusing to sacrifice to Roman gods. Portrayed in iconography as killing a dragon, George is the patron saint of England and of Boy Scouts and is venerated by Christians of the East and West — as well as by Muslims. Adalbert was the bishop of Prague who was exiled by clergy refusing to observe his clerical reforms, and exiled again after excommunicating those who violated the Church's right of sanctuary by dragging a woman accused of adultery from a church and murdering her. Consider a fitting way to honor their legacy!

On **April 23**, we remember the passing of **William Shakespeare** (1564-1616), the English playwright widely regarded as the world's greatest dramatist. His parents were Catholic at a time when practicing Catholicism in England was against the law. In his and his parents' memory, pray for those who bring beauty to our world — and to those who bravely profess their faith despite difficult circumstances!

On **April 23**, the Eritrean Orthodox Tewahedo Church celebrates the anniversary of the appointment in 2004 of **Patriarch Antonios**. In a spirit of ecumenism, pray for him and for the 3 million people he serves!

On **April 23**, the Palmarian Catholic Church — a small, traditionalist church — celebrates the anniversary of the installation in 2016 of Joseph Odermatt as **Pope Peter III**. In his honor, pray for him and for the 1,000 people he serves!

On **April 24**, we remember the passing of **St. Wilfrid** (c. 633 – c. 709), the Northumbrian abbot and bishop who reportedly introduced the Rule of St. Benedict to the Isles and chose to be consecrated in Gaul due to the lack of validly-consecrated bishops in Northumbria. Wilfrid lived ostentatiously, always traveled with a large retinue, founded a see in West Sussex, and constantly championed Roman customs over local practices. In his memory, consider your own views on the tension between local customs and the rites and practices imposed by "universal" organizations!

On **April 24**, the Church celebrates **St. Fidel of Sigmaringen** (1577-1622), the "lawyer of the poor," who divided his wealth between the poor and seminarians in need. On his day, reflect on his words: "Woe to me if I should prove myself but a halfhearted soldier in the service of my thorn-crowned Captain!"

Sunday, April 25, 2021
FOURTH SUNDAY OF EASTER
(white)

It's the Easter season: The **paschal candle** remains in close proximity to the ambo!

Today is **Good Shepherd Sunday**: Point to the ancient imagery of the shepherd-king, and challenge listeners to be good shepherds of others!

The thread in today's scriptures: Today we hear two perspectives on Jesus' death: Peter accuses the leaders of the people of crucifying Jesus, "the stone rejected by the builders" (Acts 4:11; Ps. 118:22), but Jesus speaks of himself as the good shepherd who laid down his life for his sheep (Jn. 10:11 & 15). As a result of the latter, those of us who are part of the flock "may be called the children of God" (1Jn. 3:1).

Holy humor: Perhaps you've heard this one: What did the sheep say to the abusive shepherd? You're...herding me! [Segue into the image of Jesus as Good Shepherd—and how it was that the leaders and elders of the people tried to "herd" him.]

Looking for a visual aid for your homily or object lesson? Consider a stuffed animal of a lamb! What does it mean to be a sheep? We listen to and follow the Shepherd! What does it mean to be a shepherd? We care for the "sheep"! It's easy for us to love our pets [hold the stuffed animal closely, with affection]; are we sharing the same love and affection with the many "sheep" we meet throughout the week?

On **April 25**, when it doesn't fall on a Sunday, the Church celebrates **St. Mark** (+c. 68), to whom the second gospel is attributed. In his honor, thumb through his short work on the life of Jesus!

On **April 25**, we remember the passing of **Bernard Philip Kelly** (1907-1958), the English layman who, when not working as a banker or raising his large family, penned philosophical essays and book reviews for *Blackfriars* for 25 years. He developed the social and economic theory of distributism, reflected on the poetry of Gerard Manley Hopkins, and outlined an informed, Christian approach to Eastern religions. In his memory, explore elements of an Eastern philosophy and/or religion!

On **April 26**, the Church celebrates **St. Paschasius Radbertus** (c. 785 – c. 860), the Carolingian theologian and abbot of Corbie known for his work, *On the Body and Blood of the Lord*, the first lengthy treatise on the sacrament of the Eucharist in the Western world. He affirmed that the Eucharist contains the true, historical body of Jesus—a view that was refuted by his predecessor, Ratramnus, who wrote a work with the same name and advanced that the Eucharist is strictly metaphorical. In Paschasius' memory, reacquaint yourself with that important controversy in Eucharistic theology!

On **April 26**, the Church celebrates the birth in 1936 of **Joan Chittister**, the Benedictine nun and theologian known for her works on virtue and monasticism and for her advocacy on feminism and women's role in society. Forbidden by the Vatican in 2001 to address the Women's Ordination Worldwide conference, she did so anyway. In her honor, pray for all women and men who bravely and boldly advocate for Jesus' and Paul's vision of a "discipleship of equals"!

On **April 27**, we remember the passing of **Dorothee Steffensky-Sölle** (1929-2003), the German liberation theologian who coined the term Christofascism to describe fundamentalists. Steffensky-Sölle attempted to bridge theology to practical life, and her best-known work, *Suffering*, offered a critique of "Christian masochism" and "Christian sadism." In her memory, consider the extent to which your own theology and spirituality press against or reinforce conventional thinking on matters of religion and spirituality!

On **April 28**, the Church celebrates **St. Peter Chanel** (1803-1841) and **St. Louis-Marie Grignion de Montfort** (1673-1716). Peter was a Marist missionary and protomartyr of the South Seas, whose death led to the conversion of the island of Futuna. Louis-Marie was an early writer in the field of Mariology, who promoted consecration to Jesus in Mary.

Take a moment today to entrust the missionaries of the Church to Jesus and Mary!

On **April 28**, we remember the passing of **Jacques Maritain** (1882-1973), the French Catholic philosopher who revived Aquinas, authored over 60 books, and was influential in the drafting of the Universal Declaration of Human Rights. A mentor and close friend of Paul VI, who wanted to name him a cardinal, Maritain was especially interested in metaphysics, being, and the apprehension of being through intuition and sense experience. In his memory, re-read the Universal Declaration of Human Rights and/or consider the extent to which your knowledge allows you to "Thomisticize" and/or "measure [your] knowing spirit by the real"!

On **April 28**, we remember the passing of **James Hal Cone** (1938-2018), the American theologian known for his works on Black theology and Black liberation theology. Cone noted that Jesus advocated for the same ideals espoused in the Black Power movement—and that White American churches preached a gospel based on White supremacy, antithetical to the gospel of Jesus. In his memory, reflect on how your words and actions oppress and/or liberate persons of different races, cultures and socioeconomic levels!

On **April 29**, the Church celebrates **St. Catherine of Siena** (1347-1380), the 24th of 25 children, who died at the young age of 33. She's the patroness of Europe and Italy, and is often depicted holding a lily. Draw attention to her dedication to Christ from an early age (a model for children!), her care of the sick and poor, her contemplative life, and her influence in the Church!

On **April 29**, we remember the passing of **Augusta Theodosia Drane** (1823-1894), the English Dominican nun and writer who anonymously published a moral essay long attributed to John Henry Newman. Her major works included histories of St. Dominic, St. Catherine of Siena, St. Thomas More, and an overview of Christian schools and scholars. In her memory, pray for the countless anonymous women whose lives and works have inspired the Church throughout the centuries!

On **April 30**, the Church celebrates **St. Pius V** (1504-1572), the pope whose white Dominican habit would change the papal wardrobe to the present day. In honor of this reformer of the Church, consider the possible reforms needed in your own celebrations of the Church's liturgies!

On **April 30**, the Romanian Greek-Catholic Church (in union with Rome) celebrates the anniversary of the installation in 2006 of **Lucian Mureşan** as Major Archbishop of Făgăraş and Alba Iulia. In a spirit of ecumenism, pray for him and for the 504,000 Romanian Greek-Catholics he serves!

April 30 is also a big day in Latin America: It's *el día del niño* (Children's Day)! If you have a *Latino* community, and if you won't be doing anything to celebrate the day on April 30, consider hosting children's games and activities after your Sunday Mass. Pull in volunteers to organize games, children's music, food and drink. If your budget allows, rent a moonwalk or contract a clown, a balloon artist and/or a magician!

On **May 1**, the Church celebrates **St. Joseph the Worker**, a recent addition to the liturgical calendar, to counteract May Day celebrations of workers in communist nations. In his honor, bring attention to the sanctity and dignity of human labor as a source of holiness!

On **May 1**, we remember the passing of **John Major** (1467-1550), the Scottish philosopher, theologian and historian known for his skeptical, logical approach to the Bible and his premise that people and councils should be placed above kings and popes. In his memory, consider the place of logic and/or skepticism in your own approach to the scriptures!

On **May 1**, the Southern Baptist Convention celebrates the birth in 1973 of President **James David Greear**. In a spirit of ecumenism, pray for him and for the 15 million Baptists he serves!

Sunday, May 2, 2021
FIFTH SUNDAY OF EASTER
(white)

It's the Easter season: The **paschal candle** remains in close proximity to the ambo!

The thread in today's scriptures: The apostles found it hard to believe that a person so evil as Saul (Acts 9:26) could bear fruit in his life (Jn. 15:4-5). After his conversion — after turning to the Lord (Ps. 22:28) — Saul/Paul kept God's commandments and remained in Christ, and Christ in him (1Jn. 3:24)! Like Saul/Paul, may we turn to and remain in God, that we might bear fruit in our lives!

Holy humor: In the church, we hear words like "divinity" and "humanity." We all know that God is divine, and that we are human. I recently saw a very clever church sign that said, "God is divine — d-i-v-i-n-e — and we are...dibranches!" D-i-b-r-a-n-c-h-e-s. Let me say that one more time: "God is 'divine,' and we are...dibranches!" [Segue into today's gospel: Jesus is "divine" and we are "dibranches"!]

Looking for a visual aid for your homily or object lesson? Consider a dry branch! Hold it up, say that you found it and that it's the branch of an apple or orange tree (i.e., a tree that bears fruit). If you plant it in the ground, will it bear fruit? No! The only way it will bear fruit is by remaining in the tree. So, too, must we remain in God! [Segue into the gospel image of the necessity of the branch remaining in the vine in order to bear fruit.]

May is here! **For the intellectually-curious**, share a brief lesson on the double etymology of this month: *Maia* was the Roman goddess overseeing the plant growth occurring during this month, and it was also the month in which the ancient Romans celebrated their *maiores*, their elders! Give a May nod to the elders of your community!

It's May, the traditional month of Mary! Consider a **May Day crowning of Mary**. Add to the pageantry by inviting First Communicants to wear their white suits and dresses. Invite all to bring flowers from their gardens to honor Mary!

On **May 2**, when it doesn't fall on a Sunday the Church celebrates **St. Athanasius** (c. 293-373), whose defense of the divinity of Christ led him to be exiled five times — for 17 of his 45 years as a bishop! Use this day to focus on the Eastern Church that celebrates him, and/or on the detachment from worldly possessions that he esteemed in his *Life of Anthony*!

On **May 2**, we remember the passing of **Warren Wendel Wiersbe** (1929-2019), the American Baptist pastor and theology professor who has written and published over 150 books, including the 50+ books of his "Be" commentaries on the books of the Bible. In his honor, pause to consider the contribution that you might make to the recorded history and literature of our faith!

On **May 3**, the Church celebrates **Ss. Philip** (c. 80) **and James** (+c. 62). Philip is depicted in iconography holding loaves, due to his role in the feeding of the 5,000 (Jn. 6:5-7). "James the Lesser" was the "brother of the Lord" and the leader of the Church at Jerusalem. In their honor, pray Eucharistic Prayer I, which mentions them, and reflect on how you're nourishing others and comporting yourself as a sister or brother of the Lord!

If you serve a Latino community, **May 3** is *el día de la santa cruz* (the day of the Holy Cross) and *el día de los albañiles* (Bricklayer's Day) in Latin America. For the former, people decorate crosses and bring them to church for a special blessing: Consider how you might share a cross with your congregants and/or have a crafty congregant lead an activity in which community members can make their own crosses for display at home or to be given as gifts! For the latter, consider a blessing of all who work in building-related trades (e.g., architects, engineers, contractors, painters, electricians, plumbers, etc.) and/or a blessing of their tools and/or machinery!

On **May 3**, the Ukrainian Autocephalous Orthodox Church Canonical celebrates the birth in 1962 of **Oleh Kulyk**, who would become Patriarch Moses of Kyiv. In a spirit of ecumenism, pray for him and for the people he serves!

On **May 3**, the Syriac Orthodox Church celebrates the birth in 1965 of **Sa'id Karim**, who would become Patriarch Ignatius Aphrem II of Antioch and All the East. In a spirit of ecumenism, pray for him and for the people he serves!

On **May 3**, we remember the passing of **Catherine Mowry LaCugna** (1952-1997), the feminist theologian and author of *God For Us*, who sought to make the doctrine of the Trinity relevant to the everyday lives of believers. She died of cancer at age 44, while teaching systematic theology at Notre Dame. In her memory, consider the place of the Trinity in your own daily life!

On **May 4**, we remember the passing of **Cornelio Fabro** (1911-1995), the Italian Stigmatine priest and scholastic philosopher who founded the Institute for Higher Studies on Unbelief, Religion and Cultures. Part of the scholastic revival of Thomism, he also studied anthropocentrism, analyzed the relationship of Kierkegaard's thought to Christian philosophy, and critiqued "progressive" theology. In his memory, find a way to probe the skepticism, the existentialism, and the culture of unbelief that are associated with modern philosophy!

In some places, **May 5** is *cinco de mayo*, the day on which some Mexicans and Mexican Americans celebrate the victory of the Mexican Army over the French at the Battle of Puebla in 1862. This day, largely promoted by beer companies, is admittedly more popular in the United States than in Mexico, but, if it's a significant day for your community, find some way to celebrate it—perhaps with Mexican food, drink, music and decorations!

On **May 5**, the Ukrainian Greek Catholic Church (in union with Rome) celebrates the birth in 1970 of **Major Archbishop Sviatoslav Shevchuk**. In a spirit of ecumenism, pray for him and for the 4.5 million Ukrainian Greek Catholics he serves!

On **May 6**, we remember the passing of **Cornelius Jansen** (1585-1638), the Dutch Roman Catholic bishop of Ypres in Flanders (modern-day Netherlands), who taught scripture at Louvain and is now known as the father of the theological movement of Jansenism. 75 years after his death, the opposition to his Augustinian theology would become the litmus test for obedience to the Roman papacracy, by the Jesuits who enjoyed political and theological power in the church at that time. In his memory, pray for all who insist on rigid conformity by others to their own theologies and worldviews — and to all who suffer as a result!

On **May 6**, we celebrate the birth in 1939 of **Kenneth Hartley Blanchard**, the American author best known for co-authoring *The One Minute Manager*. The CSO (Chief Spiritual Officer) of his own company, he also co-authored *Lead Like Jesus: Lessons from the Greatest Leadership Role Model of All Time*. In his honor, consider the ways in which you need to grow as you endeavor to…lead like Jesus!

On **May 7**, we remember the passing of **Agnellus of Pisa** (c. 1195-1236), the Italian Franciscan friar considered the founder of the Franciscan Order in England. The first Franciscan minister provincial in England, he saw the growth of the order to 43 friaries in the English province before his death. Pause to consider how you are helping to grow the presence of Independent Catholicism in our world!

On **May 7**, we remember the passing of **Diether von Isenburg** (c. 1412-1482), the German cleric whose election as archbishop of Mainz was not confirmed by Pius II or Emperor Frederick III due to his unceasing desire to reform the Church. The archbishop selected by the pope captured Mainz, killed 400 citizens and exiled 400 others, including Johannes Gutenberg. When the papist archbishop died 13 years later, Diether was again elected archbishop and confirmed by the reform-minded Sixtus IV. Pray today for those praying and pleading for patience amid suffering!

On **May 7**, we remember the passing of **Franz von Sickingen** (1481-1523), the German knight who provided his castles as a refuge for Martin Luther and other reformers, shielding them from the attacks of the Dominicans of Cologne. In his memory, find a way to show your care and concern for those who are persecuted!

On **May 7**, we remember the passing of **Jean Vanier** (1928-2018), the Canadian philosopher, theologian and humanitarian who founded

L'Arche, an international federation of communities for people with developmental disabilities and those who assist them. He authored over 30 books on religion, tolerance, disability and normality and is credited with saying, "We must do what we can to diminish walls, to meet each other. Why do we put people with disabilities behind walls?" In his honor, consider the ways in which you erect and/or tear down the walls that separate us from the most determined among us — and commit yourself to honoring them by replacing such words in your vocabulary as "disabled" and "disability," with more chosen words, like "determined" and "special abilities"!

On **May 8**, we remember the passing of **Josip Juraj Štrosmajer** (1815-1905), the Croatian politician and bishop who was a vocal opponent of unlimited papal power and of purported papal infallibility. He left the First Vatican Council after making a three-hour speech deemed heretical by many in attendance. He promoted religious unification through the use of a single Slavonic rite for Catholic and Orthodox churches. In his memory, consider how you are promoting unity and/or being prophetic!

Sunday, May 9, 2021

SIXTH SUNDAY OF EASTER

(white)

It's the Easter season: The **paschal candle** remains in close proximity to the ambo!

The thread in today's scriptures: Peter preaches an impartial God of universal love, who sends the Spirit on all (Acts 10:34-35 & 44), revealing to the nations God's saving power (Ps. 98:2). As a result, we are called to remain in Christ's love (Jn. 15:10) and love one another (1Jn. 4:7, Jn. 15:17).

Holy humor: Do you know what the difference is between love and marriage? (If you're married, you know this.) What's the difference between love and marriage? Love is blind, and marriage is...an eye-opener! [Segue into God's "blind," universal, impartial love — and the "blind" love with which we're called to love all those people with whom we share this planet!]

Looking for a visual aid for your homily or object lesson? Consider a glass of water in your right hand and a crystal vessel of sacred chrism in your left hand (so that they appear to your audience in the order of water then chrism). The two primary symbols of Baptism, in which we are baptized with water and sealed with the Spirit, we tend to think of them in that order—but our ways are not necessarily God's way (Is. 55:8) and vice versa! Note how the Spirit defies expectations in today's first reading (cross your forearms, so that the chrism appears to your audience to the left of the water). Whereas the Jewish people saw God as *their* God, God defies our expectations, revealing God's self in today's first reading as a God who shows no partiality (Acts 10:34) and is a God of all nations and all lands (Acts 10:35; Ps. 98:4). How might God be calling us to defy others' expectations by loving *not* just those who love us—but *all* people?

On **the second Sunday of May**, U.S. society celebrates **Mother's Day**. Each of us has a mother and various mother figures in our lives: Let's celebrate them today!

- Involve women in all liturgical ministries today!
- Incorporate intercessions for mothers—living and deceased.
- Share a special blessing for mothers and mother figures (e.g., stepmothers, godmothers, aunts, teachers, coaches), lead all present in an applause, and share with all mother figures a red, long-stemmed rose or some other symbol of your community's love for and gratitude to them!
- For the intellectually-curious, note that the ancient Greeks celebrated Cybele—the mother of Greek gods—with a spring festival, and/or share a brief lesson on Mother Jarvis' concern that, prior to Mother's Day, there was no day in the U.S. to honor women.

On **May 10**, the Church celebrates **St. Damien de Veuster** (1840-1889), who dedicated his ministry to those who suffered leprosy and were exiled to Moloka'i. Consider your own stance toward the "lepers" of your family, community, and/or society, and commit yourself to a concrete act of reaching out and assisting them!

On **May 10**, we remember the passing of **Walker Percy** (1916-1990), the American author known for his philosophical novels and his exploration of "the dislocation of [the human person] in the modern age." He and his wife, Mary Bernice, converted to Catholicism together, and his career as a Catholic writer began nearly ten years later with an article in *Commonweal* magazine condemning Southern segregation and demanding a larger role for Christian thought in Southern life. Three months before his death, he made his profession as a secular Benedictine oblate. In his memory, find a way to take a stand against vestiges of segregation that are based on such categories as race, religion, economic status, sex, sexuality and gender identity!

On **May 10**, we celebrate the birth of **Rhee Timbang**, the supreme bishop of the Philippine Independent Church. An advocate for gender equality, he consecrated in 2019 the first woman bishop in the church's 117-year history. Pray for him and for the more than one million Independent Catholics he serves!

On **May 11**, we remember the passing of **Yves René Marie Simon** (1903-1961), the French moral and political philosopher who was recognized as one of the world's "most original and distinguished political theorists." More openminded than many Thomists and scholastic philosophers, Simon ardently defended the compatibility of Thomistic virtues and moral action with liberal, Western democracy, arguing that French Catholics erred in believing that their Catholic faith supported adherence to monarchs. In his memory, pray for all who find themselves in monarchical churches that reflect more the vision and structures of the ancient and medieval Roman Empire, than the reign of God!

On **May 11**, the Independent Sacramental Movement remembers the passing of **Salomão Barbosa Ferraz** (1880-1969), the Anglican priest who founded the Free Catholic Church and was consecrated to the episcopacy by Carlos Duarte Costa. Salomão was later received into the Roman church by John XXIII, named a titular bishop, and participated in the Second Vatican Council. He was a husband and the father of seven children—a rare example of a legitimate, married bishop in the Roman church at that time. In his honor, pray for the reconciliation of churches, that we might all recognize our oneness in Christ!

On **May 12**, the Church celebrates **Ss. Nereus and Achilleus**, the first-century eunuch chamberlains of Emperor Domitian's niece, Flavia Domitilla. They were later banished with her to the island of Ponza and beheaded. In their honor, pray for all who serve others and "stick out their necks" for them!

On **May 12**, we remember the passing of **George Eglinton Alston Dix** (1901-1952), the British Benedictine monk, liturgical scholar, and Anglican papalist who advocated for reunion of the Church of England with the Roman church. In contrast with traditional Roman Catholic theology on the form and matter of the Church's sacraments, he argued in his 1945 work, *The Shape of the Liturgy*, that the four-action "shape" of the liturgy (offertory, prayer, fraction and communion) matters more than the words that are said. Pause today to thumb through his works and reflect on your own views of church and liturgy!

On **May 12**, we remember the passing of **Erik Homburger Erikson** (1902-1994), the German-American developmental psychologist and psychoanalyst known for his theory of psychological development and his coining of the phrase "identity crisis." In his memory, pray for all who suffer from mistrust, shame, guilt, inferiority, role confusion, isolation, stagnation and/or despair!

On **May 13**, the Church celebrates **Our Lady of Fatima**, the 1917 apparition of Mary to shepherd children in 20th-century Portugal. Faithful to her command to pray for sinners, find a moment today to pray the rosary!

On **May 13**, we remember the passing of **Jaroslav Jan Pelikan** (1923-2006), the American Lutheran pastor and scholar of medieval intellectual history, Christianity, and Christian doctrine. He authored more than 30 books, including his five-volume *The Christian Tradition: A History of the Development of Doctrine*, and his later works crossed from the scholarly realm into popular reading. Late in life, he "returned" to the Orthodox Church that he discovered through his study. In his memory, pause and consider Jesus and/or Mary through the centuries!

On **May 13**, the Lutheran World Federation celebrates the anniversary of the election in 2017 of President **Musa Panti Filibus**. In a spirit of ecumenism, pray for him and for the 74 million Lutherans he serves!

On **May 14**, the Church celebrates **St. Matthias** (+c. 80), the man chosen from 120 disciples to replace Judas Iscariot (Acts 1:18-26). Pray Eucharistic Prayer I, which mentions him, and use this day to reflect on how you are forming your own "replacement(s)." Identify the people who could one day do what you currently do, and empower them in their education and formation!

On **May 14**, we remember the passing of **Dominique-Marie Varlet** (1678-1742), the Roman Catholic bishop of Babylon who, without the permission of the Roman papacracy, shared valid lines of apostolic succession with four archbishops of Utrecht. Take a moment today to thank God for the tremendous courage and pastoral sensitivity of this giant in the Independent Sacramental Movement!

On **May 15**, the Church celebrates **St. Isidore the Farmer** (c. 1070-1130, not to be confused with St. Isidore of Seville, who is celebrated on April 4). In honor of the patron saint of farmers, share a prayer for all who raise and harvest the foods we all enjoy!

On **May 15**, we remember the passing of **Peter Maurin** (1877-1949), the French social activist and co-founder of the Catholic Worker Movement who "indoctrinated" Dorothy Day with such ideas as Catholic Worker farms and "houses of hospitality" for the poor. In his memory, consider your own stance toward the poor and those most in need!

On **May 15**, we celebrate the birth in 1956 of **Chung Hyun Kyung**, the South Korean lay Presbyterian theologian whose research interests have included feminist and ecofeminist theologies, Christian-Buddhist interfaith dialogue, and the theologies and spiritualities of Asia, Africa and Latin America. Pause today to learn something new about another theological or spiritual tradition!

Sunday, May 16, 2021
THE ASCENSION OF OUR LORD
(white)

Consider when you'll celebrate the Solemnity of the Ascension: If you celebrate it on the 40th day of Easter, know that many people may be unable to join you for a Thursday liturgy. By transferring the celebration to this Sunday, all will be able to celebrate this mystery of our faith!

It's the Easter season: The **paschal candle** remains in close proximity to the ambo!

For the intellectually-curious, there are various lessons today!

- Provide a brief lesson on the ascension in scripture: it's not contained in the earliest version of Mark, it can only be inferred in Matthew, and it may have taken place as soon as Easter Day in Luke's account. Also, be sure to note that the Acts of the Apostles, which contains an ascension account, was written by Luke!

- Anthropologist Joseph Campbell pointed out that, even if the risen Christ blasted off from the earth at the speed of light, he'd still be in the Milky Way nearly 2,000 years later! What are more mature understandings that we might have of this mystery, rather than a merely simplistic conception of the resurrected Christ ascending to be atop the "bowl" of the heavens in the ancient cosmology?

Note the **exclusive language** of today's first reading: Why should we presume that there were no women among the "men of Galilee" — since Jesus' mother and other women were among Jesus' disciples?

You'll need to **choose the second reading** you'll proclaim: Ephesians 1, which speaks of Christ being seated at God's right hand in heaven, or Ephesians 4, which says that Christ descended into the lower regions of the earth before ascending "far above all the heavens."

Note: **The introductory line of today's second reading is misleading.** The Letter to the Ephesians is a pseudonymous letter, written in Paul's name and spirit, but not written by Paul. Rather than confuse your listeners, begin with, "A reading from the Letter to the Ephesians"!

The thread in today's scriptures: Matthew concludes his gospel with the risen Christ's admonition to baptize and teach others to observe his commandments (Mt. 28:19-20; note the connections to last Sunday's scriptures), and we hear the ascension account of Luke's second volume (Acts1:1-11). The psalmist sings of the ascension of the messiah to his throne (Ps. 47:2-9), and the pseudonymous author of the Letter to the Ephesians affirms that God "worked in Christ, raising him from the dead and seating him at God's right hand in the heavens" (Eph. 1:20).

Holy humor: The story is told of the priest who was speaking with the small children of her congregation. Before bidding them farewell, she asked if any of the children had any questions for her. Little Rebecca was eager to share what she had discovered this week. She asked, "Do you know why God created the world with only one hand?" The priest was a bit surprised. "God only created the world with one hand?" Little Rebecca continued, "Yes! God created the world with God's left hand — and do you know why?" Deciding to play along, the priest asked, "And just how do we know that God created the world with God's left hand?" Little Rebecca was quick to answer: "Because Jesus was…sitting on God's right hand!" [Segue into today's celebration of Jesus' ascension into heaven.]

Looking for a visual aid for your homily or object lesson? Consider a large bowl and plate, and/or a cross! Ancient depictions of the universe (indeed until some 500 years ago) suggested that the heavens were like an inverted bowl over the flat plate of the earth. So, too, it's time to see this mystery of faith anew. Instead of thinking of Christ as "somewhere up there" (an admittedly androcentric conception by people on one side of a "flat" earth), open your eyes: Christ is hidden in the faces of those around you! Medieval mystics suggested that the two beams of the cross lift our attention "vertically" toward God and "horizontally" toward those around us: Consider how this feast has traditionally taken our eyes in a "vertical" direction when, perhaps more appropriately, this celebration should take our eyes in a "horizontal" direction — in the direction of the presence of Christ around us!

On **May 18**, the Church celebrates **St. John I** (+526), the elderly pope imprisoned by an Arian king. Pray in a special way for the elderly, the imprisoned, and those who are persecuted by others!

On **May 19**, we remember the passing of **Alcuin of York** (c. 735-804), the Northumbrian scholar, mathematician and poet in Charlemagne's court later named an abbot and "the most learned person anywhere to be found." He penned several works, including the famous *Life of St. Willibrord*, important in the Old Catholic tradition. In his memory, reacquaint yourself with his *Life of St. Willibrord*!

On **May 19**, we remember the passing of **Max Ferdinand Scheler** (1874-1928), the German "first man of the philosophical paradise" who developed Husserl's phenomenology and greatly influenced contemporary philosophy. Karol Wojtyla (John Paul II) defended his doctoral dissertation on Scheler, who suggested that philosophical knowledge cannot be achieved without sharing in the primal essence of love, which opens us to other "beings-of-value." In Scheler's memory, pause to consider the values and "disvalues" (negative values) that currently direct your life—and the value that you might be attaching to the realization of lower values at the expense of higher values!

On **May 19**, we remember the passing of **Jacques Ellul** (1912-1994), the French philosopher, sociologist and lay theologian who was a noted Christian anarchist and who authored 58 books and a thousand articles during his lifetime. A dominant theme of his work was the threat that technology poses to religion and human freedom. In his memory, consider the ways in which technology limits your freedom and the freedom of those whom you love!

On **May 20**, the Church celebrates **St. Bernardine of Siena** (1380-1444), the orphaned "apostle of Italy" who cared for plague victims, preached devotion to the Holy Name of Jesus, and hosted "bonfires of vanities" to burn unnecessary luxuries. In his memory, encourage acts of care for "untouchables," share a lesson on the IHS Christogram, and/or encourage congregants to share with those in need the extra food in their pantries and the extra clothes in their closets!

On **May 21**, the Church celebrates **St. Christopher Magallanes** (1869-1927) **and Companions,** the 22 priests and 3 laypersons martyred during anticlerical government reforms in Mexico (1915-1928). Christopher was killed without trial—and after absolving his executioner. Take a moment today to pray for your enemies and for their forgiveness; better yet, find a way to reach out to them today in love!

On **May 22**, we remember the passing of **St. Constantine I** (272-337). Known as "Constantine the Great" and "the Equal to the Apostles," he reunited the Roman Empire and is now considered a saint in the Orthodox tradition. For centuries, it was believed that he experienced a radical conversion leading to a personal crusade to convert his empire to his mother's religion. Pray today for all civil leaders who have been sympathetic to our Christian/Catholic beliefs and traditions!

On **May 22**, the Church celebrates **St. Rita of Cascia** (c. 1381-1457), a victim of domestic abuse, who, as an Augustinian nun, shared the sufferings of Jesus. Pray for all victims of domestic violence — and promote acts of charity for organizations that assist them!

On **May 22**, we remember the passing of **Victor Marie Hugo** (1802-1885), the French poet, novelist and dramatist who wrote *Les Misérables*, is considered one of France's greatest and best-known writers, and whose likeness is on French currency. Largely raised by his Catholic mother, he received a Catholic Royalist education. As a young man, his views became increasingly anti-Catholic and anti-clerical, particularly in light of the Church's indifference to the plight of the working class. The Catholic press responded with some 740 published attacks on *Les Misérable*. In his memory, pray for and/or connect with those who cherish the Church's message of social justice — even if they have challenges with the clericalism, structures and stances of the Church!

Sunday, May 23, 2021
PENTECOST
(red)

We're still in the Easter season: The **paschal candle** remains in close proximity to the ambo — and is removed from the sanctuary at the conclusion of today's Mass. Consider carrying it out of your worship space as part of the procession during the hymn of sending forth!

Think through the **Pentecost décor** of your worship space!

- Decorate your worship space with splashes of **red**!
- Be sure your **Pentecost vestments** are ironed or steamed — and that they coordinate with any other shades of red in your worship environment.
- Consider **banners** with images of the fire and/or dove that represents the Holy Spirit.

- Consider **floral arrangements** that symbolize the diversity of the persons who experienced the Pentecost event, with a variety of flowers of differing shapes, sizes and colors. Consider flowers with intriguing, flame-shaped and/or flame-colored blooms.

- Bring to mind the appearance of the Holy Spirit as a rushing wind by creating **ribbon banners** on portable stands lining your outer aisles, by placing banners outdoors, and/or by hanging bells and/or chimes in trees. When making ribbon banners, always vary the colors, widths and lengths of the ribbons.

- As always, **decorate the entrance to your worship space and even outdoors**, so that the spirit of the celebration is obvious to congregants as they approach your worship space! Also, don't forget the look of other spaces, like your Blessed Sacrament chapel, parish hall and classrooms!

- **Invite congregants to wear red**, or, if you have a multicultural community, invite congregants to dress in native dress, and proclaim the scriptures — particularly the first reading — in a more multilingual way!

There is no more appropriate way to celebrate the coming of the Holy Spirit than with the **sacrament of Confirmation**: Consider planning well in advance for a celebration of Confirmation on this special day!

Note: There is a **special set of scriptures** for the Vigil of Pentecost, which includes four options for the first reading!

The Church shares four "great sequences" each year: Today's is the *Veni, Sancte Spiritus*. Consider having a gifted cantor sing or chant a setting of this, before segueing into the Gospel Acclamation!

The thread in today's scriptures (for the Mass during the Day): Luke shares the story of the coming of the Spirit at Pentecost (Acts 2:1-11). John tells a different story, of how the Johannine Jesus breathed forth the Spirit on his friends on Easter night (Jn. 20:19-23). Both point to the same truth: The Spirit is present and active in Christ's Church, endowing us with gifts (1Cor. 12:3-7) and renewing the face of the earth (Ps. 104:30) through those who've received the gift of the Spirit!

Holy humor: You've likely heard the joke about how you make holy water, right? How do you make holy water? You take water, and you…boil the hell out of it! But have you heard what you get when you mix holy water and…vodka? What do you get when you mix holy water and vodka? A holy…spirit! [Segue to how it is that this day celebrates a different type of holy spirit: God's sustaining Spirit in our world!]

Looking for a visual aid for your homily or object lesson? Consider a glass of milk, a bottle of chocolate syrup, and a tall spoon! Hold up the glass of milk, and tell your listeners "This glass of milk represents…you!" Everyone knows the taste of milk. Invite forward an altar server, have him/her taste the milk, and tell you what it tastes like. It tastes like…milk! Now hold up the chocolate, and say "This chocolate represents…the Holy Spirit!" (Your listeners can now guess where this is going!) Pour the chocolate into the glass, and have the altar server taste the milk again. What does it taste like? (Be sure to prepare your altar server in advance, so that s/he is not confused.) Because the chocolate pierced the milk and settled on the bottom of the glass, the milk still tastes like…milk. What do you have to do to the chocolate? You have to stir it up! Like the glass of milk, we all receive the Spirit in the sacraments of the Church…but we ourselves need to "stir up" the Spirit! As you stir the chocolate into the milk, list a few ways listeners can "stir up" the Spirit in their lives (e.g., prayer, reading scripture, going to church, performing good works). Finally, ask the altar server to taste the milk one last time. What does it taste like? Chocolate milk! End with these words: "Sisters and brothers, we've all received the gift of the Spirit. If your life tastes like 'milk,' it's time to…stir up the Spirit!"

On Pentecost, we refresh the special dismissal that we heard during the Easter Octave: Be sure your deacon knows how to **chant the double Alleluia of the dismissal**.

After today, we return to Ordinary Time — beginning with the 8th Week in Ordinary Time this week — but we won't see the color green on a Sunday until June 13.

The school year is winding down: Be sure to have an **end-of-year blessing for all students — and all who serve them** — in thanksgiving for the past year of learning and growth, and asking for God's blessing over them during the summer break! Also, find a fitting way to **celebrate the graduates in your community** — perhaps by inviting them to wear their caps and gowns to Mass, sharing scholarships with them, and/or having a reception with cake and punch to honor them!

On **May 23,** we remember the passing of **Laurentius Surius** (1523-1578), the German Carthusian hagiographer and church historian known for his collection of the acts of the Church councils and the lives of the saints. In his memory, consider how you are capturing and telling the stories of your community and its saints!

On **May 23,** we remember the passing of **Franz von Baader** (1765-18541), the German Catholic philosopher, theologian, physician and mining engineer who revived the Scholastic school as a means of countering growing empiricism and atheism in Europe. He is known for introducing to academia the works of Meister Eckhart, the Dominican who suffered the inquisitorial process and was condemned for heresy by the Roman church. In his memory, explore the mystical works of Meister Eckhart, whom von Baader attempted to popularize!

On **May 23**, the Romanian Greek-Catholic Church (in union with Rome) celebrates the birth in 1930 of **Major Archbishop Lucian Mureşan**. In a spirit of ecumenism, pray for him and for the 504,000 Romanian Greek-Catholics he serves!

On **May 24**, we remember the passing of **Georges Darboy** (1813-1871), the archbishop of Paris who argued for the episcopal independence of the French church and strongly opposed purported papal infallibility at the First Vatican Council. He stirred controversy by suppressing the Jesuits in his diocese, and Pius IX refused him the cardinal's hat due to his liberal writings. He was among the hostages who were executed when the Paris Commune was about to be overthrown in 1871. In his memory, pray for all victims of violence, oppression, and passive-aggression!

On **May 25**, the Church celebrates **St. Bede the Venerable** (c. 672-735), **St. Gregory VII** (c. 1015-1085), and **St. Mary Magdalene de'Pazzi** (1566-1607). Bede challenges us to consider how we are recording history. Gregory VII was a reformer who, because of his disputes with the emperor, is a model for getting along with those who think very differently from us. Mary Magdalene de'Pazzi developed a love of prayer from an early age (a model for children!) and can be lifted up as a model of prayer, penance, eucharistic devotion, and love for the poor!

On **May 25**, the Roman Catholic Church celebrates the birth in 1953 of **Francesco Moraglia**, the Latin Patriarch of Venice. In a spirit of ecumenism, pray for him and for the Roman Catholics he serves!

On **May 26**, the Church celebrates **St. Philip Neri** (1515-1595), the Italian priest and "third apostle of Rome" who founded the Congregation of the Oratory for secular priests. In his memory, consider the ways in which you support and encourage the clergy around you!

On **May 26**, the Church celebrates **St. Peter Sanz** (1680-1747), the Catalan Dominican friar and bishop who was tortured and beheaded by imperial authorities in China. Pray for all who suffer the cruelty of others!

On **May 26**, we remember the passing of **Georg Hermes** (1775-1831), the German Catholic theologian whose works were posthumously condemned by the Roman church but were later championed by his students who joined the Old Catholic Church. Their efforts were in vain, and the condemnation of his works was reiterated by Pius IX—only solidifying their opposition to the oppressive papacracy of the Roman church. In his memory, pray for all who are harshly judged, even after death!

On **May 27**, the Church celebrates **St. Augustine of Canterbury** (+c. 604), the first bishop of Canterbury: Pray today for our sisters and brothers of the Anglican tradition!

On **May 27**, we remember the passing of **John Calvin** (1509-1564), the French priest, theologian and reformer who wrote commentaries on most books of the Bible, championed the absolute sovereignty of God in matters of salvation, and championed new forms of liturgy and church governance. In his memory, grow in wisdom by increasing your knowledge of God and yourself!

On **May 29,** the Syro Malabar Catholic Church (in union with Rome) celebrates the anniversary of the installation in 2011 of **George Alencherry** as Major Archbishop of Ernakulam-Ankamali. In a spirit of ecumenism, pray for him and for the 5.1 million Syro Malabar Catholics he serves!

On **May 29**, we remember the passing of **Andrew Greeley** (1928-2013), the Roman Catholic priest, sociologist and novelist who interpreted American Catholicism through his research and fiction. Greeley's explicit treatment of sex and sexuality, as well as of the Roman church's sexual abuse scandal, earned him the scorn of critics. In his memory, pray for all whose words and actions are not always charitably received by those they love!

Sunday, May 30, 2021
THE MOST HOLY TRINITY
(white)

Decorate your worship space with a white that matches your vestments, and integrate Trinitarian symbols (e.g., the triangle, or three interlocking figures). Be careful to avoid heretical images of the Trinity: To depict an old man, Jesus, and a bird pushes congregants to tritheistic notions!

Beware the **exclusive language** in today's first reading: God created man *and woman*. Today's psalm is riddled with masculine references to God that can easily be remedied by proclaiming the psalm in the second person (e.g., "all your works are trustworthy. You love justice and right"), and Paul uses the androcentric expression of "*Abba*, Father" for God. Is there really any legitimate reason to use the word "sons of God" in Romans 8:14, rather than "children of God"?

The thread in today's scriptures: An anachronistic Moses speaks of God's wonders, noting that there is no other god (Dt. 4:35 & 4:39). God created the three-tiered universe of the heavens, the earth and the seas (Ps. 33:6-9) — then chose Israel as God's own (Ps. 33:12)! Paul speaks of the creating, redeeming and sustaining acts of God (Rom. 8:14-1). The anachronistic Matthean Jesus bids farewell to his friends with instructions for them to baptize all nations with a Trinitarian formula (Mt. 28:19).

Holy humor: [Warning: This joke takes some practice to ensure its smooth delivery.] The story is told of how the pope some centuries ago had decided to expel all Jewish people from Rome. Naturally, there was an uproar from the Jewish community. So the pope made a deal: He would have a religious debate with the rabbi of the Jewish community; if the rabbi won, the Jewish people could stay; but if the pope won, the Jewish people would have to leave. The very smart rabbi who was chosen to debate the pope had one simple request: To make it more interesting, neither side would be allowed to talk! The pope agreed. The day of the great debate came, and the rabbi sat opposite the pope. The pope raised his hand and showed three fingers [raise three fingers of your right hand], and the rabbi looked back at the pope and raised one finger [raise one finger of your left hand]. The pope waved his fingers in a circle around his head [wave your right hand in a horizontal circle], and the rabbi pointed to the ground where he sat [point to the ground with your left hand]. The pope pulled out a host and a chalice of wine [hold up a chalice in your right hand], and the rabbi pulled out an apple [hold up an apple in your left hand]. Exasperated, the pope stood up and said, "I give up! You're too good! Your people can stay!" [Put down the chalice and apple.] Afterwards, the cardinals asked the pope what happened. The pope said, "First, I held up three fingers to represent the Trinity [raise three fingers of your right hand], and he responded by holding up one finger [raise one finger of your left hand] to remind me that there was still one God common to both our religions. Then I waved my finger around me to show him that God was all around us [wave your right hand in a horizontal circle], and he responded by pointing to the ground and showing that God was also right here with us [point to the ground with your left hand]. I pulled out the host and the wine to show that God absolves us from our sins [hold up the chalice in your right hand], and he pulled out an apple to remind me of our original sin [hold up the apple in your left hand]. He had an answer for everything! What could I do?" [Put down the chalice and apple.] Meanwhile, the Jewish community crowded around the rabbi and asked him what happened. "Well," said the rabbi, "First he said to me that we had three days to leave [raise three fingers of your right hand], so I told him that not one of us was leaving [raise one finger of your left hand]. Then he told me that this whole city would be cleared of Jews [wave your right hand in a horizontal circle], and I let him know that we were staying right here. [point to the ground with your left hand]." "And then?" asked a woman. "I don't know," said the rabbi. "He took out his lunch [hold up the chalice in your right hand], so I took out mine [hold up the apple in your left hand]!" [Segue into the theological complexities with which we've surrounded the Trinity and the many and varied perspectives that exist on the Trinity.]

Looking for a visual aid for your homily or object lesson? Consider involving all present in the very Catholic symbol of…the sign of the cross! Ask listeners how many times in their lives they've made the sign of the cross. Every time we do so, we express our belief in the great mystery of how God created, redeemed and continues to sustain us and our world! [Alternatively, you might warn of the heretical, tritheistic tendencies of some Trinitarian images that picture God as an old man, Jesus and bird on a cloud!]

For the intellectually-curious, share a lesson on solid Trinitarian theology, definitions from Trinitarian theology, and Trinitarian heresies. Many missals commit the heresy of tritheism by depicting the Father, Son and Holy Spirit as an old man, Jesus and a bird on a cloud. How far this is from the *mysterium tremendum et fascinans* for which we use the codename "God"!

It's **Memorial Day** weekend: Include prayers for all who made the ultimate sacrifice for our freedom!

On **May 31**, the Church celebrates the **Visitation of Mary**: Repeat Elizabeth's words as you pray the second Joyful Mystery of the rosary!

On **June 1**, the Church celebrates **St. Justin** (c. 100 – c. 165), the early apologist who used philosophy to shed light on the mysteries of our faith: Honor him with a brief refresher of his defenses of our beliefs!

On **June 1**, we remember the passing of **Karl Paul Reinhold Niebuhr** (1892-1971), the Reformed theologian and ethicist who has been called the most influential American theologian of the 20th century. He battled with religious liberals over the optimism of their Social Gospel and with conservatives over their naïve view of scripture and their narrow definition of "true religion," and he frequently wrote on the intersection of religion, politics and public policy. In his memory, find a moment today to reacquaint yourself with his life and works!

On **June 1**, we remember the passing of **Thomas Berry** (1914-2009), the Catholic Passionist priest, cultural historian and eco-theologian—or "geologian," as he preferred to be called—who was a leading voice in eco-spirituality. A leader in the tradition of de Chardin, he advocated for an interdependent "communion of subjects" in an evolving universe, something that cannot be achieved without the assistance of political, economic, educational and religious systems. In his memory, consider your own stance toward the earth from which we were created!

On **June 2**, the Church celebrates **Ss. Marcellinus and Peter** (+c. 304), the third-century Roman priest and exorcist venerated by the Church after their martyrdom at the hands of Severus. In their memory, pray Eucharistic Prayer I, which mentions them, and pray for those "martyrs" who witness to God's love through their generous sharing of self!

On **June 2**, we celebrate the birth in 1957 of **Gregory A. Boyd**, the American theologian, pastor and author who is a leading voice in the Neo-Anabaptist movement for Christian pacifism and a non-violent understanding of God. He writes widely on Christianity and politics, debunking the myth of a "Christian nation." In his honor, consider your own notions of God's purported violence and the place of peace in Jesus' liberating message!

On **June 2**, we remember the passing of **Anthony de Mello** (1931-1987), the Indian Jesuit priest and psychotherapist who drew from mystical traditions of the East and the West for his works on spirituality. In his memory, dust off his works and enrich your preaching and teaching!

On **June 3**, the Church celebrates **St. Charles Luwanga** (1860-1886), the Ugandan catechist who was burned alive with his 21 companions for spreading the faith in Uganda: Pray for and find a way to support the Church's missions in foreign lands!

On **June 4**, the Armenian Apostolic Church celebrates the anniversary of the enthronement in 2013 of Boghos Manousian as **Patriarch Nourhan Manougian of Jerusalem**. In his honor, pray for him and for the 9 million people he serves!

On **June 5**, the Church celebrates **St. Boniface** (c. 675-754), the Anglo-Saxon monk who evangelized Germany. People came to believe in him when he chopped down an oak tree dedicated to Thor—and wasn't immediately struck down. In his honor, reflect on the "sacred cows" that are presumably immune from question or criticism in our own faith tradition, to see if you, too, might grow in a deeper understanding of our faith and our world!

Sunday, June 6, 2021
THE BODY AND BLOOD OF CHRIST
(white)

Decorate your worship space with a white that matches your vestments, and integrate eucharistic symbols, like wheat and grapes and/or a loaf of bread and a cup!

The Church shares four "great sequences" each year: Today's is the *Lauda Sion*. Consider having a gifted cantor sing or chant a setting of this, before segueing into the Gospel Acclamation!

Note: **The introductory line of today's second reading is misleading**. The Letter to the Hebrews is a pseudonymous letter, written in Paul's name and spirit, but not written by Paul. To avoid this confusion, you might proclaim, "A reading from the Letter to the Hebrews."

The thread in today's scriptures: Moses used blood to seal the covenant between God and the Israelites (Ex. 24:6-8), foreshadowing the new covenant "cup of salvation" (Ps. 116:13) that is the saving blood of Christ (Heb. 9:13-15). In today's gospel, Mark shares the Last Supper story of Jesus sharing his "body" and his "blood of the covenant" (Mk. 14:22-24).

Holy humor: Have you heard the story of the Last Supper? On the night before he died, Jesus was enjoying his last supper with his friends. And he took bread, blessed it, broke it, gave it to his friends, and said, "This is my body." Then he took a cup of wine, and, giving thanks, he said, "This is my blood." And then he opened a jar of mayo...and Judas said, "I'm gonna stop you right there!" [Say, "Wait, I'm going to stop right there. Today's celebration of the Body and Blood of Christ isn't about bread, wine and mayo. It's about bread and wine: the Body and Blood of Christ!" Segue into the eucharistic motifs of each reading.]

Looking for a visual aid for your homily or object lesson? Consider a loaf of bread and a chalice! Hold up the bread when you speak of manna, wheat, bread, or the body of Christ, and hold up the chalice when you speak of the cup or of the blood of Christ!

Consider hosting a traditional *Corpus Christi* **procession** on this day! It could be as simple as a procession around the inside or outside of your worship space after the Prayer after Communion. Use a host that was consecrated at today's Mass, to make clear how our adoration of the Eucharist outside Mass flows from our liturgical action. Have your altar servers lead the procession with incense, cross and candles!

In honor of this Solemnity, consider having **a blessing of your community's eucharistic ministers!**

June is here! **For the intellectually-curious,** share a brief lesson on the double etymology of this month: Juno was the Roman goddess who was the patroness of marriage and of women's well-being; June was also the month in which the ancient Romans celebrated their *juvenis*, their young people! Give a June nod to the married couples, women, and/or young people of your community!

On **June 6**, when it doesn't fall on a Sunday, the Church celebrates **St. Norbert** (c. 1080-1134), the German nobleman-turned-priest whose near-death experience of lightning transformed his life. Consider how your life might change if you had a similar near-death experience — and begin to live in that way today!

On **June 6**, we remember the passing of **Karl Josef von Hefele** (1809-1893), the Roman Catholic bishop and German theologian known for his seven-volume work on the Church's councils. At the advent of the First Vatican Council, he published his *Causa Honorii Papae*, which argued for the moral and historical impossibility of purported papal infallibility, based on his vast knowledge of Church history. At the council, he voted against the promulgation of the proposed dogma. In his memory, spend a bit of time researching the complex contexts from which purported papal infallibility and other dogmas of the Church arose!

On **June 6**, we remember the passing of **Carl Gustav Jung** (1875-1961), the Swiss psychiatrist and psychoanalyst who influenced the fields of psychiatry, anthropology, archaeology, literature, philosophy and religious studies. He delved into individuation and coined such terms as synchronicity, the collective unconscious, extraversion and introversion. In his memory, dust off a few works on human personality and consider the correlations of various personality traits with religious behaviors!

On **June 8**, we remember the passing of **Henri Arnauld** (1597-1692), the Roman Catholic bishop of 42 years who ultimately chose to support his brother, Antoine, suffering the displeasure of Louis XIV when he refused to sign the *Formulary of Submission for the Jansenists*. He attempted to stall the tempest caused by the Archbishop of Paris' insistence that the nuns of Port-Royal-des-Champs sign the formulary, suggesting that they resist or take refuge in subtleties. In his honor, consider how you shield and protect others!

On **June 8**, we remember the passing of **Gerard Manley Hopkins** (1844-1889), the English Jesuit priest whose posthumous fame established him as one of the leading Victorian poets. In his memory, discover his sonnets of desolation!

On **June 8**, we celebrate the birth in 1928 of **Gustavo Gutiérrez Merino**, the Peruvian Dominican priest, philosopher and theologian regarded as one of the formulators of liberation theology. Focusing the movement on love of neighbor, particularly love of those who suffer poverty as a result of unjust social structures, he lifted up the ministry of Jesus to the rejected and despised as a model for the contemporary Church. In his memory, consider whether your words and actions manifest a "preferential option for the poor"!

On **June 9**, the Church celebrates **St. Ephrem the Syrian** (c. 306-373), the fourth-century, Syriac-Aramean deacon especially venerated by the Eastern Church. He is the patron saint of spiritual directors and spiritual leaders. In his memory, pray for all who have provided you spiritual direction throughout the years — and for the necessary gifts to help others discern the presence and activity of God in our world!

On **June 10**, we remember the passing of **Carl Gustav Adolf von Harnack** (1851-1930), the Baltic German Lutheran theologian and church historian who drew attention to the Greek influence that forever changed the direction of Christianity. He rejected the historicity of the Gospel of John, criticized the Apostles' Creed, and promoted the Social Gospel. In his memory, pause to critically reflect on those aspects of your faith that you may not have questioned in the past!

On the Friday after the Solemnity of the Body and Blood of Christ — the Church celebrates the **Solemnity of the Most Sacred Heart of Jesus**. For a deeper understanding of this mystery, challenge yourself to read Karl Rahner's more mature, contemporary views on this very medieval devotion. After all, what we celebrate is the mystery of Jesus' love!

On **June 11**, the Church celebrates **St. Barnabas**, who, due to his missionary endeavors, was considered an "apostle" by St. Luke. He parted ways with Paul over issues of circumcision and observance of the Mosaic law. In his honor, pray Eucharistic Prayer I, which mentions him, and highlight the diversity of the Christian/Catholic community and the need to sometimes "agree to disagree" with those we love!

On **June 12**, the Czechoslovak Hussite Church celebrates the birth in 1958 of **Patriarch Tomáš Butta**. In a spirit of ecumenism, pray for him and for the 39,000 people he serves!

On **June 12**, we remember the passing of **James Farl "J.F." Powers** (1917-1999), the novelist and short-story writer who often drew inspiration from developments in the contemporary Roman Catholic church. In his memory, consider the inspiration that you draw from contemporary events — and the ways in which you might help to interpret those events through the lens of our Catholic faith!

Sunday, June 13, 2021
Eleventh Sunday in Ordinary Time
(green)

We're back to Ordinary Time: Think about your **worship environment**!

- Decorate your worship space with a **medium green**, lighter than the green used for Winter Ordinary Time and more evocative of the grass and leaves we see outdoors at this time of year.
- Be sure to have **matching medium green vestments** for this season — and be sure they're ironed or steamed.
- Complement your décor with **green plants** with medium green leaves, and **rearrange the green plants periodically**, for variety.
- **Continue the decoration** into the entrance to your worship space, outdoors, and into other spaces on the grounds, including your Blessed Sacrament chapel, parish hall and classrooms!
- Five months of Ordinary time remain during this liturgical year: **Consider changing shades of green**! Use a yellow-green after Labor Day, as autumn approaches, then use a darker green for the final, darker weeks of Summer/Fall Ordinary Time, with matching vestments to mirror these changes!

The thread in today's scriptures: Ezekiel speaks of the tender shoot growing into a majestic cedar that houses all kinds of birds (Ez. 17:23), and Jesus speaks of the mustard seed becoming "the largest of plants" (Mk. 4:31-32). If we are "planted in the house of the Lord" (Ps. 92:14), aspiring to please god (2Cor. 5:9), we, too, will grow and flourish "like a cedar of Lebanon" (Ps. 92:13)!

Holy humor: In today's gospel, Jesus tells a joke that falls flat with 21st-century listeners. In Jesus' day, mustard shrubs were…weeds! It was as if Jesus told the story of a family that planted dandelion seeds in its yard! The sowing of mustard seeds in gardens was forbidden by the Jewish *Mishnah*, since they grow into "useless, annoying weeds." Nevertheless, poor people grew mustard plants for their inexpensive spice and medicinal uses. With their perfect "front yards," the righteous would have been offended by Jesus' suggestion that a forbidden weed could be like God's reign! God's reign, comprised of the rejected "mustard seeds," more closely resembles back-alley weeds, than manicured lawns and gardens! God's reign if more like the cypselae of a dry dandelion, than the petals of a beautiful rose!

Looking for a visual aid for your homily or object lesson? Consider a shoot from a local nursery, or a bottle of mustard seeds from a local supermarket! The former can be tied to the first reading, and the latter to the gospel. If you choose the latter, hold a mustard seed between your thumb and forefinger and ask whether those in the back pew can see it — or invite your hospitality ministers to share a mustard seed with each person present. If God can transform that tiny seed into a sizeable shrub, God can likely transform our lives as well!

On **June 13**, when it doesn't fall on a Sunday, the Church celebrates **St. Anthony of Lisbon** — or Padua, if you prefer (1195-1231), the Portuguese nobleman renowned for his Franciscan preaching. For the intellectually-curious, share a brief lesson on his life and why his name is invoked to find lost items ("Tony, Tony, look around: Something's lost and must be found"). In his honor, host the traditional blessing of St. Anthony loaves, share a loaf with each family, and invite them to share it together and to be inspired by Anthony's example of assisting the poor!

On **June 13**, we remember the passing of **Martin Buber** (1878-1965), the Austrian-born Jewish philosopher nominated seven times for the Nobel Peace Prize and best known for distinguishing I-Thou and I-It relationships. A translator of Hasidic lore, he emphasized the Hasidic ideal of living in the unconditional presence of God, with no distinction between daily habits and religious experience. In his memory, pause to consider how you treat people as objects and/or the ways in which you sometimes fail to have a heightened sense of God's presence and activity in your life!

On **June 13**, the Independent Sacramental Movement celebrates the birth in 1930 of **Emmanuel Milingo**, the former Roman Catholic archbishop of Lusaka, Zambia, who shared valid lines of apostolic succession with persons outside the Roman church. Take a moment today to thank God for his courage — and for the courage of so many former Roman Catholic bishops and priests who continue to share the Church's sacraments outside the structures and strictures of Rome!

On **June 13**, the Southern Baptist Convention celebrates the anniversary of the installation in 2020 of President **James David Greear**. In a spirit of ecumenism, pray for him and for the 15 million Baptists he serves!

On **June 14**, we remember the passing of **Gilbert Keith "G.K." Chesterton** (1874-1936), the English writer, poet, biographer, philosopher and lay theologian best known for his reasoned apologetics, his fictional priest-detective, Father Brown, and his biographies of such figures as St. Francis of Assisi and St. Thomas Aquinas. In his memory, familiarize yourself with his works and reflect on how you might bridge his words to your life!

On **June 14**, we remember the brutal murder of **Benjamin Estrope "Benjie" Bayles** (+2010), the 43-year-old Filipino activist and lay leader of the Philippine Independent Church who became a national symbol for the 1,200+ extrajudicial killings and even more "disappearances" suffered by the Filipino people in recent history. He courageously denounced abuses and human rights violations by the Philippine army. In his memory, consider your own courage in speaking out against the many human rights abuses in our world!

On **June 15**, we remember the passing of **Evelyn Underhill** (1875-1941), the English Anglo-Catholic writer and pacifist known for her numerous works on religion and mysticism. Due to her 1911 work, *Mysticism*, she was one of the most widely-read writers on the subject in the first half of the 20th century. In her memory, reflect on your own stance toward the mystical elements of life and religion!

On **June 15**, the Syro-Malankara Catholic Church (in union with Rome) celebrates the birth in 1959 of **Major Archbishop-Catholicos Moran Mor Baselios Cleemis**. In a spirit of ecumenism, pray for him and for the 500,000 Syro-Malankara Catholics he serves!

On **June 16**, we remember the passing of **Johannes Tauler** (c. 1300-1361), the German Dominican priest, theologian and mystic. A disciple of Meister Eckhart and a medieval Christian universalist, he was known for his sermons, which were widely disseminated. Pause to consider the message you share with others — and how you might better share your words and thoughts with others!

On **June 16**, we remember the passing of **Peter Joseph Elvenich** (1796-1886), the German Catholic theologian and philosopher who defended the condemned works of his teacher, Georg Hermes. His work was in vain, he was removed from his teaching post, and, after the Vatican Council, he affiliated himself with the Old Catholic Church. In his memory, pause to consider how you are defending those who lack a voice in our world!

On **June 16**, we remember the murder of **Joselito Agustín** (1976-2010), the Filipino radio journalist and lay leader of the Philippine Independent Church who was gunned down for speaking against and jeopardizing the political futures of mayoral candidates in Bacarra, Ilocos Norte, Philippines. He courageously spoke out in favor of worker rights and against government corruption. In his memory, pray for the many prophets in our world who continue to speak truth to power!

On **June 17**, the Ukrainian Autocephalous Orthodox Church Canonical celebrates the anniversary of the installation in 2005 of Oleh Kulyk as **Patriarch Moses of Kyiv**. In a spirit of ecumenism, pray for him and for the people he serves!

On **June 19**, the Church celebrates **St. Romuald of Ravenna** (c. 950-1027), the self-indulgent young man who became a monk after the death of his father in a duel. In his honor, consider the place of solitude, meditation and contemplative prayer in your life!

On **June 19**, we remember the passing of Lord Acton, **John Emerich Edward Dalberg** (1834-1902), the English Catholic historian, politician and writer known for his remark, "Powers tends to corrupt, and absolute power corrupts absolutely. Great [people] are almost always bad [people]." Lord Acton succeeded John Henry Newman as editor of a Roman Catholic paper, sharing his wealth of historical knowledge. Though Roman Catholic, he was hostile to ultramontane pretensions. His independence of thought brought him into conflict with the Roman church's hierarchy, which censured his paper. In his memory, pray for all who foster Independent Catholic thought in our world!

On **June 19**, **Juneteenth** is celebrated in Texas: an opportunity for us to show our solidarity with our African-American sisters and brothers who have endured far too many injustices throughout history!

Sunday, June 20, 2021

TWELFTH SUNDAY IN ORDINARY TIME

(green)

The thread in today's scriptures: The psalmist and the author of Job imagined God to be the master of the sea and storms (Ps. 107:25; Job 38:8-11). Similarly, Mark shows Jesus' control over the wind and sea (Mk. 4:39-41). The same God who causes ships to sink to the depths and rise to the heavens on turbulent waves (Ps. 107:25-26) raised Jesus from the grave and lifted him to heaven (2Cor. 5:15). As surely as all storms pass, all "old things" will pass in our lives, too, and we will become new creations in Christ (2Cor. 5;17)!

Holy humor: Try a few storm jokes, then segue into—all joking aside—God's power over the destructive forces of this world, as suggested in today's readings!

- What do you call a walking stick that makes you walk faster? A hurri-cane!
- Where do squirrels go in a hurricane? All over the place!
- I asked my Hindu friend whether she planned to evacuate for the hurricane, and she replied, "Na-ama-ste"!
- Maybe we should name hurricanes after politicians—then we wouldn't have to worry about them coming through with anything!
- [This one may hit too close to home] A man walked into a bar and asked for a corona and two hurricanes. The bartender said, "That'll be $20.20."
- What happened to the sailboat in the category 5 hurricane? Mast destruction!

Looking for a visual aid for your homily or object lesson? Consider a toy boat! Move it as you speak of the storms in today's readings, emphasizing how waves make boats go up and down. Paul imagined a similar movement: God sent Jesus from the heights of heaven and raised him again from the depths of death—hope for all who endure the "storms" of life!

On **the third Sunday of June**, U.S. society celebrates **Father's Day**!

- Incorporate intercessions for father — living and deceased!
- Share a special blessing for fathers and father figures (e.g., stepfathers, godfathers, uncles, teachers, coaches), lead all present in an applause for them, and share with them a keychain, a parish koozie, or some other symbol of your community's love of and gratitude for them!

On **June 20**, the Greek Melchite Catholic Church (in union with Rome) celebrates the birth in 1946 of **Patriarch Youssef Absi**. In a spirit of ecumenism, pray for him and for the 1.5 million Greek Melchite Catholics he serves!

On **June 21**, the Church celebrates **St. Aloysius Gonzaga** (1568-1591), the patron saint of youth. He died serving victims of the plague. In his honor, host a special blessing of youth, that they might be inspired by the lives of the saints in the same way that the young Aloysius was!

On **June 21**, the Greek Melchite Catholic Church (in union with Rome) celebrates the anniversary of the election in 2017 of **Youssef Absi** as Patriarch of Antioch, Alexandria and Jerusalem. In a spirit of ecumenism, pray for him and for the 1.5 million Greek Melchite Catholics he serves!

On **June 22**, the Church celebrates **St. Paulinus of Nola** (353-431) and **Ss. John Fisher** (1469-1535) **and Thomas More** (1478-1535). Paulinus and his wife, Therasia, gave their family's riches to the poor and lived an active/contemplative life by serving the lost and wayward who occupied the first floor of their two-story "monastery." Thomas More and John Fisher were known for their integrity in the court of Henry VIII. On this day, consider the privilege you enjoy (e.g., education, resources, relationships) — and how it is that you're using that privilege to advance God's reign!

On **June 22**, we remember the passing of **Yves Marie-Joseph Congar** (1904-1995), the French Dominican priest and theologian best known for his influence on ecumenism at the Second Vatican Council and for reviving theological interest in the Holy Spirit. He promoted the role of laity in the Church, criticized the Roman Curia and its clerical pomp, advocated for a "collegial papacy," and encouraged openness to ideas from the Eastern Orthodox Church and Protestantism. Following the publication of an article in support of the worker-priest movement in France, he was barred from teaching and publishing, and his book, *True and False Reform in the Church,* was forbidden. In his memory, pray for all who follow the promptings of the Spirit and advocate for the ideas espoused by Congar!

On **June 24**, the Church celebrates the **Solemnity of the Nativity of St. John the Baptist**. Decorate your worship space with large, clear vases of water (turned slightly more blue with food coloring), and pray Eucharistic Prayer I, which mentions him. For the intellectually-curious, share a lesson on the timing of this celebration, six months before Christmas Eve. Challenge congregants to be heralds of the king! If you haven't recognized your Proclaimers of the Word recently, today might be an appropriate day to share with them a special blessing and a token of your appreciation for their ministry!

On **June 24**, the Roman Catholic Church celebrates the anniversary of the appointment of **Pierbattista Pizzaballa** as Latin Patriarch of Jerusalem. In a spirit of ecumenism, pray for him and for the Roman Catholics he serves!

On **June 25**, we remember the passing of **Abraham von Franckenberg** (1593-1652), the Silesian mystic, poet and hymn writer who drew inspiration from alchemy, the Kabbalah and medieval mysticism. Many of his writings focused on unity with God through denial of self and all worldly things. In his memory, consider the sources that you incorporate into your own spirituality and the additional sources that might help you better grow in your relationships with God and others!

On **June 26**, we remember the passing of **Hans Urs von Balthasar** (1905-1988), the Swiss theologian who was considered one of the most important Catholic theologians of the 20th century and who died before being elevated to his cardinalate in the Roman Catholic Church. He is best known for his works on theological aesthetics, theodramatics of the paschal mystery, his theo-logic on the relationship of Christology to ontology, and his 15-volume systematics. In his memory, take a moment to see what wisdom from his works might enrich your life and ministry!

Sunday, June 27, 2021

THIRTEENTH SUNDAY IN ORDINARY TIME

(green)

Choose the gospel you'll proclaim: The longer version has nearly 11 more verses with the interpolation of the woman with her twelve-year hemorrhage. Even if you choose the shorter gospel, you can speak of her in your homily.

Beware the **exclusive language** in today's first reading. Is there really any reason to proclaim that "God formed *man*...in the image of *his* own nature *he* made *him*" when you could just as easily (and more inclusively) say, "God formed humankind...in the image of God's own nature God made us"? Note the five other instances of "his" in the first reading and responsorial psalm: The second can be deleted and all others can easily be rendered "God's."

The thread in today's scriptures: The book of Wisdom tells us that "death entered the world" (Wis. 2:24) despite the fact that "God did not make death" (Wis. 1:13), and, in today's gospel, Jesus raises Jairus' daughter from the dead (Mk. 5:35-42)! Jesus urges Jairus to have faith (Mk. 5:36) and credits the healing of the woman afflicted with a hemorrhage to her faith (Mk. 5:34). The psalmist speaks of God's faithful ones (Ps. 30:5), and Paul notes that the Corinthians excelled in faith (2Cor. 8:7). We might imagine Jairus' daughter singing with the psalmist, "I will praise you, Lord, for you have rescued me" (Ps. 30:2), and her father similarly proclaiming, "You changed my mourning into dancing" (Ps. 30:12)!

Holy humor: Perhaps you've heard the story of the man who went on a vacation with his wife and mother-in-law to Jerusalem. During the trip, his mother-in-law suddenly died. The American embassy told the couple that they could fly the body back to the United States for some $5,000, or they could bury her in Jerusalem for $30. The man replied, "Shipping is expensive, and we could organize a beautiful ceremony here...but I hear they buried a man here 2,000 years ago, and he came back to life in three days. We're not taking any chances!" [Segue into the contrast to this man, provided by Jesus' merciful stance toward the woman and girl in today's gospel — raising the daughter of Jairus from the dead!]

Looking for a visual aid for your homily or object lesson? Consider a report card! In today's second reading, Paul grades the Corinthians, noting that they received "A's" in faith, discourse, knowledge, earnestness and in the love Paul had for them (2Cor. 8:7). Ask your listeners what "grades" they would receive in each category. What other categories might Jesus "grade" — and what "grades" would they receive in those categories?

On **June 27**, when it doesn't fall on a Sunday, the Church celebrates **St. Cyril of Alexandria** (c. 375-444), who advanced the view that Mary is the Mother of God (*theotokos*), over the archbishop of Constantinople's "Nestorian" view that Mary is the Mother of Christ (*Christotokos*). Cyril inspired the Chalcedonian teaching on the two natures (viz., human and divine) of Christ. On this day, reflect on the great diversity of high and low Christologies and Mariologies throughout the Church, and challenge yourself to see Christ and/or Mary from a different perspective!

On **June 27**, we remember the passing of **Gerhoh of Reichersberg** (1093-1169), the canon, provost and Gregorian reformer known as one of the most distinguished theologians of 12th-century Germany. Held in high esteem by Eugene III, Gerhoh lost favor when he initially hesitated to support Alexander III and was forced to flee Rome. In his memory, consider how your own support or lack of support of others has led to friction and tension!

On **June 27**, we remember the passing of **Peter Ludwig Berger** (1929-2017), the Austrian-born American sociologist and Protestant theologian known for his work in the sociology of knowledge and religion. His co-authored work, *The Social Construction of Reality*, is considered one of the most influential texts in the sociology of knowledge, and his religious works explored the secularization and desecularization of a pluralistic, relativistic world. In his memory, deepen your own knowledge of the mutual influence of sociology and religion!

On **June 28**, the Church celebrates **St. Iraneus** (c. 130 – c. 202), the second-century Greek bishop who helped bring Christianity to present-day southern France. According to tradition, he received the faith from Polycarp, who, in turn, received it from John the Evangelist. Iraneus regarded all four now-canonical gospels as essential, and he countered Gnosticism with his three pillars of orthodoxy: scripture, tradition, and apostolic succession. In his memory, pray for those who shared the faith with you — and for those who handed on the faith to them!

On **June 28**, we remember the birth in 1950 of **Gary Robert Habermas**, the American New Testament scholar, philosopher of religion, and apologist who has catalogued and communicated trends among scholars in New Testament studies and the historical Jesus. The author of several works, he has frequently lectured on the resurrection of Jesus. In his honor, update your own knowledge of the trends in New Testament studies and/or in studies of the historical Jesus!

On **June 28**, we remember the passing of **Mortimer Jerome Adler** (1902-2001), the American Aristotelian/Thomistic philosopher and author of *How to Think About God*, whose spiritual journey took him from the Jewish religion to the Episcopal Church to the Roman Catholic Church — which he resisted for many years due to its limited views on such issues as abortion. In his memory, pray for those on winding spiritual paths who might welcome the refreshing waters of Independent Catholicism!

On **June 29**, the Church celebrates the **Solemnity of Ss. Peter** (+c. 64-68) **and Paul** (+c. 62-64), two preeminent figures in the early Church! Pray Eucharistic Prayer I, which mentions them, and meditate today on the greatness — but also the great humanness — of both saints!

On **June 29**, we remember the passing of **Henry of Ghent** (c. 1217-1293), the Italian "Solemn Doctor" and scholastic philosopher who sided with secular priests in their disputes with mendicants at the University of Paris — particularly on the issue of mendicants needing to confess to their parish priests, rather than to the priests of their orders. Henry had a hand in the creation of the 219 condemnations that were shared by the bishop of Paris. In his memory, pray for all zealous defenders of "orthodoxy"!

On **June 30**, the Church celebrates the **first martyrs of the Roman church** — those who were killed in 64 A.D. when Nero needed a scapegoat to assume the blame he was receiving for a fire that broke out in Rome. According to the stories that were shared, some were crucified, others were covered in animal skins and torn apart by dogs, and still others were tied to posts and set on fire. In their memory, consider your own courage for professing our faith!

On **June 30**, we remember the passing of **Raymond Lull** (c. 1232 - c. 1315), the Majorcan mathematician, philosopher and secular Franciscan credited with the first major work of Catalan literature. A pioneer of computational theory, he had a considerable influence on Leibniz. In his memory, consider the ways in which you are being pioneering, and/or challenge yourself in this respect!

On **July 1**, the Church celebrates **Bl. Junípero Serra** (1713-1784), the Franciscan friar who established the California missions, traveling thousands of miles on foot despite a leg injury. Lift him up as a model for overcoming obstacles in life!

On **July 1**, the Old Catholic Church celebrates the anniversary of the consecration in 2000 of **Joris August Odilius Ludovicus Vercammen** as Archbishop of Utrecht. Pray today for continued blessings for Archbishop Vercammen in his ministry to the people of God!

On **July 2**, we remember the passing of **Eliezer "Elie" Wiesel** (1928-2016), the Romanian-born Holocaust survivor, writer, political activist and Nobel Laureate who strongly defended human rights and drew attention to victims of oppression. In his memory, consider how you might better be a messenger of peace, atonement and human dignity!

On **July 3**, the Church celebrates **St. Thomas the Apostle** (+c. 53), the twin known for his doubts and the only apostle believed to evangelize outside the Roman Empire. Pray Eucharistic Prayer I, which mentions him, push yourself beyond your comfort zone, and encourage those with doubts!

On **July 3**, we celebrate the birth in 1946 of **Jean-Luc Marion**, the French Catholic theologian who writes on modern and contemporary philosophy and religion. A student of Derrida and known for his work, *God Without Being*, Marion philosophizes on such concepts as love, self-love, self-idolatry, intentionality and gift. In his honor, pause to consider how your love of others may be nothing more than your love of your own ideas as expressed in the "chance cause" of others!

On **July 3**, we remember the passing of **Sydney Eckman Ahlstrom** (1919-1984), the American historian who specialized in the religious history of the United States. In his memory, thumb through his work, *A Religious History of the American People*, to remember again aspects of American religious history you may have forgotten!

On **July 3**, we remember the passing of **Bernard Häring** (1912-1998), the German priest and moral theologian who authored 80 books and 1,000 articles, and who achieved notoriety with his three-volume work, *The Law of Christ*. As a young priest, he was conscripted into the German army and, though forbidden by Nazi authorities, shared sacraments with soldiers. As a *peritus* at Vatican II, he was part of the commission that prepared the pastoral constitution *Gaudium et spes*. In his memory, reacquaint yourself with his dialogical approach to moral theology, which esteems the ways in which God awakens and speaks to our conscience!

Sunday, July 4, 2021
FOURTEENTH SUNDAY IN ORDINARY TIME
(green)

The thread in today's scriptures: Ezekiel noted that the rebellious Israelites would recognize that a prophet had been among them (Ez. 2:5), and Jesus noted that prophets are "not without honor except in [their] native place" (Mk. 6:4). The psalmist well knew "the mockery of the arrogant" and "the contempt of the proud" (Ps. 123:4). Paul was a prophet, enjoying an abundance of revelations, but "a thorn in the flesh" kept him from being proud or elated (2Cor. 12:7). Instead, Paul was "content with weaknesses, insults, hardships, persecutions, and constraints for the sake of Christ" (2Cor. 12:10).

Holy humor: Do you know any good prophet jokes? Share two or three, then segue into today's scriptures! A few examples follow:

- Why didn't Jesus start a charity? Because charities are...not-for-prophets!
- Did you hear about Jesus' personal trainer? He was making a big...prophet!
- Why couldn't Elisha join the [insert the name of a 501(c)(3)] or the [insert the name of another 501(c)(3)]? Because they're...non-prophet organizations!
- I talked to an atheist today. Turns out he's part of a non-prophet organization! [Or, turns out he supports non-prophet organizations!]
- Why are less and less people buying into religion? Prophets are down!

Looking for a visual aid for your homily or object lesson? Consider a plastic, five-gallon bucket! It is said that those who harvest crabs need not put lids on buckets of crabs — because the crabs will pull one another down! Today's readings share various ways in which people — including prophets — are "pulled down." Ask listeners who and what pulls them down, and how, if they were honest, they have pulled down others — including the "prophets" among us!

July is here! **For the intellectually-curious,** share a brief lesson on the etymology of this month, named after Julius Caesar (100-44 B.C.), the Roman dictator after whom the Julian calendar was named. Speak of the difficulties presented by this calendar, which led to the Church's institution of the Gregorian calendar and the Church's attempt to (incorrectly) date it to the birth of Jesus of Nazareth. July and August are the two months named after Roman emperors, which, when inserted into the Roman calendar, caused the seventh (September), eighth (October), ninth (November) and tenth (December) months of the year to become the ninth, tenth, eleventh and twelfth months we now know!

On **July 4**, the U.S. celebrates **Independence Day**: Use the proper contained in the Proper of Saints, highlight human freedom, and reflect on the *e pluribus unum* ("from many, one") theme of the second Prayer over the Gifts. After Mass, host a July 4 barbeque with hamburgers and hotdogs, and with games for the kids!

On **July 4**, the Latin American Church celebrates **Our Lady Refuge of Sinners** (a feast celebrated by dioceses of California on July 5 and by the

U.S. Church on August 13). The "New Eve" and *Refugium Peccatorum* is the patroness of California and parts of Mexico: If you serve a *Latino* community, pray the Litany of Loreto, which invokes her!

On **July 4**, the Chaldean Catholic Church (in union with Rome) celebrates the birth in 1948 of **Catholicos-Patriarch Louis Raphaël Sako**. In a spirit of ecumenism, pray for him and for the 640,000 Chaldean Catholics he serves!

On **July 5**, the Church celebrates **St. Anthony Zaccaria** (1502-1539) and **St. Elizabeth of Portugal** (c. 1271-1336). Anthony was the doctor-turned-priest who popularized the 40-hour devotion of Eucharistic exposition and established three religious orders to reform society and abuses in the Church. Isabel, the wife of the king of Portugal, was known for her peacemaking skills and is a patron saint of Third Order Franciscans. Consider your own commitment to peacemaking and the reform of Church and society!

On **July 5**, we remember the passing of **Helmut Richard Niebuhr** (1894-1962), one of the most important Christian ethicists of 20th-century America. The younger brother of Reinhold Niebuhr, he was part of the neo-orthodox school of American Protestantism and was one of the main sources of the "Yale School" of postliberal theology. In his memory, find a moment today to reacquaint yourself with his life and works!

On **July 5**, we remember the passing of **William Reed "Bill" Callahan** (1931-2010), the Jesuit priest whose advocacy for social justice, LGBTQ Catholics, and the ordination of women led to his expulsion from the Roman church in 1991. He went on to found the Quixote Center, Priests for Equality, and Catholics Speak Out, ministering to dissident Catholics and "following the example of Jesus, who was never willing to shut up." In his memory, pray for the modern-day prophets who model the necessary courage to stand up against powerful religious institutions!

On **July 6**, we remember the passing of **Jan Hus** (c. 1372-1415), the Czech priest, theologian and philosopher who called out simony and spoke against the sale of indulgences. Excommunicated, he was arrested and brought before the Council of Constance where he proclaimed, "I would not for a chapel of gold retreat from the truth!" He sang psalms as he was burned at the stake for "heresy." Consider your own courage and willingness to question the practices of the Church that may run contrary to gospel values!

On **July 6**, the Church celebrates **St. Maria Goretti** (1890-1902), the patroness of teenage girls and rape victims. Use this day to advocate for self-determination and against sexual abuse!

On **July 6**, the Roman Catholic Church celebrates the anniversary of the installation in 2013 of Manuel José Macário do Nascimento Clemente as **Manuel III**, the Latin Patriarch of Lisbon. In a spirit of ecumenism, pray for him and for the Roman Catholics he serves!

On **July 8**, we remember the passing of **Eugene III** (c. 1080-1153), the pope who confirmed the privilege granted by Sergius I to the cathedral chapter of Utrecht, allowing it to elect its own bishop without the permission or oversight of the pope. Consider how you empower others to make decisions and exercise "local control"!

On **July 8**, we remember the passing of **Joseph René Vilatte** (1854-1929), the Frenchman later known as Mar Timotheus I, who lived on the fringes of various religious traditions and is often referred to as the first Independent Catholic bishop in the U.S. Ordained by the Episcopal Church, he ministered to the Belgian Catholics in Wisconsin who had broken from the Roman church and who had sympathies more aligned with the Old Catholic Church. As Metropolitan of North America for the Malankara Orthodox Syrian Church, he built the small St. Louis Cathedral in Green Bay. When asked how one might define Independent Catholics, he replied that, in contrast to Roman Catholics, Old Catholics, etc., "we are Catholics without qualification." In his memory, seek to be less denominational and more *catholic* — more universal and inclusive — in your love for God and others!

On **July 9**, we remember the passing of **Angelus Silesius** (c. 1624-1677), the German Franciscan priest, physician, mystic and poet who converted from Lutheranism, studied medieval mystics, wrote 55 pamphlets on Catholicism, and explored themes of mysticism, quietism and pantheism in 1,676 poems in German couplets. His words were popularized in 18th-century Lutheran, Catholic and Moravian hymns. In his memory, consider how you might better help others to lift up their hearts in prayer!

On **July 9**, the Church celebrates **St. Augustine Zhao Rong** (1746-1815) **and Companions** — the 87 Chinese Catholics and 33 Western missionaries who lost their lives for failing to renounce their Christian faith between 1648 and 1930. Consider your own commitment to your Church and your ministry!

On **July 9**, we remember the passing of **Jaime Luciano Balmes y Urpiá** (1810-1848), the Spanish metaphysician, theologian and sociologist deemed the Prince of Modern Apologetics. In his memory, consider your own willingness to contribute to the apologetics of the Independent Catholic movement!

Sunday, July 11, 2020

FIFTEENTH SUNDAY IN ORDINARY TIME

(green)

Choose the second reading you'll proclaim: The longer version contains four extra verses that form two long, run-on sentences on how we are chosen and destined as part of "our inheritance toward redemption as God's possession."

Note: **The introductory line of today's second reading is misleading**. The Letter to the Ephesians is a pseudonymous letter, written in Paul's name and spirit, but not written by Paul. Rather than confuse your listeners, begin with, "A reading from the Letter to the Ephesians"!

The thread in today's scriptures: The priest Amaziah told Amos to "go, prophesy to my people Israel" (Amos 7:15), and Jesus sent out the Twelve to preach repentance, anoint and cure the ill, and cast out demons (Mk. 6:7-13). We, too, are chosen in Christ (Eph. 1:11) to proclaim God's peace and salvation (Ps. 85:9-10)!

Holy humor: Perhaps you've heard the story of the cowboy whose horse died on the trail. The cowboy journeyed for three days on foot before arriving at a small town where he asked if anyone had an extra horse he could buy. No luck. He walked for two more days before arriving at the next town, where he again asked whether anyone had an extra horse he could buy. A man there said that his brother owned a stable that was a two-day journey away. The cowboy walked to that stable, and, nearly dying of exhaustion, said to the stable owner, "I hear you have a horse for sale." The stable owner replied, "I do have a horse, but he don't look so good." The cowboy said, "I've been walking for a week. I'm tired, dirty and exhausted. I'll take him!" The cowboy bought the horse, jumped on it, and rode it out of the stable — where the horse immediately collided with a tree! The farmer walked back to the stable and complained, "You sold me a blind horse!" The stable owner shot back: " I told you he don't look so good!" [Segue into the journey that each person has through life, the journey to which Jesus called the Twelve, and how Jesus sent them out — inviting them to have faith in and rely on God!]

Looking for a visual aid for your homily or object lesson? Consider a walking stick, and a backpack containing food, a coat, and some cash and a credit card or two. Holding the walking stick, with the backpack over your shoulder, declare that you are now ready to…follow Christ! Before you "leave," review Jesus' checklist: "He instructed them to take nothing for the journey but…a walking stick." Hold up the walking stick and say, "Check! I've got the walking stick." Reread the last line, pausing after the words, "no food." Stop to ask your listeners if those words mean that you have to leave behind the cookies or crackers or chips, etc. that you have in your backpack. The audience will, of course, delight in seeing you empty your bag. Reread the pericope again, pausing after the words "no sack." Ask your listeners if those words mean that you have to leave behind the backpack. They'll say yes, and you reply, "No problem. Let me just take out my coat and my money first." They'll know where this is going. With the coat and money in your hands, reread the pericope, pausing after the words, "no money in their belts." What will you need to leave behind? The cash and credit cards! Reread it one final time, pausing after "a second tunic." What will you need to leave behind? The coat! The lesson: Have faith and rely on God! [You might later ask listeners to take a dollar or coin out of their pocket or purse (if indeed people still carry these!): What message does each U.S. bill and coin contain? The reminder that…"in God we trust"!]

On **July 11**, when it doesn't fall on a Sunday, the Church celebrates **St. Benedict of Nursia** (c. 480 – c. 547), the hermit-turned-monk who established the fundamentals of monastic life. The opening line of his rule says, "Listen carefully." In his memory, reflect on how it is that the English words "listen" and "silent" contain the same letters, and consider how silence and solitude might assist you in your own journey of spiritual growth!

On **July 12**, we remembers the passing of **Desiderius Erasmus** (1469-1536), the Dutch Catholic priest and Christian humanist who was the greatest scholar of the northern Renaissance. Though faithful, he was critical of the abuses of the Roman church, and he raised questions that would be influential in the Protestant Reformation and Catholic Counter-Reformation. In his memory, we pray for all who abuse the power and positions they currently enjoy.

On **July 12**, we remember the passing of **Jean Charlier de Gerson** (1363-1429), the French scholar, educator, reformer and poet who served as chancellor of the University of Paris and was one of the most prominent theologians at the Council of Constance. He championed conciliarism as a means to overcome the competing claims of rival popes, and he defended Joan of Arc and her supernatural vocation. In his memory, consider how you're bringing people together and defending their dignity and rights!

On **July 12**, the Eritrean Orthodox Tewahedo Church celebrates the birth in 1929 of **Patriarch Antonios**. In a spirit of ecumenism, pray for him and for the 3 million people he serves!

On **July 13**, the Church celebrates **St. Henry** (973-1024), the childless German king and Holy Roman Emperor invoked against infertility. Lift up in prayer those who struggle to bring to birth the families they desire!

On **July 13**, we remember the passing of **Wilhelm Emmanuel von Ketteler** (1811-1877), the German theologian and bishop of Mainz whose social teachings influenced Leo XIII's *Rerum novarum*. He opposed the formulation of purported papal infallibility as inopportune, and he proposed the founding of prayer societies for the reconciliation of Catholics and Protestants. In his memory, pray that unity might one day be restored to the Body of Christ!

On **July 13**, we remember the passing of **Joseph Langen** (1837-1901), the German priest and theologian who was excommunicated with Döllinger and others for not accepting the dogma of purported papal infallibility. As an Old Catholic priest, he published various works on scripture and the New Testament world and was famous for the sound scholarship of his *History of the Church of Rome*. He was instrumental in the German Old Catholic Church and contributed to the Old Catholic *International Theological Journal*. In his memory, consider your own possible contributions to scholarship!

On **July 14**, the Church celebrates **St. Kateri Tekakwitha** (1656-1680), the first Native American to be canonized. Scarred by smallpox, Kateri was embarrassed by her appearance, and she died at age 24, after years of self-mortification. She is the patroness of ecology and the environment, of people in exile, and of Native Americans. Reflect on and pray for these important causes today!

On **July 15**, we remember the passing of **Anselm of Laon** (+1117), the French theologian who helped pioneer biblical hermeneutics and co-wrote a "gloss" on the scriptures — an interlineal and marginal incorporation of scriptural interpretations — which is hailed as one of the great intellectual achievements of the Middle Ages. Known for expelling Peter Abelard from his cathedral school in 1113, Anselm's style of writing inspired the theological "handbooks" of Peter Abelard and Thomas Aquinas. In his memory, increase your knowledge of biblical hermeneutics throughout the centuries!

On **July 15**, the Church celebrates **St. Bonaventure** (c. 1217-1274), the Franciscan philosopher and theologian who was captivated by medieval, Pseudo-Dionysian suggestions that God is self-diffusive Good —

goodness that just keeps overflowing, like a cup of coffee, resulting in all that exists. In his memory, reflect on and share God's self-diffusive goodness!

On **July 16**, the Church celebrates **Our Lady of Mount Carmel**: Consider sharing scapulars as a symbol of our desire to keep Christ and the saints close to our hearts!

On **July 16**, the Roman Catholic Church celebrates the birth in 1948 of **Manuel José Macário do Nascimento Clemente**, the Latin Patriarch of Lisbon. In a spirit of ecumenism, pray for him and for the Roman Catholics he serves!

On **July 16**, we remember the passing of **Stephen Richards Covey** (1932-2012), the American educator and author known for his bestsellers, including *First Things First*, *Principle-centered Leadership*, and *The Seven Habits of Highly Effective People*. In his memory, consider your own mission in life, the many roles you juggle, and ways in which you might schedule greater effectiveness into your life and ministry!

Sunday, July 18, 2021
SIXTEENTH SUNDAY IN ORDINARY TIME
(green)

Note: **The introductory line of today's second reading is misleading**. The Letter to the Ephesians is a pseudonymous letter, written in Paul's name and spirit, but not written by Paul. Rather than confuse your listeners, begin with, "A reading from the Letter to the Ephesians"!

The thread in today's scriptures: Jeremiah pronounced a "woe" to the shepherds who misled and scattered their flocks (Jer. 23:1). Jesus was moved with pity because the people "were like sheep without a shepherd" (Mk. 6:34), so he brought them together and taught them. The pseudonymous author of the letter to the Ephesians noted that Jesus brought near those who were once far off (Eph. 2:13). He is the good shepherd, leading us to green pastures and refreshing our souls (Ps. 23:2-3)!

Holy humor: Perhaps you've heard this joke before. How do you turn eight scattered sheep into ten sheep? By…rounding them up! [Segue into today's themes of Jesus bringing near and rounding up his "sheep," versus the shepherds who misled and scattered them.]

Looking for a visual aid for your homily or object lesson? Consider a crozier, shepherd's staff or walking stick! Shepherds used a single tool to guide sheep and to chase away predators. How sad that the "shepherds" of Jeremiah's day were misleading and scattering their sheep! Our words and actions have similar dual powers: We can use our words and actions to gather people in and bring them closer to one another — and we can use our words and actions to scatter others and make them run from us!

On **July 18**, when it doesn't fall on a Sunday, the Church celebrates **St. Camillus de Lellis** (1550-1614), a patron saint of hospitals, nurses and the sick. In his memory, reach out to someone in need of healing and health!

On **July 20**, the Church celebrates **St. Apollinaris** (+c. 175), the patron saint of those suffering from epilepsy and gout — the causes of pain and fear in far too many lives. Pray for and reach out to those affected by such maladies!

On **July 21**, we remember the passing of **Peter Lombard** (c. 1096-1160), the scholastic theologian and bishop of Paris who authored the *Four Books of Sentences*, which became the medieval textbook of theology. His view on marriage as consensual and needing to be consummated had a significant impact on the Church's later interpretations of the sacrament. In his memory, thumb through a summary of his lengthy *Sentences*!

On **July 22**, the Church celebrates **St. Mary Magdalene** (or St. Mary of Magdala), the "apostle to the Apostles": Find a way today to share the inclusive love of the Church with our sisters who have been the backbone of the Church for centuries — and help to empower them for ministry!

On **July 22**, the Jacobite Syrian Christian Church celebrates the birth in 1929 of **Catholicos Baselios Thomas I of India**. In a spirit of ecumenism, pray for him and for the 1.2 million people he serves!

On **July 22**, the Armenian Apostolic Church celebrates the birth in 1948 of **Boghos Manousian**, who would become Patriarch Nourhan Manougian of Jerusalem. In his honor, pray for him and for the 9 million people he serves!

On **July 22**, the Romanian Orthodox Church (recognized by the Ecumenical Patriarch of Constantinople) celebrates the birth in 1951 of **Dan Ilie Ciobotea**, who would become Patriarch Daniel of Romania. In a spirit of ecumenism, pray for him and for the 17 million Romanian Orthodox Catholics he serves!

On **July 23**, the Church celebrates **St. Bridget** (+c. 525), the patroness of Europe and of widows: Reach out to a widow or widower, and share with him/her God's love!

On **July 23**, we celebrate the birth of Father **Günter Esser**, the Director of Old Catholic Studies at the University of Bonn, who was part of conversations in 2006 with a small group of U.S. Old/Independent Catholic clergy that discussed the (im)possibility of union with Utrecht. Take time today to delve more deeply into the rich tradition of Old Catholicism and to pray about how we might continue to grow in our relationship with one another!

On **July 24**, the Church celebrates **St. Sharbel Makhlüf** (1828-1898), the Lebanese Maronite Catholic monk known for his holiness. Devotion to him is popular throughout Mexico: If you serve a Mexican community, be sure to send congregants home with an(other) image of him!

On **July 24**, we celebrate the birth in 1940 of **Stanley Hauerwas**, the American theologian and ethicist who has written on a diverse range of subjects and who was named "America's Best Theologian" by *Time* magazine in 2001. A fierce critic of capitalism, militarism and fundamentalism, he often draws from a number of theological perspectives, including Methodism, Anabaptism, Anglicanism and Catholicism. In his honor, consider the sources that shape your own theology and help you to critique the systems that surround us!

On **July 24**, we remember the passing of **Joseph Leo Cardijn** (1882-1967), the Belgian cardinal who earlier in life founded the Young Christian Workers. Imprisoned during World War II and becoming increasingly aware of social inequalities, he dedicated his life to social activism and bringing the Gospel to the working class. In his memory, pause to consider your own efforts on behalf of social justice and the working class!

On **July 24**, we remember the passing of **Lawrence Edward Boadt** (1942-2010), the American Paulist priest and scripture scholar who authored *Reading the New Testament* and other works. He advocated for improved relationships between Christians and Jews. In his memory, explore more deeply the world inhabited by our ancient Hebrew and Jewish ancestors!

Sunday, July 25, 2021

SEVENTEENTH SUNDAY IN ORDINARY TIME

(green)

Note: **The introductory line of today's second reading is misleading.**
The Letter to the Ephesians is a pseudonymous letter, written in Paul's
name and spirit, but not written by Paul. Rather than confuse your
listeners, begin with, "A reading from the Letter to the Ephesians"!

The thread in today's scriptures: Elisha fed 100 people with 20 barley
loaves (2Kgs. 4:42-44), foreshadowing Jesus' multiplication of the loaves
and fish (Jn. 6:1-15). Indeed, the hand of the Lord feeds us and answers
all our needs (Ps. 145:16)! May we who come together to be nourished by
Word and Sacrament work to preserve the unity of the Body of Christ
(Eph. 4:4-6)!

Holy humor: The priest instantly realized her mistake: She was
launching into her homily on the multiplication of the loaves and fish,
and she realized that she had just said that Jesus fed five people with two
fish and 5,000 loaves of bread. Oops! She collected — and corrected —
herself. She continued, "Actually, the story said that there were 5,000
people." Little Joey's face registered surprise and confusion. The priest
paused and looked in her direction, and Joey said, "It shouldn't be hard
to feed 5,000 people; he had 5,000 loaves of bread!" [Segue into the story's
suggestion that five loaves fed a multitude. Are we to understand this
story only literally, as a nice magic trick by Jesus to turn five loaves into
5,000, or did his sharing of those two fish and five loaves inspire those
gathered to more generously share with others the food, drinks and
snacks that they had brought along with them into the wilderness on that
hot day?]

Looking for a visual aid for your homily or object lesson? Consider a
penny and a check for one million dollars! Hold them up together at the
beginning of your homily and ask which your listeners prefer: a check
for one million dollars or a penny doubled each day for a month. If they
choose the former, they'll have a million dollars (presuming you have
enough funds in your account to cover the check); if they choose the
latter, they'll have more than three million dollars at the end of the
month! Did you ever wonder what type of math Jesus practiced? Today's
gospel suggests it was…multiplication! Imagine for a moment what this
world would be like if we all committed ourselves to multiplying love
and peace and forgiveness in this world!

On **July 25**, when it doesn't fall on a Sunday, the Church celebrates **St. James the Greater** (+44), one of Jesus' close friends and a witness of some of Jesus' greatest signs. He is the patron saint of Spain, Nicaragua and Guatemala, and his shrine in Spain was a popular pilgrimage destination in the Middle Ages. He was invoked during the Crusades as *Santiago Matamoros* (St. James the moor-slayer): Make an inclusive gesture today to reach out to our Muslim sisters and brothers!

On **July 25**, we remember the passing of **Thomas à Kempis** (1380-1471), the German/Dutch canon who followed Geert Groote and wrote *The Imitation of Christ*, one of the most popular and best-known Christian devotional books. Consider how you are imitating Christ!

On **July 26**, the Church celebrates Mary's parents, **Ss. Joachim and Anne**. Bring attention to the Protogospel of James and its stories about them, and invoke them as patron/matron saints of grandparents! In some places, St. Anne is also invoked as the saint who can help a single woman find a suitable spouse. The traditional rhyme to her is: "Saint Anne, Saint Anne, help me find a man!"

On **July 26**, the Jacobite Syrian Christian Church celebrates the anniversary of the appointment of **Catholicos Baselios Thomas I of India** in 2002. In a spirit of ecumenism, pray for him and for the 1.2 million people he serves!

On **July 29**, the Church celebrates **St. Martha**, a model for active ministry and the matron saint of domestic servants, homemakers, cooks and single laywomen. Pray for and lift high those who follow in her footsteps!

On **July 30**, the Church celebrates the "golden-worded" **St. Peter Chrysologus** (c. 400/06 – c. 450), known for his 176 extant homilies: Consider the way in which you're recording and sharing your own "golden words" of inspiration!

On **July 30**, we remember the passing of **Rudolf Karl Bultmann** (1884-1976), the German Lutheran theologian who was a prominent voice in the liberal Protestant Christian movement and a major figure in early-20th-century biblical studies. Bultmann attempted to demythologize the New Testament and disregard historical analysis of Jesus' life in favor of the "thatness" of Jesus (i.e., *that* Jesus existed, preached and died). In his memory, reflect on some of the myths that you might continue to cling to with respect to Jesus!

On **July 31**, the Church celebrates **St. Ignatius of Loyola** (1491-1556), the founder of the Jesuits and the author of *Spiritual Exercises*: Find some time and space to "retreat" today and focus on spiritual exercises meaningful to you!

On **July 31**, we remember the passing of **Warren Gamaliel Bennis** (1925-2014), the American scholar and author widely regarded as a pioneer in the field of leadership studies. He suggested that future challenges will be best met by institutions that are less hierarchical and more democratic and adaptive. In his memory, pause to consider the experience, self-knowledge and personal ethics you bring to your life and ministry — and the ways in which you might grow in each!

In **August**, we remember the passing of **Callixtus III** (+c. 1180), the abbot elected "antipope" of the Roman church in 1168. Emperor Frederick played the rival popes as pawns against one another, finally uniting the empire under Alexander III with the condition that Callixtus III be given an abbacy and that all cardinals previously named by him be incorporated into the College of Cardinals. The occasion was celebrated with a feast in honor of Callixtus III by Alexander III. In his memory, consider ways in which you might make peace with your enemies!

On **August 1**, the Church celebrates **St. Alphonsus Liguori** (1696-1787), the lawyer whose lost case propelled him to found the Redemptorists, a community of priests dedicated to preaching, hearing confessions, and administering the sacraments: Consider ways in which you and your community might improve your own "Redemptorist" mission!

On **August 1**, the Ancient Church of the East celebrates the birth in 1946 of **Shlemun Giwargis**, who would become Catholicos Patriarch Addai II of Baghdad and Basra. In a spirit of ecumenism, pray for him and for the people he serves!

On **August 1**, we celebrate the birth in 1949 of **Bruno Forte**, the noted Italian Roman Catholic theologian and archbishop who oversaw the preparation of "Memory and Reconciliation," which led to John Paul II's famous liturgy of asking God's forgiveness for 2,000 years of sins by the Roman church. Known for his works on Trinitarian theology and his defense of Jesus' historical resurrection, he is considered "one of the more noted theological minds in the Italian hierarchy." In his honor, pause to consider — and ask forgiveness for — the sins you have committed against others!

Sunday, August 1, 2021
EIGHTEENTH SUNDAY IN ORDINARY TIME
(green)

Note: **The introductory line of today's second reading is misleading.** The Letter to the Ephesians is a pseudonymous letter, written in Paul's name and spirit, but not written by Paul. Rather than confuse your listeners, begin with, "A reading from the Letter to the Ephesians"!

The thread in today's scriptures: The Israelites grumbled against Moses and Aaron, and God sent them manna and quail (Ex. 16:2-4 & 12-15): bread from heaven (Ps. 78:24)! In a rare exchange between Jesus and the crowd, the crowd refers back to story of the grumbling Israelites and grumbles when Jesus suggests that he is "the bread that came down from heaven" (Jn. 6:31). Do you grumble from time to time? Perhaps it's time to "put away the old self…and put on the new self (Eph. 4:22 & 4:24)!

Holy humor: The story is told of the Hollywood star who was shopping on Rodeo Drive when she came across a man begging on a street corner. The man held out his cupped hand and pleaded, "I haven't eaten in four days." She paused, looked at him over her sunglasses, and replied, "I wish I had your willpower!" [Segue into the fact that food and water are essential for life, then to how it is that many of us, like the Israelites, are focused on such physical things while our spiritual lives languish for lack of spiritual nourishment!]

Looking for a visual aid for your homily or object lesson? Consider a handful of white paint chips — or some other flaky, white material that might help people to visualize manna! Imagine waking up in the morning to find your lawn covered with the flaky, white — but very delicious! — excretions of night insects. The Israelites asked, "What is this? — which is literally what the Aramaic word *manna* (*man hu*) means. To their surprise, God was providing for them in an unexpected way!

August is here! **For the intellectually-curious,** share a brief lesson on the etymology of this month, named after Augustus Caesar (63 B.C. to 14 A.D.), the Roman emperor (and grandnephew of Julius Caesar) who ruled the Roman empire during the first half of Jesus' life. July and August are the two months named after Roman emperors, which, when inserted into the Roman calendar, caused the seventh (September), eighth (October), ninth (November) and tenth (December) months of the year to become the ninth, tenth, eleventh and twelfth months we now know!

On **August 1**, we celebrate the birth in 1955 of **Emilie M. Townes**, the African-American Christian social ethicist and theologian who was the first Black woman to be elected president of the American Academy of Religion in 2008. She is the author of various works on womanist ethics, spirituality and justice. In her honor, take a moment today to deepen your own knowledge of womanist theology!

On **August 2**, the Church celebrates **St. Eusebius of Vercelli** (+c. 370) and **St. Peter Julian Eymard** (1811-1868). Eusebius advocated for the divinity of Christ and of the Holy Spirit, and urged merciful treatment of repentant bishops who had signed the Arian creed: Consider your own stance toward and (in)ability to forgive the repentant. Peter Julian, the "apostle of the Eucharist," dissuaded sculptor Auguste Rodin from giving up art: Consider how you're encouraging others in the development and sharing of their gifts—and of their understanding and reception of the Eucharist!

On **August 2**, we remember the passing of **Gioacchino Ventura dei Baroni di Raulica** (1792-1861), the Italian Jesuit and Theatine orator and philosopher known for his eloquence and his papal funeral orations. He advocated for the separation of church and state, and his diatribe against monarchs and for the union of religion and liberty earned a spot on the *Index of Forbidden Books*. In his memory, pray for all who continue to stand against theocracy and autocracy!

On **August 3**, we remember the passing of **Mary Flannery O'Connor** (1925-1964), the American novelist whose writings reflected her Catholic faith. She examined questions of morality and ethics, and highlighted the acceptance or rejection of characters with limitations and imperfections. In her memory, take a few moments to expand your knowledge of her works!

On **August 3**, the Salvation Army celebrates the anniversary of the installation in 2020 of **General Brian Peddle**. In a spirit of ecumenism, pray for him and for the 1.6 million people he serves!

On **August 4**, when it doesn't fall on a Sunday, the Church celebrates **St. John Marie Vianney** (1786-1859), the patron saint of parish priests! He was internationally known for transforming his community of Arx, France, and 20,000 would come to visit him each year, causing him to spend 16 to 18 hours each day in the confessional. In his memory, pray for your parish priests, and consider how you are transforming your community and serving the needs of those around you!

On **August 5**, the Church of God in Christ celebrates the birth in 1940 of **Presiding Bishop Charles Edward Blake, Sr**. In a spirit of ecumenism, pray for him and for the 6.5 Christians he serves!

On **August 6**, the Church celebrates the **Transfiguration of the Lord**. Luke's account is the only story that speaks of the disciples napping after their journey up the mountain: Stop to consider whether you're getting enough rest these days, whether you're seeing Christ transfigured in otherwise-ordinary moments of your day, and how you've "come down the mountain" after the mountaintop experiences in your life!

On **August 6**, we remember the passing of **Jacqueline-Marie-Angélique Arnauld** (1591-1661), the Abbess of the Abbey of Port-Royal des Champs, who was instrumental in the reform of several monasteries. Raised by Cistercian nuns, she desired to be the superior of a convent from a young age and was named coadjutrix to the abbess at age 12. Her biography was largely the story of her community's heroic resistance in the face of tribulations caused by the Roman church. In her memory, pray for all who display courage in the face of resistance and obstacles!

On **August 7**, the Church celebrates **St. Sixtus II** (+258) **and Companions** and **St. Cajetan**. Sixtus II was bishop of Rome for less than a year before his martyrdom, but is known for reconciling the Western church of Europe and the Eastern churches of Africa on the issue of Baptism. Stop today to consider how you are bringing together and reconciling your sisters and brothers! Cajetan founded the Theatines, an order of clerics who performed works of charity, promoted reception of the sacraments, and called clergy to their vocations in a time when many hierarchs in the Church were morally compromised. Pause to consider the example that you're providing others!

Sunday, August 8, 2021
NINETEENTH SUNDAY IN ORDINARY TIME
(green)

Note: **The introductory line of today's second reading is misleading**. The Letter to the Ephesians is a pseudonymous letter, written in Paul's name and spirit, but not written by Paul. Rather than confuse your listeners, begin with, "A reading from the Letter to the Ephesians"!

The thread in today's scriptures: Exhausted, Elijah prayed for death — but an angel brought him bread and water to sustain him for 40 days and

40 nights (1Kgs. 19:4-8). In today's gospel, the Johannine Jesus proclaims that he is "the living bread that came down from heaven" enabling those nourished by him to "live forever" (Jn. 6:51). If we live the values suggested by the author of the letter to the Ephesians (Eph. 4:31-32), others will "taste and see the goodness of the Lord" through us (Ps. 34:9)!

Holy humor: Never underestimate the spiritual power of a nap and a snack! Remember that Elijah was mad at God and lashed out—saying that he wanted to die! After a nap and a snack, he was good to go—for 40 days!

Looking for a visual aid for your homily or object lesson? Consider a hearth cake and a jug! Imagine being sustained by such little nourishment for 40 days and 40 nights! Of course, the Bible is a book of theology, not of history, and such stories are not meant to be literally understood. Speak of ways in which people are nourished and sustained today—particularly the ways in which we are nourished and sustained by God and others!

On **August 8**, when it doesn't fall on a Sunday, the Church celebrates **St. Dominic of Guzmán** (1170-1221), founder of the Dominican Order, whose friars preached the goodness of the body in contrast to the Albigensian belief that matter—and specifically the body—is evil. His order would become synonymous with the torture and deaths of the Inquisition. Pray for the self-righteous who persecute others, and find ways to reinforce the goodness of the body and its functions in a world that continues to look askew at things created good by God!

On **August 8**, we remember the passing of **Antoine Arnauld** (1612-1694), the French Roman Catholic patristic theologian, philosopher and mathematician who was one of the leading intellectuals at Port-Royal-des-Champs. He attracted controversy by pointing out the relaxed morals of the Jesuits of his day and by suggesting that frequent communion was a deviation from the ancient Christian practice of celebrating the eucharist on the Lord's Day alone. For more than 20 years, he couldn't appear publicly in Paris. In his memory, pray for outcasts of every kind and those who are scorned—particularly in your family and among those you know!

On **August 8**, we remember the passing of **Augustin Theiner** (1804-1874), the German priest, theologian and historian who had access to several sources while serving as prefect of the Vatican's secret archives during the First Vatican Council. His book against the Jesuits was forbidden in the papal states, and he was deposed from his office for communicating the previously-secret order of business of the Council of

Trent to opponents of purported papal infallibility. Despite these acts and his later correspondence with Old Catholic scholar Johann Friedrich, he was buried adjacent to St. Peter's Basilica, in the German cemetery for those who served the Roman church. In his memory, pray for all the "insiders" of other churches who help us to better know and understand the inner workings of those institutions!

On **August 8**, we remember the passing of **Raymond Edward Brown** (1928-1998), the American Sulpician priest and prominent biblical scholar known for his studies of the Johannine community and of the life and death of Jesus. The historical investigation of the Bible was forbidden by the Roman church in 1893, but authorized in 1943, and Brown became one of the first Catholic scholars to apply historical-critical analysis to the Bible at that time. He opposed literalism and was scorned by traditionalists who suggested that he denied the inerrancy of scripture and cast doubt on the historical accuracy of numerous articles of the Catholic faith, including the virginal conception of Jesus. In his memory, explore his works and/or reflect on the elements of scripture that may be more fantastical than historical!

On **August 9**, we remember the passing of **Pierre d'Ailly** (1351-1420), the French cardinal, theologian, astrologer and chancellor of the University of Paris who supported conciliarism as a way to depose rival popes and end the Great Schism. In his memory, work to overcome division and help others to see the value of collective wisdom!

On **August 9**, the Church celebrates **Edith Stein** (1891-1942). Also known as **St. Teresa Benedicta of the Cross**, Edith was raised in an observant Jewish family. She is known for converting to atheism, then to Catholicism, before dying in Auschwitz. Pray today for those whose doubts and beliefs are taking them in various directions, and for all who continue to extinguish tremendous light in this world!

On **August 9**, we celebrate the birth in 1937 of **Justo L. González**, the Cuban-American Methodist historian and theologian known for his contributions to the development of Hispanic theology and Latin-American theology. His two-volume work, *The Story of Christianity*, is a popular text on Church history. In his honor, enrich your preaching and teaching with his thought!

On **August 9**, the Salvation Army celebrates the birth in 1957 of **General Brian Peddle**. In a spirit of ecumenism, pray for him and for the 1.6 million people he serves!

On **August 10**, the Church celebrates **St. Lawrence** (225-258), whose words to those roasting him to death ("Turn me over; I'm done on this side") has made him the patron saint of...comedians! Pray Eucharistic Prayer I, which mentions him, consider how you employ humor in your ministry, and search for a joke to tickle the funny bones of those around you!

On **August 11**, the Church celebrates **St. Clare of Assisi** (1194-1253), the contemplative whose purported act of bilocation resulted in her renown as matron saint of television: Consider how much time you spend watching television — and how you might better use technology to "bilocate" and reach more people!

On **August 11**, we remember the passing of **Nicholas of Cusa** (1401-1464), the German cardinal, philosopher, theologian, mathematician, astronomer and prolific writer hailed as the "first modern thinker." As bishop, he enacted reforms in his diocese — some of which were nullified by papal decree — and he discouraged pilgrimages to the "bleeding hosts" of Wilsnack. In his memory, consider what reforms might be necessary in your life and in the life of your community!

On **August 11**, we remember the passing of **John Henry Newman** (1801-1890), the Anglican priest and Roman Catholic cardinal who was an important and controversial figure in 19th-century England. In his memory, learn a bit about his works or listen to a recording of his hymns "Lead, Kindly Light" and "Praise to the Holiest in the Height." More recently added to the Roman canon, he was canonized on October 13, 2019!

On **August 12**, the Church celebrates **St. Jane Frances de Chantal** (1572-1641), the wealthy widow whose newly-formed congregation admitted women refused by other congregations due to their health or age. Consider your own biases against those who enjoy less health and/or vigor, and find a way to let them know they are loved and appreciated!

On **August 12**, we remember the passing of **Francisco de Vitoria** (c. 1486-1546), the Spanish philosopher, theologian and jurist who founded the School of Salamanca. He is remembered for his contributions to just war theory and international law. In his memory, take a moment to reacquaint yourself with the Church's social teachings on just war.

On **August 12**, we remember the passing of **Walter Jackson Ong** (1912-2003), the Jesuit language professor, philosopher and religious historian who explored the impact on human consciousness of the shift from orality to literacy. In his memory, consider the written records generated and maintained by your community, and challenge yourself to better capture your history through "craft literacy" — like the scribes of old!

On **August 13**, the Church celebrates **Ss. Pontian** (+235) **and Hippolytus** (+235): Pontian was a bishop of Rome exiled by the emperor, and Hippolytus was a bishop—known for the invaluable information we now have from the *Apostolic Tradition*—who, ironically, led a schism against Pontian, whose day he now shares! Pray for reconciliation with those who seem most against you!

On **August 13**, the U.S. Church celebrates **Our Lady Refuge of Sinners** (a feast celebrated by the Church of Latin America on July 4). She is the patroness of California. If you serve a *Latino* community, pray together the Litany of Loreto, which invokes her!

On **August 14**, the Church celebrates **St. Maximilian Kolbe** (1894-1941), the polish Franciscan who volunteered to die in place of a stranger at Auschwitz. Invoke the patron saint of prisoners on behalf of those who are incarcerated, and consider how you're doing with respect to the corporal work of mercy of visiting the imprisoned!

Sunday, August 15, 2021

TWENTIETH SUNDAY IN ORDINARY TIME

(green)

On **August 15**, the Roman Church celebrates the **Solemnity of the Assumption of Mary**—the last dogma proclaimed by the bishop of Rome. This day is not universally celebrated by Independent Catholics due to its tie to the Roman church's novel proclamations of purported "papal infallibility" and universal jurisdiction of the pope—the same issues that filled bishops and priests of the 1800's with a desire to return to the beliefs of the ancient—or Old—Catholic Church. Pause today to consider the extent to which your Mariology—your views on Mary—are rooted in the beliefs of the ancient Church and/or are influenced by the novelties introduced by hierarchs of more-recent memory! If you celebrate this day, call to mind the German custom of blessing fruits and herbs on this day by decorating your worship space with baskets overflowing with ripe fruits and vegetables, calling to mind Mary's fertility. Fill pots with pungent herbs that stimulate the senses. Leave them in place through the Queenship of Mary on August 22.

Due to the division that Marian dogmas have caused in the Church, the following suggestions are intended for a celebration of the 20th Sunday in Ordinary Time instead.

176

Note: **The introductory line of today's second reading is misleading**. The Letter to the Ephesians is a pseudonymous letter, written in Paul's name and spirit, but not written by Paul. Rather than confuse your listeners, begin with, "A reading from the Letter to the Ephesians"!

The thread in today's scriptures: Wisdom invites all to a banquet of rich foods and fine wines (Prov. 9:1-6), where those who forsake foolishness might "taste and see the goodness of the Lord" (Ps. 34:9). Jesus also provides a feast, saying, "my flesh is true food, and my blood is true drink" (Jn. 6:55). May we seek to live "not as foolish persons, but as wise" (Eph. 5:15) — not continuing in ignorance or getting drunk on wine, but being filled with the Spirit (Eph. 5:17-18)!

Holy humor: The story is told of the 98-year-old Irish mother superior who lay on her deathbed. The nuns gathered around her bed, trying to comfort her. The nuns gave her some warm milk to drink, but she refused it. One of the nuns took the glass back to the kitchen and poured a generous amount of Irish whiskey into the warm milk. Back at the mother superior's bed, the nun held the glass to her lips. Mother superior drank a little, then a little more, and, before they knew it, she had drunk the whole glass of milk and whiskey! The nuns pleaded, "Mother Superior, please give us some wisdom before you die." Mother Superior straightened up and shared this wisdom: " Don't...sell...that cow!" [Segue into enjoying the rich fare offered by Wisdom — and the wisdom that flows from a life filled with the Spirit!]

Looking for a visual aid for your homily or object lesson? Consider a bottle of wine! Explain the significance of wine for ancient people seeking "spiritual" experiences. How might we seek a different sort of "high," one that comes from being "filled with the Spirit" (Eph. 5:18)?

On **August 15**, we remember the passing of **Hermann of Wied** (1477-1552), the German archbishop of Cologne who pushed for the punishment of Martin Luther, then, after a quarrel with the papacy, broke from Roman church. The people of Cologne failed to support his reforms and theological innovations, leaving him deposed and excommunicated in the last year of his life. In his memory, pray that more people might experience Saul/Paul conversions and come to embrace those they previously persecuted!

On **August 16**, the Church celebrates **St. Stephen of Hungary** (c. 975-1038), the founder and first king of Hungary, who established Christianity there. He is the patron saint of kings, masons, and children who are dying. In his honor, consider how you might be the hands and heart of Christ for the thousands of children who daily die — and for their heartbroken families!

On **August 16**, we remember the passing of **John Courtney Murray** (1904-1967), the Jesuit theologian known for his advocacy for religious freedom, his efforts to reconcile Catholicism and religious pluralism, and his key role in persuading bishops at Vatican II to adopt *Dignitatis humanae*, the Council's Declaration on Religious Liberty. He had previously helped to draft the 1943 *Declaration on World Peace*, he promoted a close post-war constitutional agreement between the Roman church and the German state, and, in 1954, the Vatican forbade him from writing on religious freedom. In his memory, re-read *Dignitatis humanae* and/or consider your own stance toward issues of religious pluralism and freedom!

On **August 17**, we remember the passing of **Henri Brémond** (1865-1933), the French Jesuit priest and philosopher suspended for attending the funeral of his friend, modernist George Tyrrell. He authored several books on Catholicism, including his renowned *A Literary History of Religious Sentiment in France*. Several of his books explored his interest in English topics, including English public schools, the evolution of Anglican clergy, and the psychology of John Henry Newman. In his memory, reacquaint yourself with the life and works of Brémond!

On **August 18**, we remember the passing of **Walafrid Strabo** (c. 808-849), the Alemannic Benedictine monk known for his exposition on the Mass and the psalms, and for his rhymed poems on scripture, theology, rulers of his day, and, most famously, his garden. In his memory, incorporate poetry into your prayer and/or pause for the meditative exercise of creating your own poem!

On **August 19**, the Church celebrates **St. John Eudes** (1601-1680), who founded seminaries to equip future priests with the necessary knowledge and skills to help people grow in their relationship with God and others. Reflect on how you're empowering others and helping them to grow in their knowledge and skills for ministry in the Church!

On **August 19**, we remember the passing of **Blaise Pascal** (1623-1662), the French mathematician, physicist, inventor, writer and Catholic theologian who died before reaching his 40th birthday. By age 23, he self-identified as a Jansenist Catholic, and his famous *Provincial Letters* are set in the conflict between the Jansenists and the Jesuits. Because of his chronic poor health, he pleaded with his sister, Jacqueline, not to enter the Jansenist convent at Port-Royal-des-Champs. Later, he frequently visited the convent and donated her share of their inheritance to the community there. In his memory, pray for and find a way to support the expressions of religious life that exist outside mainstream religions!

On **August 19**, we remember the passing of **Johann Friedrich** (1836-1917), the Catholic priest and German theologian who was an early leader in the Old Catholic movement. As secretary to the leading German cardinal at the First Vatican Council, he played an important role in opposing the dogma of purported papal infallibility by supplying historical and theological material for opposing bishops. He was excommunicated in 1871 but continued to serve as a priest and professor. In 1874, he established the Old Catholic theological faculty at the University of Bern. In his memory, reach out to those who continue to exercise their ministry outside the churches they once loved!

On **August 19**, we celebrate the birth in 1944 of **Jack Canfield**, the American author and motivational speaker who co-authored the bestselling *Chicken Soup for the Soul* series. More than 500 million copies have been sold of his 250 books. In his honor, infuse your teaching and preaching with a story or two from his works!

On **August 19**, the Coptic Catholic Church (in union with Rome) celebrates the birth in 1955 of **Patriarch Ibrahim Isaac Sidrak of Alexandria**. In a spirit of ecumenism, pray for him and for the 175,000 Coptic Catholics he serves!

On **August 19**, the Philippine Independent Church celebrates the birth in 1966 of **Emelyn Dacuycuy**, the first woman consecrated bishop by the church in its 117-year history. She shared, "Gender is just a social construct, a way of ordering society and ascribing values. As a spiritual community, however, we must see beyond gender. We must see God's people as Jesus sees them—children of God and heirs of God's eternal reign." In her honor, pause to consider how you are helping to empower our sisters for ministry at all levels of our Church and society!

On **August 20**, the Church celebrates **St. Bernard of Clairvaux** (1090-1153), the abbot who wrote numerous theological and spiritual classics. Reflect on how you might better honor the legacy of "Mary's harper," "Our Lady's faithful chaplain"!

On **August 20**, we remember the passing of **Geert Groote** (1340-1384), the Dutch deacon and popular preacher who co-founded the Brothers of the Common Life and was a key figure in *Devotio Moderna*. He taught the virtues of piety and joy to all who flocked to the nearly 100 communities of his Windesheim Congregation for clergy, which played an important role in education and in the transcribing and printing of books. Pause to consider how you might grow in charism, attract more people to the Lord's work, and help them to grow in their relationship with God and with one another!

On **August 21**, the Church celebrates **St. Pius X** (1835-1914), who, despite his conservative tendencies, lowered the age of reason from 12 to 7, making him the patron saint of First Communicants. Reflect on how you might better eliminate barriers to the sacraments of the Church, particularly for the youngest among us!

On **August 21**, we remember the passing of **Alexander of Hales** (c. 1185-1245), the "Irrefutable Doctor," who played a key role in the development of medieval Scholasticism and the Franciscan School. He quoted Aristotle, cited works not frequently cited by others, and he shared his agreement and disagreement with such theological authorities as Anselm and Augustine. He also formulated the question that became a focal point of philosophical and theological inquiry: Would Christ have become incarnate if humanity had never sinned? In his memory, reacquaint yourself with his life and works!

On **August 21**, we remember the passing of **Noël Alexandre** (1639-1724), the French Dominican theologian and ecclesiastical historian who was the pensioned preacher to King Louis XIV. Later banished and deprived of his pension for his opposition to *Unigenitus*, his works are still valued by students of Church history. In his memory, pray for those who suffer loss as a result of their beliefs!

On **August 21**, the Armenian Apostolic Church celebrates the birth in 1951 of **Ktrij Nersessian**, who would become Catholicos Karekin II of All Armenians. In a spirit of ecumenism, pray for him and for the nine million people he serves!

Sunday, August 22, 2021

TWENTY-FIRST SUNDAY IN ORDINARY TIME

(green)

Choose the second reading you'll proclaim. Actually, unless you can justify how the subordination of wives to their husbands fits with Jesus' "discipleship of equals," skip the longer, first option. The husband is no more "head of his wife" than the wife is head of her husband! Imagine the problems this reading would have caused if it suggested, "Husbands, be subordinate to your wives in everything"! Knowing that such language has no place in communities that reflect Jesus' spirit, use the second option for today's second reading. Take it a step farther: Rather than assume that all marriages are comprised of a husband and wife, proclaim, "Spouses, love one another" and "love your spouse as your own body. When you love your spouse, you love yourself." The final inclusive gesture comes when you proclaim, "For this reason, spouses leave their parents to be joined with another, and the two shall become one flesh." Your listeners will thank you.

Note: **The introductory line of today's second reading is misleading**. The Letter to the Ephesians is a pseudonymous letter, written in Paul's name and spirit, but not written by Paul. Rather than confuse your listeners, begin with, "A reading from the Letter to the Ephesians"!

The thread in today's scriptures: Joshua proclaimed that he and his household would serve the Lord (Jos. 24:15). When "many of [Jesus'] disciples returned to their former way of life" (Jn. 6:66), those who remained needed to make a decision. Peter chose to turn to and follow Jesus. Similarly, God turns toward us, seeing the just and hearing their cry (Ps. 34:16). May we find ourselves turning toward one another—just as spouses do (Eph. 5:31)!

Holy humor: During a pandemic, a man was asked which he would choose after the pandemic quarantine: going on a vacation with his wife, or having a barbeque with his friends. Which would *you* choose: Going on a vacation with your spouse, or having a barbeque with your friends? Which did this man choose? Before answering directly, he asked, "…spareribs or hamburgers!" [Segue into the many choices we have to make in life, and the choices in today's readings.]

Looking for a visual aid for your homily or object lesson? Draw an invisible line in the sanctuary! Today's readings force us to make a choice: Whom will we serve? Will we follow Christ? On which side of the line will we stand?

On **August 22**, when it doesn't fall on a Sunday, the Church celebrates the **Queenship of Mary**: Pray the fifth glorious mystery of the rosary, and reflect on the place of Mary in your own theology and Mariology!

On **August 23**, the Church celebrates **St. Rose of Lima** (1586-1617), the patroness of South America, Central America, and the Philippines. She disfigured herself when others complimented her beauty. In her honor, pray for and reach out to those who struggle with their physical appearance!

On **August 24**, the Church celebrates **St. Bartholomew**, the first-century apostle who was skinned alive and beheaded for his faith. Pray Eucharistic Prayer I, which mentions him, consider how much "skin in the game" you have with respect to the faith, and pray for those whose suffering is extremely difficult to endure!

On **August 24**, we remember the passing of **Elisabeth Kübler-Ross** (1926-2004), the Swiss-American psychiatrist and pioneer in near-death studies. Her groundbreaking work, *On Death and Dying*, outlined the five stages of grief. In her memory, pray for and find a meaningful way to minister to someone who is approaching the great mystery of death!

On **August 25**, the Church celebrates **St. Louis King of France** (1214-1270) and **St. Joseph Calasanz** (1556-1648). Crowned at age 12, Louis dedicated his reign to the promotion of justice and peace, feeding and housing the poor, and negotiating peace with England. He tried to prevent the private wars that plagued his country, and he introduced the presumption of innocence in criminal procedure. In his memory, consider the ways in which you might better promote justice and peace in our world. Joseph was the Spanish priest who founded the Pious School to provide free education to the children of the poor. Together with St. Camillus de Lellis, he served Christ in the "distressing disguise" of plague victims, and his religious order, the Piarists, were last of the religious Orders of solemn vows approved by the Church. As a new school year dawns, find a way to contribute in his memory to the education of those in need!

On **August 25**, we remember the passing of **Hubert Augustus Rogers** (1887-1976), the bishop of the African Orthodox Church who was named coadjutor archbishop of the North American Old Roman Catholic Church in 1942 by Carmel Henry Carfora, whom he succeeded in 1958. During an era of segregation, Rogers was the first Black man to lead a predominantly-White Independent Catholic jurisdiction in the U.S. In his memory, consider how you might help our sisters and brothers from diverse backgrounds to grow in their relationship with God and others through the rich tradition of Independent Catholicism!

On **August 26**, the Philippine Independent Church celebrates **Our Lady of Balintawak**, an image of Mary from a revolutionary's dream, who saw her dressed as a Filipina farmer, in the white, blue and red colors of the Filipino flag, crying, "Liberty! Liberty!" and leading by the hand a boy dressed as a Katipunan guerilla. As a result of the vision, the revolutionaries chose not to return to Manila and were kept safe from capture. In honor of this day, imagine ways in which you might help to inculturate images of Mary and Jesus in ways that are meaningful to the people you serve!

On **August 26**, we remember the passing of **William James** (1842-1910), the philosopher and "Father of American psychology" whose work influenced several 20th-century intellectuals. His renowned work, *The Varieties of Religious Experience*, suggests that religious experience should take precedent over religious institutions, and that "over-belief" in things that can't be proven helps us to live fuller, better lives. In his memory, seek out an opportunity today to share with someone of your own religious experiences!

On **August 27**, the Church celebrates **St. Monica** (c. 331-387), who suffered a promiscuous, alcoholic husband and a son whose lifestyle greatly pained her. Pray for and reach out to distressed spouses and parents!

On **August 27**, we celebrate the birth in 1952 of **Miguel Ángel Ruiz Macías**, the Mexican spiritual writer who uses the pen name "Don Miguel Ruiz" for his works on indigenous Mexican spirituality. In 2018, he was named one of the 100 Most Spiritually Influential People, and his bestseller, *The Four Agreements*, was a *New York Times* bestseller for more than a decade. In his honor, enrich your teaching and preaching with insights from indigenous religious traditions!

On **August 27**, we remember the passing of **Hélder Pessoa Câmara** (1909-1999), the Brazilian archbishop and advocate of liberation theology who championed human rights and democracy during the country's military regime. He once said, "When I give food to the poor, people call me a saint; when I ask why they are poor, people call me a communist." In his memory, consider your own words and actions on behalf of the poor and marginalized!

On **August 28**, the Church celebrates **St. Augustine of Hippo** (354-430), one of the four great fathers of the Western Church, who suggested that, contrary to the teaching of the Eastern Church, we all bear the consequences of the sin of Adam and Eve. On this day, consider the wisdom of the Eastern tradition—and the consequences of Augustine's views on the development of such Western novelties as infant baptism and limbo!

On **August 28**, the Serbian Orthodox Church (recognized by the Ecumenical Patriarch of Constantinople) celebrates the birth in 1930 of **Miroslav Gavrilović**, who would become Patriarch Irinej of Serbia. In a spirit of ecumenism, pray for him and for the 12 million Serbian Orthodox Catholics he serves!

Sunday, August 29, 2021
TWENTY-SECOND SUNDAY IN ORDINARY TIME
(green)

Beware the **exclusive language** of today's first reading: Why would anyone choose to say "the God of your fathers" when s/he could just as easily say "the God of your ancestors"? To avoid all the exclusive references in today's psalm, you do well to recast the psalm in the second person: "You who do justice will live in the presence of the Lord. You who walk blamelessly and do justice, who think the truth in your heart and slander not with your tongue." *Et cetera*. James twice refers to God as Father; if you lead an inclusive community, replace the first instance with "God" and delete "and the Father" from the second instance, which shares a ditheistic image.

Note: After a long hiatus, during which we heard John's Bread of Life discourse, we're finally back to the gospel of Mark today!

The thread in today's scriptures: Moses noted that other nations would see Israel's "wisdom and intelligence" in following the statutes and decrees that Moses shared with the Israelites (Dt. 4:6-8). Today's psalm gives examples of what it means to live by God's law (Ps. 15:2-5). Jesus points out the ridiculous situation that arose as a result of the Pharisees' scrupulous following of the letter of the law (Mk. 7:1-8). Rather than scrupulous adherence to the 613 Mosaic laws, we certainly do better to "welcome the word that has been planted in [us] and is able to save [our] souls" (Jas. 1:21). Let's be "doers of the word" (Jas. 1:22)!

Holy humor: Today, I'm going to share with you the two rules you need to follow to be extremely successful in life! Are you ready? These are the two rules you need to follow to be extremely successful in life. Rule #1:

Don't reveal everything you know…. [After an extremely long pause, to allow the joke to "sink in," segue into the contrast provided by the 613 prescriptions of the Mosaic law, and Jesus' admonition to follow the spirit of two simple laws: love God and love others!]

Looking for a visual aid for your homily or object lesson? Consider a representation of the two tablets of the Ten Commandments! Explain that God didn't merely give Moses ten commandments; instead, the Mosaic law consisted of—imagine this—j613 rules! Even worse, some people scrupulously followed as many of these laws as they could, while looking down their noses on the poor and unlearned (i.e., people like shepherds!) who weren't familiar with and/or couldn't fulfill all 613 prescriptions. Speak to the way that Jesus boiled down the 613 commandments into the spirit of two simple rules: love God and love others (Mk. 12:30-31)!

On **August 29**, when it doesn't fall on a Sunday, the Church commemorates **the Passion (formerly "the Beheading") of St. John the Baptist**: Consider the gifts and actions of this greatest of persons (Lk 7:28), which drew to him so many persons desirous of his baptism of repentance!

On **August 29**, we remember the passing of **Wayne Walter Dyer** (1940-2015), the American motivational speaker and self-help author whose first work, *Your Erroneous Zones*, was one of the bestselling books of all time. He distinguished between religion and spirituality and famously wrote: "I don't think that Jesus was teaching Christianity; Jesus was teaching kindness, love, concern, and peace. What I tell people is don't be Christian, be Christ-like. Don't be Buddhist, be Buddha-like." In his memory, find a concrete way today to be more Christ-like!

On **August 30**, the Indian Orthodox Church celebrates the birth in 1946 of **Paulose Mar Milithios**, who would become Catholicos Baselios Mar Thoma Paulose II. In a spirit of ecumenism, pray for him and for the 2.5 million people he serves!

On **August 30**, we celebrate the birth in 1976 of Father **Robert W. Caruso**, author of *The Old Catholic Church*. Reacquaint yourself with his work, and pray for our sisters and brothers of the Union of Utrecht of Old Catholic Churches!

On **August 30**, we remember the passing of **Don Richard Riso** (1946-2012), the American author on the Enneagram's nine impressionistic sketches of personality types and their implications for spirituality. In his memory, consider the broad strokes of your own personality and the degree to which you manifest various healthy and unhealthy personality traits!

On **September 1**, we remember the passing of **Izidor Guzmics** (1786-1839), the Hungarian theologian known for his Hungarian translations of ancient writers and for his work, *On Religious Unity among Christians*. He also founded a school and built an asylum for 150 children. In his memory, pray for Christian unity, and consider how you're serving the children of your community!

On **September 1**, we remember the passing of **Gregorio Aglípay y Labayán** (1860-1940), the Filipino priest and revolutionary who was excommunicated by the Roman church for serving as vicar general of the revolutionary army. He served as the first supreme bishop of the Philippine Independent Church, which grew to over one million adherents during his lifetime. After unsuccessfully campaigning for president of the Philippines in 1940, he married at age 79, the year before his death, to set an example for his clergy. In his memory, pray for our sisters and brothers in the Philippines who continue to honor his life and legacy!

On **September 2**, the U.S. celebrates **Labor Day**: Pray the Proper Mass for Labor Day or the Mass "for the Sanctification of Human Labor," pray for those currently without employment, and thank the volunteers of your community for their labor of love!

On **September 2**, we remember the passing of **Johann Nikolaus von Hontheim** (1701-1790), the priest and professor who used the pseudonym Febronius to denounce papal pretensions, papal absolutism in Germany, and the interference of the Roman church in the affairs of the empire. Threatened with censure and excommunication, he was forced to retract what he wrote — then to say that he had done so of his own free will. In his memory, pray for the victims of bullying and all who must act anonymously for fear of reprisals!

On **September 2**, we remember the passing of **Viktor Frankl** (1905-1997), the Austrian neurologist and Holocaust survivor whose bestselling *Man's Search for Meaning* encourages readers to find meaning — and a reason to continue living — in even the most brutal forms of existence. In his memory, consider the hope and meaning that you share with others!

On **September 3**, the Church celebrates **St. Gregory the Great** (c. 540-604), the mayor of Rome who gave half his fortune to the poor, and the other half for the establishment of seven monasteries. His name is associated with reforms: of the calendar, church governance, clerical behavior, and liturgy. Consider your own vocation to reform!

On **September 4**, we remember the passing of **Gilbert de la Porrée** (c. 1085-1154), the scholastic logician and theologian from Poitiers (present-day France) whose commentary on Boethius was widely misinterpreted as a Trinitarian heresy. Brought to trial before Eugene III, Gilbert aptly defended his works, and his knowledge of scriptures eclipsed that of his prosecutor, Bernard of Clairvaux — but he was forced to edit parts of his work to express the official position of the Roman church. In his memory, consider the ways in which others might misunderstand you — or that you might misunderstand others!

On **September 4**, we remember the passing of **Johann Baptist von Hirscher** (1788-1865), the German priest and theologian whose works on moral theology were censured as part of the Roman church's reaction against rationalistic morality. His catechism advanced the teaching of religion in Germany and gave rise to lively discussions, requiring him to vigorously defend it. His book, *The Notion of a Genuine Mass*, was included on the *Index of Forbidden Books* for its relegation of sacrifice to the background. Accused of being "an enemy of Rome and everything Roman," of opposing celibacy and the breviary, and of promoting a German national church, he continued to defend himself through the publication of pamphlets. Those closest to him knew him as a holy, zealous catechist with pure intentions, who spurred a religious awakening in Baden. In his memory, pause to consider how you are contributing to the spiritual and religious awakening of those around you!

On **September 4**, we remember the passing of **Henri-Marie Joseph Sonier de Lubac** (1896-1991), the French Jesuit who played a key role in shaping the Second Vatican Council and is now considered one of the most influential Catholic theologians of the 20th century. His *Meditations on the Church* had a profound influence on *Lumen gentium*. Pius XII's *Humani generis* is believed to be directed at de Lubac and other theologians of the "new theology," which respected lay competencies and addressed contemporary concerns through patristic sources. After three of his books were condemned, de Lubac turned conservative, co-edited a journal with Joseph Ratzinger, and was named a non-bishop cardinal of the Roman church by John Paul II. In his memory, pray for all whose prophetic spirit is dulled by the vicissitudes of life!

Sunday, September 5, 2021
TWENTY-THIRD SUNDAY IN ORDINARY TIME
(green)

Be sure the coming of Autumn is reflected in **your worship environment**!

- Consider switching out your medium green vestments of Summer Ordinary Time, for **yellow-green vestments** that reflect the changing season! Be sure they match the décor of your worship space — and that they're ironed or steamed!

- **Incorporate elements from the natural world** into your evolving Ordinary Time décor: first fruits from the harvest, colored leaves, and other signs of the season.

- As you change the shade of green, **change the shape and placement of fabric** as well. If you started Ordinary Time with simple vertical fabric, try changing to a draped placement or a series of smaller widths of fabric hung together on a large rod.

- Complement with **green plants containing yellow-green leaves**.

Beware the exclusive language in today's scriptures. "The God of Jacob" was also the God of Leah, Rachel, Bilhah and Zilpah. In the psalm, "the fatherless" can easily be rephrased "the orphan." In James, "a man" with gold rings and fine clothes could just as easily be "a person."

The thread in today's scriptures: Isaiah shares a vision of the reigning God proleptically coming to save us, make us whole, and bring us joy (Is. 35:4-7). The liberation, nourishment and healing in today's psalm characterizes this coming (Ps. 146:6-10). The Marcan Jesus is depicted as embodying the inbreaking reign of God, since, because of him, "the deaf hear and the mute speak" (Mk. 7:37). We, too, manifest the inbreaking of God's reign when we defy the distinctions of this world and "show no partiality" — just as God chose the poor of the world (Jas. 2:1-5)!

Holy humor: Perhaps you've heard it said: "True friends don't judge each other." That's right: True friends don't judge one another. Instead, they judge *other* people! [Segue into the human tendency to judge others, as expressed in today's second reading.]

Looking for a visual aid for your homily or object lesson? Find a way to express the human tendency to judge "books" by their "covers"! Many preachers have tried the gimmick of inviting a shabbily-dressed "poor" person into their congregations today, to see people's reactions. Do we welcome the person in the same way as the well-dressed, well-showered and groomed person? So as not to place people on the "hot seat," pull out a few children's books, and see if listeners can infer what's inside each, based on the cover. Segue into the way in which we similarly judge people by how they look and dress — hence the warning: "Don't judge a book by its cover"!

September is here! **For the intellectually-curious**, note that the remaining months of the calendar year are named for the seventh (*septem*), eighth (*octo*), ninth (*novem*) and tenth (*decem*) months of the Roman calendar! Four months remain this year: Are you accomplishing the goals you had for 2020?

This is **Labor Day weekend**: Expect lower Mass attendance than usual. Consider planning a barbeque, picnic, or "white party" for those desirous of building community!

On **September 5**, when it doesn't fall on a Sunday, the Church celebrates **St. Teresa of Calcutta** (1910-1997), who dedicated her life to the poorest of the poor. Consider your own stance toward the poor, and find a unique way today to recognize your relationship to our sisters and brothers with much less means!

On **September 6**, we remember the passing of **Joachim Jeremias** (1900-1979), the renowned German Lutheran theologian and scholar of Near Eastern and New Testament studies. The author of several publications, he attempted to reconstruct the historical context of Jesus and to provide a deeper understanding of Jesus' life and teachings. In his memory, update your own understanding of the New Testament context in which Jesus lived and ministered!

On **September 8**, the Church celebrates **the birth of Mary**. Consider a unique way to celebrate this day, perhaps with a small birthday cake and/or prayer of gratitude to God for the birth of Jesus' mother!

On **September 8**, we remember the passing of **Sergius I** (c. 650-701), the pope who consecrated Willibrord as bishop to the Frisians and — very significantly — extended to him the special privilege of allowing Utrecht to elect his successors without the permission or oversight of the pope. Consider how you equip, support and empower others to spread the Word as co-workers in the Lord's vineyard!

On **September 8**, we remember the publication in 1713 of *Unigenitus*, the papal bull condemning 101 propositions of Pasquier Quesnel as "false, captious, ill-sounding, offensive to pious ears, scandalous, pernicious, rash, injurious to the [Roman] Church and its practices, contumelious to Church and State, seditious, impious, blasphemous, suspected and savoring of heresy, favoring heretics, heresy, and schism, erroneous, bordering on heresy, often condemned, heretical, and reviving various heresies, especially those contained in the famous propositions of Jansen." (They really pulled out the thesaurus for that sentence!) *Unigenitus* would become a litmus test for obedience to the Roman papacracy, as it purportedly warned against "false prophets...[who] secretly-spread evil doctrines under the guise of piety and introduce ruinous sects under the image of sanctity." In memory of this day, pray for all within the Independent Catholic tradition who, inspired by those who've gone before us, have risked the ill perceptions of others in order to help the People of God to grow in holiness!

On **September 9**, the Church celebrates **St. Peter Claver** (1581-1654), the Spanish Jesuit who preached missions to plantation owners and ministered to the needs of African slaves in Colombia. Consider new ways to share God's love with oppressors and the oppressed!

On **September 9**, we remember the passing of **Henry Parry Liddon** (1829-1890), the Anglican theologian who communicated with Old Catholic and Russian Orthodox clergy in an attempt to create closer bonds between them and the Anglican Church. Intriguingly known for his pulpit oratory and his defiance to modern thought and scholarship, he was a pioneer in ecumenical relations. In his memory, consider how your own words and actions contribute to ecumenism in our world!

On **September 9**, the Church of Jesus Christ of Latter-day Saints celebrates the birth in 1924 of President **Russell Marion Nelson**. In a spirit of ecumenism, pray for him and for the 16 million Mormons he serves!

On **September 10**, we celebrate the birth in 1943 of **Neale Donald Walsch**, the American actor, screenwriter, and author of the longtime international bestseller, *Conversations with God*. Raised Catholic, he informally studied comparative religion and attempted to unify all theologies to help people relate to God from a modern perspective. In his honor, reflect today on how you are "one with God and one with life," in a shared global state of being!

Sunday, September 12, 2021

TWENTY-FOURTH SUNDAY IN ORDINARY TIME

(green)

Beware the **exclusive language** in today's scriptures. In the first reading, substitute "person" for "man." Rephrase the psalm in this way: "I love the Lord who has heard my voice in supplication and listened on the day I called." The other two instances of "he" can just as easily read "God."

The thread in today's scriptures: Deutero-Isaiah shares the song of the suffering servant (Is. 50:5-9), who, not being recognized by the people, suffered distress and sorrow (Ps. 116:3). Wondering whether people recognized him, the Marcan Jesus asked, "Who do people say that I am?" (Mk. 8:27). Peter recognized Jesus as the anointed, the messiah, the Christ! Jesus responded by foretelling his suffering and death (Mk. 8:31). Do we "walk the walk," or do we merely "talk the talk"? Would others recognize us by our works (Jas. 2:14)?

Holy humor: Have you heard the story of the woman who went to a fortune teller and was told that she would suffer incredible heartbreak in 12 years? To cheer herself, she went out and bought herself…a puppy! [Pause for a moment to let that sink in, then segue into the prediction of suffering in today's scriptures.]

Looking for a visual aid for your homily or object lesson? Consider a small curtain rod with a curtain! In today's gospel, Jesus' identity as the Christ is revealed. The English word "reveal" comes from a Latin root that literally means to pull back the veil (or curtain). Traditional weddings begin with the big "reveal," when the veil is removed from the bride's face. In the same way, the "veil" is lifted in today's gospel, and we are able to more clearly see who Jesus really is!

U.S. society celebrates **Grandparents' Day** today: Mark this day with special prayers for all grandparents, living and deceased, and share a special blessing and gift with all grandparents in attendance! Even better, invite grandparents to bring their grandchildren to Mass today, and take photos after Mass of grandparents with their grandkids! Print and share free copies of the photos next Sunday!

On **September 13**, the Church celebrates "golden-tongued" **St. John Chrysostom** (347-407), a head and reformer of the Eastern church. How much do you know about the rich traditions of the Eastern church? Take a moment today to increase your knowledge of this saint and his heritage!

On **September 13**, we remember the passing of **Dante Alighieri** (c. 1265-1321), the Italian poet who composed a *comedia* later considered divine — the most important poem of the Middle Ages. His depictions of heaven, purgatory and hell have influenced imaginations to the present day. In his memory, pause to consider the influences on your own ideas of the afterlife!

On **September 13**, we remember the passing of **William Farel** (1489-1565), the French theologian who invited John Calvin to remain in Geneva, causing the city to become the "Protestant Rome," a refuge for persecuted reformers of the Church. Farel dedicated his life to the formation of missionaries. Pray for all missionaries and for all who help prepare them for ministry, and consider your own role in empowering others to preach the Good News!

On **September 14**, the Church celebrates the **Exaltation of the Cross**: Lift high the cross as the symbol of our redemption!

On **September 15**, the Church celebrates **Our Lady of Sorrows**. Pray in a special way for all whose hearts are pierced by suffering!

This is a week of celebrating freedom in Latin America: **September 15** is **Independence Day in Costa Rica, El Salvador, Guatemala, Honduras and Nicaragua. September 16** is **Independence Day in Mexico. September 18** is **Independence Day in Chile.** If you serve a *Latino* community and/or have congregants who descend from these nations, find a fitting way to celebrate their *fiestas patrias*! Invite people to wear traditional dress and to share traditional foods. Decorate with *papel picado* and traditional decorations. Play traditional music. Share the *grito*. Your attempts to honor their culture and heritage will be much appreciated!

On **September 16**, the Church celebrates **Ss. Cornelius** (+253) **and Cyprian** (+258). Cornelius advocated for welcoming back to the Church repentant individuals who had previously renounced their faith, and Cyprian spent much of his life in hiding due to persecution. Pray Eucharistic Prayer I, which mentions them, and, in light of Sunday's gospel on the prodigal son, consider your own stance toward those who express contrition — and your own desire to escape suffering and pain!

On **September 16**, we remember the passing of **Michael Baius** (1513-1589), the Belgian theologian and leader of the anti-scholastic reaction of the 16th century, whose presence at the Council of Trent was not allowed before intervention by the King of Spain. His positions on St. Augustine's theology brought him into conflict with Rome, and 79 of his propositions were condemned by Pius V. Despite this and subsequent condemnations, he retained his professorship and was named chancellor of the

University of Louvain. His name is most often associated with Cornelius Jansen, the young Blaise Pascal, and the theologians of Port-Royal-des-Champs. In his memory, pray for all who inspire others to think "outside the box"!

On **September 17**, we remember the passing of **Heinrich Bullinger** (1504-1575), the Swiss pastor who was one of the most influential theologians during the 16th-century Reformation of the Church. Nearly 12,000 letters to and from him exist. In his memory, consider how you are reaching out and staying in touch with friends old and new!

On **September 17**, the Church celebrates **St. Robert Bellarmine** (1542-1621), who prayed for his opponents during a time of deep division in the Church. Honor him by thinking through non-defensive, systematic ways in which you might articulate your own beliefs with those who have differing views!

On **September 17**, we remember the passing of **Hildegard of Bingen** (1098-1179), the German Benedictine abbess, writer, composer and mystic who created the oldest surviving morality play. Named a Doctor of the Church in 2012, she is considered the founder of scientific natural history in Germany. In her memory, delve deeper into her life and works!

On **September 17**, we remember the passing of **Adrienne von Speyr** (1902-1967), the Swiss Catholic physician, writer, theologian, mystic and stigmatist who authored over 60 books on spirituality and theology. She was the inspiration for much of the work of the Jesuit priest Hans Urs von Balthasar. In her memory, reach out to the women whose lives and faith have inspired you!

Sunday, September 19, 2021
TWENTY-FIFTH SUNDAY IN ORDINARY TIME
(green)

Beware the exclusive language in today's scriptures. The first reading concerns a "son of God," but could just as easily refer to God's people in the plural (e.g., "Let us beset the just, because they are obnoxious to us. They set themselves against our doings..."). In the psalm, the word "men" can be deleted with no consequence. Based on your community, you can determine whether to use the gospel phrase: "The Son of Man is to be handed over to men."

The thread in today's scriptures: The wicked suggest that God will deliver God's chosen ones from evil (Wis. 2:18). Today's psalm is a lament and a plea for deliverance by one under attack (Ps. 54:3-8). The Marcan Jesus benefited from Mark's knowledge of Jesus' suffering and death; he might just as easily have said, "the haughty have risen up against me, the ruthless seek my life; they set not God before their eyes" (Ps. 54:5). James' language is dark: jealousy, selfish ambition, disorder, every foul practice, wars, conflicts, coveting, killing, envying, fighting, and waging war (Jas. 3:16–4:3).

Holy humor: Have you heard about the man who was attacked by a group of mimes? They did...unspeakable things to him! [Segue into the attacks perpetrated against the suffering servant, the Marcan Jesus, and against modern-day prophets and martyrs!]

Looking for a visual aid for your homily or object lesson? Consider a target or a dartboard! Those who do good will naturally have "a target on their backs." The prophets endured attacks. Religious leaders had Jesus executed after excruciating suffering. Should we expect anything less?

On **September 19**, when it does not fall on a Sunday, the Church celebrates **St. Januarius** (+305), the Italian bishop credited with preventing the eruption of Mount Vesuvius. Consider the ways in which you might help prevent "eruptions" in the relationships that are boiling around you!

On **September 19**, we remember the passing of **Étienne Gilson** (1884-1978), the French philosopher and scholar of medieval philosophy who viewed Thomism as a revolt against Scholasticism. He is perhaps the only Thomist philosopher whose work and reputation have not suffered from the decline in interest in medieval philosophy since the 1960's. In his memory, reacquaint yourself with a chapter or two of his writings on the philosophy of St. Bonaventure and/or St. Thomas Aquinas!

September 20-26 is **National Migration Week**. Consider special prayers and actions in honor of the occasion, and decorate your worship space with a swath of appropriately-colored fabric—free of any inappropriate symbols—from a place like Guatemala, El Salvador, West Africa, India or China.

On **September 20**, we remember the passing of **Paschal III** (c. 1110-1168), the cardinal and "antipope" who, consecrated by the bishop of Liège, challenged the reign of Alexander III. To gain the support of the emperor, he hosted a magnificent celebration of the canonization of Charlemagne. In his memory, pray for all whose political motivations have shaped and continue to shape Church history!

On **September 20**, the Church celebrates **Ss. Andrew Kim Dae-gŏn** (1821-1846), **Paul Chong Ha-sang** (1795-1839) **and 101 Companions**, who represent the 8,000 Catholics martyred in Korea between 1839 and 1867. Consider your own willingness to lay down your life for your beliefs!

On **September 20**, we remember the passing of **Basil Christopher Butler** (1902-1986), the English Benedictine priest and internationally-respected scripture scholar who defended the traditional priority of the Gospel of Matthew and became the pre-eminent English-speaking voice at the Second Vatican Council. He wrote on spirituality, contemplative prayer, ecumenism, and the Church Fathers, and he contributed, often in fluent Latin, to many of the Council's documents. In his memory, thumb through the documents of Vatican II—particularly *The Dogmatic Constitution on Divine Revelation*, which Butler considered to be the foundation for all other Vatican II documents!

On **September 21**, the Church celebrates **St. Matthew**, the first-century tax-collector-turned-apostle to whom the first gospel is attributed. In his honor, pray Eucharistic Prayer I, which mentions him, and flip through the Gospel of Matthew and refamiliarize yourself with its themes and stories—and find one on which to reflect in a deeper way today!

On **September 21**, we remember the passing of **Luigi Taparelli** (1793-1862), the Italian Jesuit who coined the term "social justice" and whose social teachings influenced Leo XIII's 1891 encyclical, *On the Condition of the Working Classes*. In his memory, consider how your own words and actions promote social justice in our Church and in our world!

On **September 21**, we remember the passing of **Henri Jozef Machiel Nouwen** (1932-1996), the Dutch Catholic priest and theologian who wrote widely on psychology, pastoral ministry, spirituality, social justice and community. He coined the concept of the "wounded healer" and retired from academia to work with individuals with intellectual and developmental disabilities. In his memory, consider how your "growing edges" might actually be great gifts to your own ministry as a wounded healer!

On **September 22**, we remember the passing of **Josse van Clichtove** (c. 1472-1543), the Flemish priest, theologian and humanist who was entrusted with the task of collecting and summarizing all the charges against Martin Luther. Pray today for all who store up grievances against others!

On **September 23**, the Church celebrates **St. Pius "Padre Pio" of Pietrelcina** (1887-1968), the Capuchin priest who purportedly bore the stigmata until his death, when—intriguingly—the wounds of Christ were no longer visible. Consider how you and others "bear the marks of Christ" (Gal 6:17) in various ways!

On **September 23**, the Czechoslovak Hussite Church celebrates the anniversary of the installation in 2006 of **Patriarch Tomáš Butta**. In a spirit of ecumenism, pray for him and for the 39,000 people he serves!

On **September 25**, we remember the passing of **Francisco Suárez** (1548-1617), the Spanish Jesuit priest, philosopher and theologian who was one of the leading figures of the School of Salamanca and is regarded as one of the greatest scholastics after Aquinas. His work bridged the scholasticisms of the Renaissance and Baroque phases, and it influenced Leibniz, Schopenhauer and Heidegger. In his memory, reacquaint yourself with his thought and/or the main currents of the Salamanca School!

On **September 25**, we remember the passing of **M. Scott Peck** (1936-2005), the American psychiatrist known for his bestselling *The Road Less Traveled* and *People of the Lie*. He explored the notion of discipline as key for emotional, psychological and spiritual health, and he expounded on such concepts as balance, delayed gratification, acceptance of responsibility and dedication to truth. In his memory, read a chapter or two from one of his works and use it as fodder for self-reflection!

On **September 25**, we celebrate the birth in 1956 of **Miroslav Volf**, the Croatian Protestant "theologian of the bridge" who has attempted to bring Christian theology to bear on culture, politics and economics. Volf has explored dialogues between different faiths, denominations and ethnic groups. In his honor, consider the bridges you're building and/or burning!

Sunday, September 26, 2021
TWENTY-SIXTH SUNDAY IN ORDINARY TIME
(green)

The thread in today's scriptures: Defying expectations, God shared Moses' spirit with 70 elders, who instantly began to prophesy—but also with Eldad and Medad who weren't in the camp (Num. 11:25-29). Joshua pleaded with Moses to stop them! In today's gospel, John tries to prevent others from driving out demons in Jesus' name (Mk. 9:38). As humans, we set ourselves against others, mistreating them, condemning them, even murdering them (Jas. 5:4-6). We pray with the psalmist: Cleanse us from our unknown faults; from wanton sin especially, restrain your servants (Ps. 19:13-14)!

Holy humor: One day, a woman confessed to her maid, "I think my husband is having an affair with his secretary." Her maid replied, "I don't believe that for a minute. You're just trying to make me jealous!" [Segue into the very human emotion of jealousy in today's scriptures.]

Looking for a visual aid for your homily or object lesson? Consider a handheld, crossing guard's stop sign! As jealous humans, we sometimes try to impede others from doing good. We try to stop them! Like Jesus, we forget that "the enemy of my enemy is my friends"—that we're on the same "team"! When we detect such failings in others (Ps. 19:13), like Joshua and John, we have to find a Christian way of saying, "Stop!"

On **September 26**, when it doesn't fall on a Sunday, the Church celebrates **Ss. Cosmas and Damian**, the third-century brothers who practiced medicine and wouldn't accept money for their services. They are the patron saints of twins, confectioners, the blind, and of many medical professions (e.g., physicians, nurses, dentists). Pray Eucharistic Prayer I, which mentions them, and find a fitting way to honor their memory and those who continue their legacy. If your community has ties to the Franciscan tradition, call these saints to mind through your display of the San Damiano Crucifix.

On **September 26**, we remember the passing of **Frederick William Faber** (1814-1863), the English hymn writer and theologian known for his work, *Faith of Our Fathers*. An Anglican vicar, he followed his hero, John Henry

Newman, into the Roman church. He was joined by 11 men who formed a religious community that called itself the Brothers of the Will of God. In his memory, pray for all who continue to be inspired to leave behind their former religious affiliations and to found new communities that seek to realize the will of God!

On **September 26**, we remember the passing of **George Santayana** (1863-1952), the Spanish-American philosopher, poet and novelist known for his aphorisms. With a fond spot in his heart for the Catholic values, practices and worldview with which he was raised, he described himself as a "Catholic atheist." In his memory, pray for and/or reach out to someone who may no longer self-identify as Catholic, but who still shares a fondness for our Catholic values and/or traditions!

On **September 27**, the Church celebrates **St. Vincent de Paul** (1581-1660), who provided for the physical needs of the poor. Cold weather is coming: Plan a clothing drive or a collection of canned goods and imperishable foods in his honor, to benefit a local food pantry or St. Vincent de Paul Society!

On **September 27**, the Assyrian Church of the East celebrates the anniversary of the installation in 2015 of Warda Daniel Sliwa as **Catholicos-Patriarch Gewargis III** of Iraq. In a spirit of ecumenism, pray for him and for the people he serves!

On **September 28**, the Church celebrates **St. Wenceslaus** (c. 911-935) and **St. Lawrence Ruiz** (1594-1637) **and Companions**. King Wenceslaus evangelized pagan Bohemia and was murdered by his brother. Lawrence was a married father of three who fled from Manila to Japan and refused to trample Catholic images and adhere to the state religion of Japan. He and 231 Catholics were martyred in Japan in the 16th and 17th centuries. Consider the ways in which you steal life and enthusiasm from others!

On **September 29**, the Church celebrates the **Archangels Michael, Gabriel and Raphael**. They are the three biblical archangels: Michael, who led the angels in fighting the dragon (Satan) and hurling it to the earth (Rev. 12:7-9), Gabriel, who appeared to Zechariah and Mary (Lk. 1:19-20 & 26-38), and Raphael, who disguised himself as a human to heal Tobit and free Sarah from a demon (Tob. 12:15). Many people are captivated by the idea of angels and other heavenly beings. For the intellectually-curious, share a lesson on heavenly beings, the rise of angels in ancient religions, the symbolism of such numbers as seven, and the lack of agreement on the names of the other four archangels!

On **September 29**, we remember the election of **Innocent III** (died after 1180), the cardinal and "antipope" supported by Roman barons over

Alexander III. A cardinal successfully bribed the guards of his castle, and he and his supporters were imprisoned for life in a monastery. In his memory, pray and/or perform an act of charity for our sisters and brothers in prison!

On **September 30**, the Church celebrates **St. Jerome** (c. 347-420), the patron saint of scholars and librarians. In his honor, enrich your ministry through the purchase of a new biblical commentary for your personal library!

On **September 30**, the Old Catholic Church celebrates the anniversary of the consecration in 1725 of **Cornelius Johannes Barchman Wuytiers** as the eighth archbishop of Utrecht, by Bishop Dominique-Marie Varlet of the Roman church. This was the second of four consecrations performed by Varlet without the permission of Rome. Pray in a special way today for those who bravely and tenaciously follow their beliefs—despite the consequences!

On **September 30**, we remember the passing of **Monika Konrad Hildegard Hellwig** (1929-2005), the German-born British theologian who left religious life to pursue her academic career. As the research assistant to a Vatican official, she was one of the few women permitted to enter Vatican II as an observer. The author of many books, she co-signed a controversial letter in support of Charles E. Curran, who was barred from teaching Roman Catholic theology due to his dissent on the church's teachings on such issues as contraception and homosexuality. In her memory, reacquaint yourself with one of her works!

On **September 30**, the Romanian Orthodox Church (recognized by the Ecumenical Patriarch of Constantinople) celebrates the anniversary of the installation in 2007 of Dan Ilie Ciobotea as **Patriarch Daniel of Romania**. In a spirit of ecumenism, pray for him and for the 17 million Romanian Orthodox Catholics he serves!

On **October 1**, the Church celebrates **St. Thérèse of the Child Jesus** (1873-1897), the "Little Flower," who was the youngest of five daughters—all of whom became nuns. Don't be so ageist: Pray that God might continue to manifest God's self in the vocations of the young!

On **October 1**, we remember the passing of **Johann Baptista Baltzer** (1803-1871), the German Catholic priest and theologian who traveled to Rome in an attempt to prevent the condemnation of Anton Günther's writings. The Holy See subsequently suspended him and asked him to resign his professorship. Baltzer was a strenuous opponent of purported papal infallibility and later promoted the Old Catholic movement in

Silesia. In his memory, pray for all who promote and defend Independent Catholicism in our world!

On **October 1**, we remember the passing of **Romano Guardini** (1885-1968), the noted Italian-German academic whose *The Spirit of the Liturgy* was a major influence on the Liturgical Movement in Germany, and, by extension, on the liturgical reforms of Vatican II. In his memory, reacquaint yourself with his works and/or with the liturgical documents that continue his liturgical legacy!

On **October 2**, the Church celebrates **Guardian Angels**: Incorporate an image into the décor of your narthex or devotional chapel. For the intellectually-curious, share a lesson on the history of and scriptural basis for this belief!

On **October 2**, the birthday of Mahatma Gandhi, we also celebrate **International Day of Nonviolence**, a day established by the United Nations in 2007 to promote education and public awareness of nonviolence. In honor of this day, reflect on how your words, actions and preaching espouse this universal value!

Sunday, October 3, 2021

TWENTY-SEVENTH SUNDAY IN ORDINARY TIME

(green)

Choose the gospel you'll proclaim: the longer version, with four extra lines including Jesus' blessing of children, or the shorter version, which solely focuses on Jesus' response to the question of the legality of divorce.

The **exclusive language** of today's first reading provides the etiology for an androcentric, patriarchal society. There are, however, inclusive translations, including the Priests for Equality translation, which tells the following story of God's first "earth creature" [*adâm*], which was without gender until God created Woman [*isha*] from Man [*ish*]:

> Our God made the earth creature fall into a deep sleep, and, while it slept, God divided the earth creature in two, then closed up the flesh from its sides. Our God then fashioned the two halves into male and female, and presented them to one another. When the male realized what had happened, he exclaimed, "This time, this is the one! Bone of my bone and flesh of my flesh! Now, she will be Woman, and I will be Man, because we are of one flesh!"

The instance of "man" in today's psalm can just as easily be rendered "one," and "brothers" in the second reading can easily be rendered "brothers and sisters." The line from Genesis is easily made inclusive, too: "This is why people leave their parents and become bonded to one another, and the two become one flesh."

Note: **The introductory line of today's second reading is misleading**. The Letter to the Hebrews is a pseudonymous letter, written in Paul's name and spirit, but not written by Paul. To avoid this confusion, you might proclaim, "A reading from the Letter to the Hebrews."

The thread in today's scriptures: In Genesis (1:21-24), God creates a suitable partner for the first human, and, despite only bearing three sons, the first couple is apparently so fruitful (Ps. 128:3) that, according to the ancient mind, the entire human race could be traced to them. The Marcan Jesus points to the Genesis story to justify his hard-liner position that "what God has joined together, no human being must separate" (Mk. 10:9). The new *adâm*, Jesus "for a little while" was made "lower than the angels" and tasted death, "bringing many children to glory" (Heb. 2:9-10).

Holy humor: Marriage is such a beautiful thing—where two people become one. The trouble starts when they try to decide...which one! [Segue into the challenge of living in unity with others.]

Looking for a visual aid for your homily or object lesson? Consider two pieces of rope! We talk about marriage as "tying the knot." Explain how marriage brings two people—like two pieces of rope—together. As you tie the two pieces with a square knot, talk about the unity toward which we're called. To underscore the strength that comes from unity, return later to the fact that the piece of rope is composed of various threads or strands that are brought together! [If you want to introduce this object lesson with a joke, hold up a single piece of rope and tell the story of the rope that walked into a bar. The bartender said, "We don't serve rope here." So the rope went outside, tied himself in a knot [tie an overhand knot], and messed up his hair [fray the top end of the rope]. When the rope walked back into the bar, the bartender asked, "Aren't you the rope that just came in here?" And the rope said, "No, I'm...a frayed knot!"]

On **October 4**, the Church celebrates **St. Francis of Assisi** (c. 1182-1226), the patron saint of ecology. Pray his "Canticle of Brother Sun" and host a blessing of pets, with refreshment for people and pets. Knowing that water can spook some of God's creatures, consider ways of sharing God's blessing *without* holy water!

On **October 4**, we remember the passing of **Wessel Gansfort** (1419-1489), the Frisian theologian, pre-Reformation reformer and "learned light of the world" who spoke against magical and superstitious conceptions of the sacraments, the paganization of the papacy, and the supremacy of ecclesiastical tradition. When Sixtus VI offered him a bishopric, he asked instead for a copy of the Hebrew scriptures, which he read aloud to the bemusement of his fellow monks. Consider what you might do to be perceived as a "learned light" by those around you!

On **October 4**, we remember the passing of **Jacqueline Pascal** (1625-1661), the French nun who vehemently opposed the Roman church's attempt to compel assent for the condemnation of Jansenism. Her brother, Blaise Pascal, was instrumental in her conversion to Jansenism but strongly opposed her decision to join the convent of Port-Royal-des-Champs. Shortly after being compelled to provide her assent to *Unigenitus*, she died on her 36th birthday. In her memory, pray for all who find themselves in situations where they feel forced to do what they do!

On **October 4**, we celebrate the birth in 1941 of **Anne Rice**, the bestselling American author of vampire fiction and Christian literature, including *The Vampire Chronicles* and *Christ the Lord: Out of Egypt*. Raised Catholic, she attended Catholic schools, but left the Church at age 18. After decades of atheism, she returned to the Catholic Church in 1998 — though not with a full embrace of the Church's stances on gay marriage, abortion rights, and birth control. In her honor, reach out to someone who has a similarly complex relationship with the church of his/her upbringing!

On **October 5**, the Church celebrates **Bl. Francis Xavier Seelos** (1819-1867), the German Redemptorist immigrant to the U.S. who refused the bishopric of Pittsburgh to be a missionary throughout the U.S. In his honor, consider saying "no" to certain goods, so that you can say "yes" to even greater goods!

On **October 6**, we remember the passing of **St. Bruno of Cologne** (c. 1030-1101), the renowned teacher at Reims, advisor of his former student, Urban II, and the founder of the Carthusian Order. Depicted in iconography with a skull in his hand, he refused an archbishopric and vowed to renounce secular concerns. In his honor, contemplate your own death and how you will use your remaining days and years to grow in your relationship with God and others!

On **October 6**, the Church celebrates **Bl. Marie-Rose Durocher** (1811-1849), the Canadian "saint of Beloeil" and reluctant co-foundress of the Sisters of the Holy Names of Jesus and Mary. Her last years were marked by poverty, trials, sickness and slander. Pray and reach out to those who similarly suffer!

On **October 6**, we remember the passing of **Jean du Vergier de Hauranne** (1581-1643), the French Catholic priest who served as Abbot of Saint-Cyran and as spiritual director of the nuns at Port-Royal-des-Champs. He introduced to France the thought of his friend, Cornelius Jansen, and was imprisoned for his view that contrition (and not the less-perfect "attrition") could save a person. In his memory, pray for those who might misunderstand you, your intentions, and/or your desire to help others grow in their relationship with God and others!

On **October 6**, we celebrate the birth in 1958 of **Miguel De La Torre**, the Southern Baptist professor who has written over 30 books on social ethics and Latinx Studies. He achieved notoriety in 2005 when he was forced to resign his tenure over his article "When the Bible is Used for Hatred," which satirized James Dobson's outing of SpongeBob SquarePants. He continues to comment on ethical issues, Hispanic religiosity, LGBTQ civil rights, and immigrant rights. In his honor, consider your own willingness to speak a prophetic word against the powers that be!

On **October 7**, in the midst of this Month of the Holy Rosary, the Church celebrates **Our Lady of the Rosary**. Nothing is more fitting than praying the rosary on this day! Learn new mysteries. If you have a multilingual community, consider bringing the community together for a multilingual experience of the rosary!

On **October 7**, we celebrate the birth in 1931 of **Desmond Mpilo Tutu**, the South African Anglican archbishop, theologian, and Nobel Peace Prize winner known for his stand on human rights issues and against the racial segregation of apartheid. As the first Black archbishop of Cape Town, he oversaw the introduction of women priests and led negotiations to end apartheid and institute a multi-racial democracy. In his honor, consider how you are using your influence to address the most pressing human rights abuses around you!

On **October 8**, we celebrate the birth in 1940 of **Thomas Moore**, the American psychotherapist and former monk who has authored a number of popular spiritual works, including his bestselling *Care of the Soul* and *Soul Mates*. His books and lectures have covered such topics as spirituality, religion, ecology, imagination, mythology and archetypal psychology. In his honor, reflect on one of his works as a spiritual exercise!

On **October 8**, we remember the passing of **Gabriel Honoré Marcel** (1889-1973), the French Catholic philosopher and Christian existentialist who wrote over 30 plays and 12 books, including his two-volume *The Mystery of Being*. He paid particular attention to the modern struggle against our dehumanization by technology, and he hosted a weekly philosophical discussion group, where he influenced Ricœur, Levinas and Sartre. In his memory, pause to consider the possibly-dehumanizing impact of technology in your life and in the lives of those around you!

On **October 9**, the Church celebrates **St. Denis of Paris** (+c. 258) and **St. John Leonardi** (1541-1609). Denis (not to be confused with Dionysius the Aeropagite or Pseudo-Dionysius) is depicted as a decapitated bishop holding his own head and is invoked against headaches, rabies and demonic possessions. Pray for those who suffer these, and for those who are "losing their head" and acting overly emotional or irrational! John Leonardi was a pharmacist's assistant who, after being ordained to the priesthood, gathered laity interested in ministering in hospitals and prisons. They formed the Clerks Regular of the Mother of God, and John died 14 years later of the plague, which he contracted from his ministry to the ill. In his memory, consider how you are being the hands and heart of Christ to those most in need!

On **October 9**, we remember the passing of **Robert Grosseteste** (1175-1253), the English statesman, scientist, scholastic theologian and bishop who has been called the founder of scientific thought in medieval Oxford. He was an original thinker on what today is known as scientific method. In his memory, pray for all who seek to bridge theology to the many great scientific discoveries of our day!

On **October 9**, we remember the passing of **Penny Lernoux** (1940-1989), the American Roman Catholic educator, author and journalist who criticized the Roman church's policies toward Latin America. Drawn to liberation theology, she attempted to relate Christ's teachings to Latin American struggles against economic exploitation and military dictatorship. She focused her last years on the attempts of John Paul II and Joseph Ratzinger to clamp down on dissent and to fortify an authoritarian, pre-conciliar model of the church. In her memory, reacquaint yourself with the tensions between Latin American liberation theologians and the church with which they shared a love/hate relationship!

Sunday, October 10, 2021

TWENTY-EIGHTH SUNDAY IN ORDINARY TIME

(green)

Choose the gospel you'll proclaim: the shorter version that ends, "all things are possible for God," or the longer version, which continues with three additional verses containing Peter's affirmation that he and his friends gave up everything to follow Jesus, and Jesus' promise that they will receive 100-fold — "with persecutions and eternal life in the age to come."

Think through the two instances of **exclusive language** in today's second reading: Both instances of "him" might easily be rendered "God," particularly if the first instance is not interpreted to tie to the subject of the previous sentence, the Word of God, which, like God, has no gender.

Note: **The introductory line of today's second reading is misleading.** The Letter to the Hebrews is a pseudonymous letter, written in Paul's name and spirit, but not written by Paul. To avoid this confusion, you might proclaim, "A reading from the Letter to the Hebrews."

The thread in today's scriptures: The author of the book of Wisdom chose Wisdom over gold and silver, "scepter and throne," health, light and countless riches (Wis. 7:7-11). In contrast, the unnamed man in today's gospel chose his "many possessions" over "treasure in heaven" (Mk. 10:21-22). May we, too, enjoy the gift of discernment (Heb. 4:12) as we pray with the psalmist "that we may gain wisdom of heart" (Ps. 90:12)!

Holy humor: Perhaps you've seen the cartoon of the winged person in heaven carefully watching over a large pile of assorted objects: furniture, furnishings, knick-knacks, even a lawnmower. The caption reads: "When hoarders store up 'treasures' in heaven!" [Segue into the treasure of Wisdom in today's first reading, and the contrasting "treasures" in today's gospel.]

Looking for a visual aid for your homily or object lesson? Consider a piggy bank! Ask your listeners if they ever had a piggy bank. Why did they have a piggy bank? To save up the change they received and see it build up over time. The adult equivalent is the savings account: Adults know it's a good idea to save money for unexpected emergencies. Note how Jesus warned us to focus less on the "treasures" of this world — and more on the treasures of heaven. Help your listeners reflect on concrete acts by which we might store up treasures in heaven!

On **October 10**, we remember the passing of **Isabelo de los Reyes** (1864-1938), the Filipino politician, writer and labor leader who announced the formation of the Philippine Independent Church on August 3, 1902. He rallied support of the new church and directed the church's publications, including its catechism, rituals, magazine and numerous devotional and doctrinal texts. Consider how you dedicate your time, talent and treasure to the upbuilding of God's reign!

On **October 11**, we remember the passing of **Ulrich Zwingli** (1484-1531), the "soldier of Christ" and *Leutpriester* (people's priest) in Zürich who emphasized the authority of the Bible, questioned Lenten fasting, noted the corruption of Roman Catholic hierarchy, and promoted clerical marriage. In his memory, pray for all "soldiers of Christ" who courageously question the practices of our Catholic tradition!

On **October 11**, the Church celebrates **St. John XXIII** (1881-1963), the bishop of Rome who sought to model the Good Shepherd and who advocated for opening the "windows" of the Roman church, to allow in some "fresh air." In his honor, thumb through the documents of Vatican II and find a few fresh insights to enliven your ministry and your liturgy!

On **October 11**, we remember the passing of **Félix Antoine Philibert Dupanloup** (1802-1878), the French priest, prolific writer, and "Apostle to Youth" who very vocally opposed purported papal infallibility during the First Vatican Council. He was known for his imposing height, eloquence, zeal and charity, and his fiery rhetoric contributed to the canonization of St. Joan of Arc. In his memory, consider how your own preaching and teaching embody the energy, the powerful voice, and the impassioned gestures for which Félix was famous!

On **October 12**, we remember the passing of **Luis de Molina** (1535-1600), the Spanish Jesuit priest and scholastic who stirred controversy and debate through his staunch defense of free will in the debate over human liberty and God's grace. Molinism was the precursor of Jansenism, a lightning rod issue with respect to submission to the authority of the Roman papacracy. In his memory, pause to consider your own views on grace and freedom!

On **October 14**, U.S. society celebrates **Columbus Day**, which is increasingly celebrated as **Indigenous Peoples' Day** in more than 50 U.S. cities. Latin America celebrates this day as *el día de la raza* (the Day of Our People). Find a fitting way to commemorate this day, with an acknowledgement of the sins of the Church in erasing the rich cultures and religions of indigenous people!

On **October 14**, the Old Catholic Church celebrates the birth in 1952 of **Joris August Odilius Ludovicus Vercammen**, the Roman Catholic priest who joined the Old Catholic Diocese of Utrecht and was named Archbishop of Utrecht in 2000. Pray today for Archbishop Emeritus Vercammen and for all our sisters and brothers of the Old Catholic tradition!

On **October 15**, the Church celebrates **St. Teresa of Jesus** (1515-1582), the mystic and Carmelite reformer who modeled her life on the poor and crucified Christ. In her honor, go deeper into your own "interior castle" and consider how you might grow in your own "way of perfection"!

On **October 15**, the Old Catholic Church celebrates the anniversary of the consecration in 1724 of **Cornelius van Steenoven** as the 7th archbishop of Utrecht, by Bishop Dominique-Marie Varlet of the Roman church. This was an historic day: the first of four consecrations performed by Varlet without the permission of Rome! Pray in a special way today for our sisters and brothers of the Old Catholic Church, who trace the succession of their archbishop back to these consecrations by Varlet!

On **October 15**, the Bulgarian Orthodox Church (recognized by the Ecumenical Patriarch of Constantinople) celebrates the birth in 1945 of **Simeon Nikolov Dimitrov**, who would become Patriarch Neophyte of Bulgaria. In a spirit of ecumenism, pray for him and for the 11 million Bulgarian Orthodox Catholics he serves!

On **October 16**, the Church celebrates **St. Hedwig of Silesia** (1174-1243) and **St. Margaret Mary Alacoque** (1647-1690). Living 500 years apart, both are known today as patron/matron saints of orphaned children. Find a way today to honor the little ones for whom God shows a particular solicitous concern!

On **October 16**, we celebrate the birth in 1930 of **Sir John Charlton Polkinghorne**, the English Anglican priest, physicist and theologian who has authored over 25 books on the relationship between science and religion. In his honor, reacquaint yourself with any one of his works!

Sunday, October 17, 2021
TWENTY-NINTH SUNDAY IN ORDINARY TIME
(green)

We're nearing the end of Fall Ordinary Time: Does **your worship environment** reflect this? (Please don't say that you have same worship environment you had in June!)

- Consider transitioning to a **darker green** in your décor and vestments, to mirror the darkening days of this season. Be sure the greens match—and that your vestments are ironed or steamed!

- Among the plants in your worship space, intersperse tall pottery vases of **dried grasses or willow branches** that reflect nature's changes.

- Incorporate **fruits of the harvest**—particularly those grains that call to mind the sifting of "wheat" and "chaff" that will occur in the final judgment.

- Harvested **squash and pumpkins** can add variety—but be sure to clean pumpkins with a solution of water and bleach, to slow deterioration.

- **Experiment with textures, small prints, discrete woven patterns, and fabrics with a sheen.**

- Complement with **green plants possessing deeper green leaves**.

Choose the gospel you'll proclaim: the shorter version with the succinct message that those who wish to be great should serve others and strive to be last, or the longer version, with seven initial verses on the squabbling sons of Zebedee.

Note: **The introductory line of today's second reading is misleading**. The Letter to the Hebrews is a pseudonymous letter, written in Paul's name and spirit, but not written by Paul. To avoid this confusion, you might proclaim, "A reading from the Letter to the Hebrews."

The thread in today's scriptures: Like Deutero-Isaiah's suffering servant, who was crushed with affliction and infirmity as he bore the guilt of many (Is. 53:10-11), Jesus was "tested in every way" (Heb. 4:15) and foretold his suffering and the suffering of his disciples (Mk. 10:35). As we follow Jesus' counsel to sacrifice ourselves and serve others (Mk. 10:43-44), we pray with the psalmist that God might deliver us from death and harm (Ps. 33:19).

Holy humor: Perhaps you've heard the story of the factory worker who died when she fell in a large vat of coffee. The police said it came as a shock to all who knew her, but they took some relief at the fact that she didn't suffer. It was…instant. [Segue to the suffering that many endure in life, which is far from "instant," then to the suffering in today's scriptures.]

Looking for a visual aid for your homily or object lesson? Consider a crucifix! The very-Catholic image of Jesus hanging on the cross is a symbol of his suffering for our sake. He was rejected by his own friends and people, and he suffered the most excruciating and humiliating death.

On **October 17**, when it does not fall on a Sunday, the Church celebrates **St. Ignatius of Antioch** (+c. 140), the apostolic father who emphasized the humanity and divinity of Christ, and advocated for Church unity. Pray Eucharistic Prayer I, which mentions him, and consider how you're bringing greater unity (or not) to the Church!

On **October 17**, we remember the passing of **Helmut Gollwitzer** (1908-1993), the Bavarian Lutheran theologian and author who was part of the Confessing Church movement that resisted the efforts of the Nazi regime to control the Church. The diary of his experiences as a prisoner of war in Russia for four years became a bestseller in Germany, and the president of West Germany referred to it as "a great historical document." Gollwitzer later became a pacifist, opposing nuclear weapons, the arms race, and the Vietnam War. In his memory, pray the peace prayer attributed to St. Francis, meditating on how Gollwitzer and so many others have been instruments of peace—and how it is that you, too, might better bring pardon and hope to situations of injury and despair!

On **October 18**, the Church celebrates **St. Luke** (+84): Incorporate a large Book of the Gospels into today's décor. If you haven't already, on this physician's feast, consider celebrating a White Mass with a special recognition and blessing of all who work in medical professions!

On **October 18**, the Old Catholic Church celebrates the anniversary of the consecration in 1739 of **Petrus Johannes Meindaerts** as the tenth archbishop of Utrecht, by Bishop Dominique-Marie Varlet of the Roman church. This was the fourth of four consecrations performed by Varlet over the course of 15 years, without the permission of Rome. Meindaerts, who served as bishop for nearly 30 years, would later consecrate three other bishops to ensure the apostolic succession of the Old Catholic Church. Pray in a special way today for all who have the foresight to think about the legacy they are creating in this world — and for those who fail to do so!

On **October 19**, the Church celebrates **Ss. John de Brébeuf** (1593-1649), **Isaac Jogues** (1607-1646) **and Companions**. They were Jesuit priests misunderstood and martyred by early indigenous Americans. Pray for and reach out to those persons you find most difficult to understand and share with them the merciful, compassionate face of Christ!

On **October 20**, the Church celebrates **St. Paul of the Cross** (1694-1775), founder of the Passionists, a religious congregation that takes a fourth vow of spreading memory of Jesus' passion. Consider how you lift up the suffering of Jesus as a model for all who follow in his footsteps on the path to redemption!

On **October 21**, we remember the passing of **Paul Scriptoris** (c. 1460-1505), the German Franciscan mathematician and Scotist whose work on Scotus was the first book created with a printing press in Tübingen. He was banished for lecturing against transubstantiation, and he died in exile. In his memory, pause to learn about alternative perspectives in Eucharistic theology than the ancient Greek metaphysical categories of transubstantiation!

On **October 22**, the Roman church celebrates **St. John Paul II** (1920-2005), a conservative voice barring our sisters from the ministries enjoyed by women in the early Church. Find a way today to promote conversation on the place of women in the ordained ministries of the Church — both during the first quarter of the Western Church's history and in Independent Catholicism today!

On **October 22**, we remember the passing of **Paul Johannes Tillich** (1886-1965), the German-American philosopher and Lutheran theologian who is regarded as one of the most influential theologians of the 20th century. His works introduced theology and modern culture to popular audiences, and his three-volume *Systematic Theology* helped theologians explore the symbols of Christian revelation as answers to the problems of human existence raised by contemporary philosophy. In his memory, "brush up" on your knowledge of Tillich's life and works!

On **October 23**, the Church celebrates **St. John of Capistrano** (1386-1456), the Italian Franciscan who attracted so many people that he had to preach outdoors! Think through ways in which you might extend the reach of your ministry. John is also the patron of those involved in the legal profession: Consider hosting a Red Mass and/or praying for judges, lawyers, law school professors, law students and elected officials!

On **October 23**, the Church celebrates **St. Anicius Manlius Severinus Boëthius** (c. 477-524), the sixth-century Roman senator and philosopher whose *Consolation of Philosophy* expounded on human nature, virtue, evil, justice and free will — and became one of the most popular and influential works of the Middle Ages. As a translator of Aristotle, Boethius became an intermediary between classical antiquity and the following centuries. In his memory, dust off his conversations with Lady Philosophy!

On **October 23**, we remember the passing of **Francis A. Sullivan** (1922-2019), the American Jesuit theologian best known for his writings on ecclesiology and in defense of the Roman Catholic magisterium. His research on Pauline charisms was incorporated into *Lumen gentium*, and his students included Avery Dulles, Joseph Komonchak, Richard McBrien and William Levada. He questioned John Paul II's assertion in *Ordinatio sacerdotalis* that the prohibition of women's ordination has been infallibly taught, and he emphasized consensus among theologians as a criterion by which it might be determined that a doctrine is universally taught by the Church. In his honor, consider your own role in helping to define the ecclesiology of the Independent Catholic movement!

Sunday, October 24, 2021
THIRTIETH SUNDAY IN ORDINARY TIME
(green)

Note: **The introductory line of today's second reading is misleading**. The Letter to the Hebrews is a pseudonymous letter, written in Paul's name and spirit, but not written by Paul. To avoid this confusion, you might proclaim, "A reading from the Letter to the Hebrews."

The thread in today's scriptures: Jeremiah speaks of how God would gather all people — including the blind and the lame, often marginalized for their maladies, which were blamed on sin (Jer. 31:8). Whereas others tried to silence the blind Bartimaeus, Jesus approached him and restored his sight (Mk. 10:46-52), allowing him to sing with the psalmist — and with so many others who experienced Jesus' healing: "The Lord has done great things for us; we are filled with joy" (Ps. 126:3)! In this way, Jesus showed himself to be the new high priest connecting people with God and making "sin offerings...for the people" (Heb. 5:3).

Holy humor: Perhaps you've heard the joke of the blind man who walked up to Jesus and said, "Hey, Jesus, I understand that you're healing the blind. What's the catch?" And Jesus said, "You'll…see!" [Segue into the gospel story of Bartimaeus.]

Looking for a visual aid for your homily or object lesson? Consider a pair of glasses! In the 21ˢᵗ century, many of us benefit from such marvels of optometry and ophthalmology as glasses, contact lenses and laser surgery. Ask listeners to raise their hands if they've ever had any type of vision correction. Invite all to imagine what it would be like to see 2,000 years ago without any type of vision correction. Not only did Jesus restore the sight of those in need of vision correction; he also helped people to "see" themselves as connected with God (the ancient role of the priest!) and one another — in a community where no one feels marginalized!

It's **World Mission Sunday**: Consider having a special collection to support a concrete missionary endeavor, and invite congregants to be "missionaries" from afar through their support of the Church's missions!

On **October 24**, when it does not fall on a Sunday, the Church celebrates **St. Anthony Mary Claret** (1807-1870), the Spanish weaver and printer who was named archbishop of Santiago, Cuba, where he confronted racism, slavery and anti-Christian persecution. Pray and show solidarity today with those who suffer racism, work for unjust wages, and/or are persecuted for their faith!

On **October 24**, the Greek Orthodox Patriarchate of Alexandria and all Africa (recognized by the Ecumenical Patriarch of Constantinople) celebrates the anniversary of the installation in 2004 of Nikolaos Horeftakis as **Pope and Patriarch Theodore II of Alexandria**. In a spirit of ecumenism, pray for him and for the 1.4 million Greek Orthodox Catholics he serves!

On **October 25**, we remember the passing of **Geoffrey Chaucer** (c. 1342-1400), the English author widely regarded as "the Father of English Literature" and the greatest English poet of the Middle Ages. The creator of "The Canterbury Tales," Chaucer esteemed Christianity, even while recognizing that the Church contained some venal, corrupt individuals. In his memory, share with another person your understanding of the difference between Christianity and the Church!

On **October 27**, we remember the passing of **Miguel Serveto** (c. 1509-1553), the Spanish theologian, physician, cartographer and humanist who first described pulmonary circulation. Regarded as the first Unitarian martyr, Serveto was burned at the stake for denying Catholic Trinitarian and Christological theology, and aversion to his death spurred the idea of religious tolerance in Europe. In his memory, renew your own commitment to religious tolerance, ecumenism and interreligious dialogue!

On **October 27**, the Armenian Apostolic Church celebrates the anniversary of the installation in 1999 of Ktrij Nersessian as **Catholicos Karekin II of All Armenians**. In a spirit of ecumenism, pray for him and for the nine million people he serves!

On **October 27**, we remember the passing of **James Hillman** (1926-2011), the American psychologist and author who wrote widely on archetypal psychology. His bestselling work, *The Soul's Code*, suggests that the soul is revealed in imagination, fantasy, myth and metaphor—but also in psychopathology (literally, the "speech of the suffering soul"). In his memory, consider the ways in which you might better allow your soul to "speak" and breathe life into our world!

On **October 28**, the Church celebrates **Ss. Simon and Jude**, two first-century apostles about whom we know very little. St. Jude is invoked as the patron saint of hopeless causes and occupies a preeminent space in the canon of Mexican saints. St. Simon the Zealot, according to one tradition, preached and was martyred in Persia along with St. Jude. Pray Eucharistic Prayer I, which mentions them. If you serve a *Latino* community, be sure to share a prayer card or medal with St. Jude's image!

On **October 28**, we remember the passing of **Libert Froidmont** (1587-1653), the theologian and scientist who corresponded with René Descartes and posthumously published Cornelius Jansen's *Augustinus*. As a theologian, he chaired the scriptural studies department at Louvain, and, as a physicist interested in meteors, he sought to co-opt, rather than reject, new scientific discoveries. In his memory, consider your own stances toward science and emerging views on the human person and on the world we inhabit!

On **October 28**, the Old Catholic Church celebrates the anniversary of the consecration in 1733 of **Theodorus van der Croon** as the ninth archbishop of Utrecht, by Bishop Dominique-Marie Varlet of the Roman church. This was the third of four consecrations performed by Varlet without the permission of Rome. Pray in a special way today for all who continue to generously share the gift of the Spirit and the sacraments of the Church for the sake of God's holy people!

On **October 28**, we remember the birth in 1957 of **Scott W. Hahn**, the American Roman Catholic theologian who, influenced by *Opus Dei*, converted from Presbyterianism and became an ardent and conservative apologist for the Roman church. He is the author of various works and is a regular guest on EWTN. On this day, pray that the Spirit might similarly inflame the hearts of those who contribute to the upbuilding of the Independent Catholic movement in our world!

On **October 29**, we remember the passing of **Godfrey of Fontaines** (+1306-1309), the scholastic philosopher and theologian at the University of Paris who wrote on subjects ranging from moral philosophy to epistemology and metaphysics. The "Venerated Doctor" attacked mendicant orders but defended the novel theory of Thomism, formulated by a mendicant and condemned by the bishop of Paris. In his memory, pause to consider the inconsistencies in your own words and actions!

On **October 29**, we remember **the closure of the convent of Port-Royal-des-Champs** by King Louis XIV in 1709. The convent that sixty years earlier had flourished with 150 nuns had been reduced to 22, all of whom were over the age of 50 and several of whom were now ill. "For the good of the state," 200 soldiers descended on the convent, gave the nuns three hours to pack their belongings and say good-bye, then drove them in separate carriages to the different convents to which they were now scattered and exiled. Shortly thereafter, the convent cemetery was exhumed, the remains of the nuns there were dumped into a mass grave, and the convent was razed. In memory of this somber event, pray for those whose histories have been purposely erased — throughout the centuries and even still today!

On **October 29**, the Independent Sacramental Movement celebrates the anniversary of the passing of **Luis Fernando Castillo Méndez** (1922-2009), the Venezuelan priest who was the last living bishop consecrated by Carlos Duarte Costa. He served as Patriarch of the National Catholic Apostolic Church of Brazil and was persecuted by the Roman church and tortured with hot irons by the Venezuelan government, to make him deny that he was a Catholic bishop. Pray today for all who are persecuted for serving the people of God in the Independent Sacramental Movement!

On **October 30**, we remember the passing of **Gustav Adolf** (1594-1632) who was named a Roman Catholic bishop at age 34 and a cardinal at age 44. After von Bismarck appointed him Ambassador of the German Empire to the Holy See, Pius IX (who appointed him a cardinal) rejected him due to his public opposition to the pope's ultramontane position. In his memory, pray for all who are suffering the pain of friendships gone bad!

On **October 30**, we remember the passing of **Joseph John Campbell** (1904-1987), the American professor who penned groundbreaking works on comparative religion and mythology. His 1949 book, *The Hero with a Thousand Faces*, pointed to the archetypal hero shared by the "monomyth" of world mythologies. He also drew attention to the various myths surrounding Jesus of Nazareth, noting, for instance, that even if Jesus ascended from the earth at the speed of light, he would still be in our galaxy nearly 2,000 years later. George Lucas credited Campbell for his influence on the Star Wars saga. In Campbell's memory, consider the place of myth in our faith tradition and its many, fascinating stories!

Sunday, October 31, 2021

THIRTY-FIRST SUNDAY IN ORDINARY TIME

(green)

Note: **The introductory line of today's second reading is misleading.** The Letter to the Hebrews is a pseudonymous letter, written in Paul's name and spirit, but not written by Paul. To avoid this confusion, you might proclaim, "A reading from the Letter to the Hebrews."

The thread in today's scriptures: Moses exhorted the Israelites to love God with all their heart, soul and strength (Dt. 6:5). Jesus, the "high priest" who connected people with their God (Heb. 7:25-27), referred to this as the "first of all commandments," with the second being love of neighbor (Mk. 12:30-31). May we sing with the psalmist, "I love you, Lord" (Ps. 18:2) — and may that love find expression in our love for one another!

Holy humor: The story is told of the newly-ordained deacon who came to her new community and preached her first homily, titled, "Love God, and Love Your Neighbor." Everyone enjoyed it. She continued to get to know the people, and, a few weeks later, her pastor invited her to preach again. So, she shared her homily: "Love God, and Love Your Neighbor." Her pastor thought it was odd — but maybe the young deacon was so busy ministering to the needs of the people that she didn't have time to prepare a new homily. The deacon continued to get to know the people, and, a few weeks later, her pastor invited her to preach again. You guessed it: She shared the same homily: "Love God, and Love Your Neighbor." Her pastor patiently endured the homily for a third time, but quickly took her aside after Mass. She smiled and replied: "For weeks now, I've been getting to know this community, and I'd love to preach a new homily—believe me, I would. But it doesn't seem they've done anything about the first one yet!" [Segue into how easy it is to talk about loving God and others—but how difficult it might be to prove that our love for God and/or others is actually growing from week to week!]

Looking for a visual aid for your homily or object lesson? Take two wooden boards, and, before holding them up, ask how many pieces of wood are needed to build a cross. Hold up the pieces in the form of a cross. The answer is obvious: two! Note how Jesus distilled the 613 precepts of the Mosaic law into two simple commandments, symbolized by the two beams of the cross: The vertical beam reminds us of the "vertical" direction of our love—that we need to love God (who is traditionally imagined as being "up")—and the horizontal beam reminds us of the "horizontal" direction of our love for those around us. Invite listeners to point upward and beside them, making a cross with their forearms—or to simply make a cross with their index fingers. That's the essence of Jesus' distillation of the Mosaic law, and if we love God and neighbor, we're following in the footsteps of him who died on a cross!

Daylight Saving Time ends next Sunday: Be sure to spread word today, letting congregants know to "fall back" and enjoy an extra hour at home, rather than arrive an hour early for Mass!

On **November 1**, the Church celebrates **All Saints Day**! Consider hosting a heavenly-themed party and costume contest with ribbons for all participants—or minimize the stress by having halos and silver beads that congregants can wear on top of their regular attire. Use the occasion as a way to catechize. Have an All Saints photo booth. Plan some heaven-themed games. Decorate with silver foil stars and clusters of white balloons. Cover furniture with white sheets and cushions. Drape white tulle around the room, with white lights behind for a twinkling effect. Scatter white, silver and clear balloons all over the floor, to give the effect of walking on clouds. Pull out a fog machine, for an additional effect. Provide a smorgasbord of white treats: finger sandwiches on white bread, cauliflower and jicama with ranch dressing, white cheeses and crackers, marshmallows, yogurt-covered nuts, white M&Ms, macadamia nuts, white chocolate pretzels, cloudlike meringue cookies, and, of course, an angel food cake with whipped cream and coconut. You will have created a heavenly memory!

On **November 1**, we remember the passing of **Dale Harbison Carnegie** (1888-1955), the American writer and speaker known for assisting others with their public speaking and interpersonal skills. The renowned author of the bestselling *How to Win Friends and Influence People*, Carnegie believed that the best way to influence other people's behavior is by changing your own behavior toward them. In his memory, reflect on your own interpersonal skills, and consider incorporating suggestions from his works into your life and ministry!

On **November 1**, the Indian Orthodox Church celebrates the anniversary of the installation in 2010 of Paulose Mar Milithios as **Catholicos Baselios Mar Thoma Paulose II**. In a spirit of ecumenism, pray for him and for the 2.5 million people he serves!

On **November 2**, the Church celebrates **All Souls Day**, an outgrowth from the 1274 formulation of Purgatory, a place where our loved ones and friends are purportedly purged of sin. Consider hosting a Mass of remembrance in a cemetery or mausoleum, and invite all families who lost a loved one during this year. Announce this a few weeks in advance with a special envelope (since Catholics are accustomed to offering Masses for the dead) onto which congregants can write the names of their beloved departed family members and friends, for inclusion in the intentions of this day. During the presentation of gifts, bring these envelopes forward in a lovely basket, and place them near the altar during the celebration of the Liturgy of the Eucharist. The Church shares four "great sequences" each year: Today's is the *Dies Irae*. Consider having a gifted cantor sing or chant a setting of this, before segueing into the gospel acclamation. Offer a prayer for those who've gone before us, and conclude with the popular words: "Eternal rest grant unto them, O Lord...."

On **November 2**, people throughout Latin America celebrate *el día de los muertos* ("the Day of the Dead") with altars in memory of departed loved ones. They fill these altars with photos, *papel picado* (hand-cut tissue paper), yellow and orange chrysanthemums and marigolds, and foods, drinks and objects that call to mind the lives of their beloved deceased. Incorporate elements into your own celebration of All Souls Day, and point to the *esqueletos* (skeletons that are eating, drinking, playing the guitar, riding bicycles, etc.) as a reminder of the great mystery of our faith: that those who have gone before us are not dead, but are very much alive in Christ. Send congregants home with ideas for their own simple home altars in honor of deceased loved ones!

On **November 2**, we celebrate the birth in 1936 of **Rosemary Radford Ruether**, the American feminist scholar and Catholic theologian who, despite sanction by the Vatican, has been an outspoken advocate for the ordination of women in the Roman church. As a director of Catholics for Choice, she has advocated for allowing women to follow their Spirit-inspired consciences. In her honor, consider what you are doing to advance Jesus' and Paul's vision of a "discipleship of equals"!

On **November 2**, the Eastern Orthodox Church celebrates the anniversary of the installation in 1991 of Aghios Theodoros as **Ecumenical Patriarch Bartholomew I of Constantinople**. In a spirit of ecumenism, pray for him and for the 260 million Eastern Orthodox Catholics he serves!

On **November 4**, the Church celebrates **St. Charles Borromeo** (1538-1584), the doctor of civil and canon law who established seminaries and formulated a code of moral conduct for clergy. Consider ways to focus today on your own continuing education and formation!

On **November 4**, we remember the passing of **Antoine Le Maistre** (1608-1658), the French Jansenist lawyer and author who was the nephew of Antoine Arnauld, the leading Jansenist theologian in 17th-century France, and of Jacqueline-Marie-Angélique Arnauld, the abbess of Port-Royal-des-Champs, the religious community at the center of Jansenism. A talented jurist, Antoine withdrew from public affairs, greatly displeasing Cardinal Richelieu, and founded an ascetic group of hermits at Port-Royal. In his memory, lift up in prayer all who dedicate themselves to a contemplative life of prayer!

On **November 5**, we remember the passing of **Francisco de Quiñones** (c. 1482-1540), the Spanish Franciscan friar and cardinal responsible for several reforms of the Roman church in Spain, including the formulation of a breviary that was printed in 100 editions over 30 years. His breviary was later banned for its disregard of tradition. In his memory, consider how you are helping others to pray and grow in their daily relationship with God!

On **November 5**, we celebrate the birth in 1931 of **Charles Margrave Taylor**, the Canadian philosopher who has contributed to many philosophical fields, including the philosophy of religion. His work, *A Secular Age*, argues against the diminished influence of religion in light of science and technology, noting that religion continues to grow and diversify in our world. In his honor, consider your own stance toward the intersection of science, technology and religion, and the role of religion in a quickly-evolving world!

On **November 6**, we remember the passing of **Guillaume Fillastre** (1348-1428), the French cardinal, canonist and geographer who was among the first to advocate at the Council of Constance for the abdication of rival popes in favor of conciliarism at the Council of Constance. He kept a diary during the council, which shed light on the quarrels, the precedence of various "nations," and the French king's response to the proceedings. Pause today to consider the ways in which you are helping to record and share history!

Sunday, November 7, 2021
THIRTY-SECOND SUNDAY IN ORDINARY TIME
(green)

Choose the gospel you'll proclaim: the shorter version that focuses on the widow's mite, or the longer version, which begins with three verses of Jesus warning the crowds of the Pharisees.

Beware the **exclusive language** of today's readings: The "fatherless" in the third verse of the psalm might easily be the "orphan," and the line is easily recast: "The orphan and the widow are sustained, but the way of the wicked is thwarted."

Note: **The introductory line of today's second reading is misleading**. The Letter to the Hebrews is a pseudonymous letter, written in Paul's name and spirit, but not written by Paul. To avoid this confusion, you might proclaim, "A reading from the Letter to the Hebrews."

The thread in today's scriptures: The widow in today's gospel "contributed all she had," trusting that God would provide for her (Mk. 12:44), just as God provided, through Elijah, for the widow of Zarephath and her son (1Kgs. 17:10-16). The Lord "gives food to the hungry" and sustains widows and orphans (Ps. 146:7), and the pseudonymous author of the letter to the Hebrews notes that Christ "will appear…to bring salvation to those who eagerly await him" (Heb. 9:28).

Holy humor: Perhaps you've heard the joke before: What are the smallest insects in the Bible? The widow's mite and…"the wicked flee" (Prov. 28:1)! [Segue into the double entendre of the mite, the small, copper Roman coin better known as the *lepton*, worth about six minutes of an average daily wage.]

Looking for a visual aid for your homily or object lesson? Consider a small coin purse, with 57 cents! Share the story of Hattie Wiatt, first told in a sermon by Russell Conwell on December 1, 1912. According to the story, a young girl, Hattie, was waiting outside a Sunday school classroom because it was so crowded with children. The church's pastor saw Hattie and helped to accommodate her in the room, telling her that he was going to raise the necessary money to build a larger Sunday school classroom for the children. Sometime later, little Hattie died, and, after the funeral, Hattie's mother handed the pastor a small coin purse with 57 cents, explaining that Hattie had been saving her pennies to help build a new Sunday school classroom. When the pastor shared the story of Hattie's generosity, it so inspired the congregation that they quickly raised the necessary money to build a wonderful, new building with room for all the children. Jesus would say that Hattie gave more than anyone else to that building project — she gave all she had!

On **November 8**, we remember the passing of **Æthelbert of York** (+780), the Northumbrian monk, scholar and Archbishop of York who rebuilt the cathedral and taught many missionaries, including Alcuin, the biographer of Willibrord. He convened a council to depose and exile the Northumbrian king. In his memory, consider how you are contributing to the formation of others!

On **November 8**, we remember the passing of **John Duns** (c. 1265-1308), the Scottish "Subtle Doctor" of the High Middle Ages. Also known as Duns Scotus, he argued for the Immaculate Conception and developed a complex argument for the existence of God. He is also known for such concepts as haecceity, formal distinction, and the univocity of being. In his memory, refresh your knowledge of him and his works!

On **November 8**, we remember the passing of **John Milton** (1608-1674), the English poet and intellectual who created his own non-trinitarian catechism and wrestled with theological themes, including the tension between virtue and vice. Milton was not shy about sharing his dislike for Roman Catholicism and its episcopacy, referring to Rome as Babylon and to bishops as Egyptian taskmasters. He also saw England as the new Israel, led by the new Moses, Oliver Cromwell. In his memory, consider more creative expressions for your views on our church and world!

On **November 10**, we remember the passing of **George Alexander McGuire** (1866-1934), the Caribbean Episcopal priest who immigrated to the U.S. and was named chaplain-general of Marcus Garvey's Universal Negro Improvement Association. He founded and led the African Orthodox Church for 13 years, overseeing congregations in the U.S., Canada, the Caribbean and East Africa. McGuire drew on his knowledge of religion and African history to create foundational documents on Black Independent Catholic theology and ritual. In his memory, consider how you are working to correct vestiges of colonialism and slavery in our world!

On **November 11**, U.S. society celebrates **Veteran's Day**. Share a special blessing for all who have served in the military, and celebrate them with a cake or some other fitting symbol of your gratitude!

On **November 11**, the Church celebrates **St. Martin of Tours** (+397), the soldier who shared his cloak with Christ disguised as a poor man. Consider the persons around you through whom Christ might be appearing "in disguise"! Martin is the patron saint of business owners in Mexico: If you serve a *Latino* community, share a prayer of blessing with the entrepreneurs who are attempting to support themselves and their families in creative ways!

On **November 11**, we remember the passing of **Jerome Murphy-O'Connor** (1935-2013), the Irish Dominican priest and New Testament professor considered a leading authority on St. Paul. He made numerous television appearances, and he authored several books, including an archaeological guide to the Holy Land. In his memory, explore more deeply St. Paul's life, writings and theology!

On **November 12**, the Church celebrates **St. Josaphat** (1580-1623), the Lithuanian archbishop who tirelessly worked in an attempt to unite the Western and Eastern Churches. Renew your commitment today to deepening ecumenical relations!

On **November 12**, we celebrate the birth in 1936 of **Sandra Marie Schneiders**, the American professor *emerita* who has published numerous works on theology, spirituality, feminism and religious life. In her memory, consider the ways in which you might be pouring "new wine" into "old wineskins" by failing to reimagine your life and ministry!

On **November 12**, we celebrate the birth in 1942 of **John F. Haught**, the American systematic theologian who has written widely on physical cosmology, evolutionary biology and Christianity. His many works provide a space for both scientific inquiry and a biblical understanding of God, and he explores the persistence of biblical literalism, which erroneously looks to the Bible as a source of scientific truth. In his honor, consider your own views toward the "science" contained in the scriptures!

On **November 13**, the Church celebrates **St. Frances Xavier Cabrini** (1850-1917), the first American citizen to be canonized. In honor of the matron saint of immigrants, share a special prayer for all who are attempting to survive and thrive in a foreign land!

On **November 13**, we remember the passing of **Francis Thompson** (1859-1907), the English poet and mystic who dropped out of medical school to pursue his passion of writing. His poem, "The Hound of Heaven," describes the pursuit of the human person by God and has been described as "one of the most tremendous poems ever written." In his memory, pray using the words of Thompson's "The Hound of Heaven"!

Sunday, November 14, 2021

THIRTY-THIRD SUNDAY IN ORDINARY TIME

(green)

Note: **The introductory line of today's second reading is misleading**. The Letter to the Hebrews is a pseudonymous letter, written in Paul's name and spirit, but not written by Paul. To avoid this confusion, you might proclaim, "A reading from the Letter to the Hebrews."

The thread in today's scriptures: As we approach the end of Ordinary Time, we hear of the end of the world: Daniel imagines a time of unsurpassed distress, when "those who sleep in the dust of the earth shall awake; [and] some shall live forever" (Dan. 12:2), and Jesus foretells a day when the sun and moon will be darkened, the stars will fall from the sky, and people will see Christ "coming in the clouds" (Mk. 13:26). Knowing that Christ now reigns "forever at the right hand of God" (Heb. 10:12), we, like the psalmist, are undisturbed, knowing that God will not abandon God's faithful ones (16:8-10)!

Holy humor: In her book, *Forbidden*, Jana Oliver has a scene where a man is shouting in the street, "the end is near!" We've all seen cartoons and portrayals of such people in movies, right? In Oliver's work, Riley asks the man, "Is there still time for hot chocolate?" And the man blinks and replies, "Uh, maybe. I don't know." [Segue into the fact that none of us knows the day or the hour of Christ's return; hence, the need to be prepared!]

Looking for a visual aid for your homily or object lesson? Try a roll of toilet paper! Ask, "How long would a roll of toilet paper, like this, last in your home?" We're all familiar with toilet paper, and we all know when a roll of toilet paper is coming to an end. We don't need a message printed on a sheet near the roll to tell us that "the end is near." Unlike toilet paper, though, we have no idea when the end is coming. Remember in 2020, when we endured a pandemic, hurricanes, even clouds of locusts in Kenya—yet here we are! For millennia, humans have imagined the end of the world, but, unlike a roll of toilet paper, none of us can even begin to guess the day or the hour! [Note: if a roll of toilet paper could be negatively perceived within your community, try a roll of paper towels or a tube of toothpaste instead!]

On **November 14**, we remember the passing of **Georg Wilhelm Friedrich Hegel** (1770-1831), the German philosopher who sought to overcome dualisms and whose philosophy of the spirit integrated philosophy, psychology, history, art and religion. Called the "Protestant Aquinas" by Barth, he provided the basis for many great philosophical ideas of the 19th and 20th centuries. In his memory, take a moment to reacquaint yourself with Hegel's life and works!

On **November 14**, the Armenian Catholic Church (in union with Rome) celebrates the birth in 1934 of **Catholicos-Patriarch Krikor Bedros "Gregory Peter" XX Ghabroyan**. In a spirit of ecumenism, pray for him and for the 758,000 Armenian Catholics he serves!

On **November 15**, the Church celebrates **St. Albert the Great** (c. 1200-1280), the great teacher and mentor who suffered memory loss and dementia before death. Pray in a special way today for all who suffer similar maladies—and for all who so lovingly and patiently care for them!

On **November 15**, we celebrate the birth in 1932 of **Alvin Carl Plantinga**, the American philosopher whose writings on the philosophy of religion include a "free will defense" to refute the argument that a good God could not allow evil in the world. Within the study of theodicy, he is best known for his work, *God, Freedom and Evil*. In his honor, pause today to reflect on your own beliefs with respect to the presence of evil and suffering in our world!

On **November 15**, the Syriac Catholic Church (in union with Rome) celebrates the birth in 1944 of **Patriarch Ignatius Ephrem Joseph III Yonan of Antioch**. In a spirit of ecumenism, pray for him and for the 205,000 Syriac Catholics he serves!

On **November 16**, the Church celebrates **St. Margaret of Scotland** (1045-1093) and **St. Gertrude the Great** (1256-1302). Margaret raised eight children and lived a life of extraordinary charity that flowed from prayer. Gertrude was a nun whose prayer led to ecstatic, mystical experiences. Pause today to consider the state of your own prayer life. Even better, find some time and space today to focus on growing in your own prayerful relationship with God!

On **November 16**, we remember the passing of **Pierre Nicole** (1625-1695), the great Jansenist theologian whose *Les Imaginaires* suggested that the supposed heretical opinions ascribed to the Jansenists existed only in the imaginations of the Jesuits. Despite his absent-mindedness and social awkwardness, he wrote numerous popular theological works and a 14-volume work of moral theology. In his memory, encourage the gifts of the persons you're tempted to "write off"!

On **November 16**, we remember the passing of **Ignacio Ellacuría** (1930-1989), the Spanish Jesuit priest, philosopher and theologian who was assassinated with other Jesuits by Salvadoran soldiers in the closing years of the Salvadoran Civil War. His work, a significant contribution to liberation theology and liberation philosophy, met with strong opposition from the conservative religious and political forces in El Salvador. In his memory, pray for all modern-day martyrs and all who pour out their lives for the liberation of others!

On **November 17**, we remember the passing of **Giovanni Pico della Mirandola** (1463-1494), the Italian Renaissance nobleman and philosopher known for his manifesto of 900 theses on religion, philosophy, natural philosophy and magic—the first book to be universally banned by the Roman church. The founder of the Christian Kabbalah tradition, his teachings influenced Western esotericism. In his memory, research the works that have been condemned and/or banned throughout history!

On **November 17**, we remember the passing of **Jakob Böhme** (1575-1624), the "first German philosopher," mystic and Lutheran theologian who was made famous by his first, scandalous work, *Aurora*, and later influenced German idealism and romanticism. Many of his works focused on sin, evil and redemption. Pause today to consider your own views on these theological themes!

On **November 18**, we remember the passing of **Adam Marsh** (c. 1200-1259), the English Franciscan theologian and bishop who was "the most eminent master of England" after Grosseteste. The queen's spiritual director, he mediated between the court party and its opposition, rebuking both for their shortcomings, but remaining a friend of all. In his memory, consider which "bridges" you need to mend in order to be "a friend to all"!

On **November 18**, the Church celebrates **St. Rose Philippine Duchesne** (1769-1852), who cared for the Native Americans of St. Louis, Missouri. Pause today to consider your own efforts of catechesis and evangelization!

On **November 18**, we remember the passing of **Karl Hugo Prüter** (1920-2007), the Congregationalist minister who became an Independent Catholic bishop and founded Christ Catholic Church. For decades, his church was deemed the world's smallest cathedral by *Guinness Book of World Records*. He also established St. Willibrord Press to publish and distribute Independent Catholic literature. In his memory, recommit yourself to leaving a greater legacy within the Independent Catholic movement!

On **November 18**, the Coptic Orthodox Church of Alexandria celebrates the anniversary of the installation in 2012 of Wagih Subhi Baqi Sulayman as **Pope Tawadros II of Alexandria**. In a spirit of ecumenism, pray for him and for the 22 million people he serves!

On **November 20**, we celebrate the birth in 1942 of **Daniel A. Helminiak**, the American Roman Catholic priest and theologian who has written widely on such topics as neuroscience, human sexuality, and the psychology of spirituality. He is renowned for his bestseller, *What the Bible Really Says about Homosexuality*, which argues that the Bible does not condemn, but is actually indifferent to, same-sex relationships. In his honor, share a copy of his book with someone who might be in need of a bit of good news on what the Bible *really* says about his/her sexuality and/or the sexuality of his/her children and grandchildren!

On **November 20**, we celebrate the birth in 1943 of **Luke Timothy Johnson**, the American Benedictine New Testament scholar and historian of early Christianity. He has written widely on Luke-Acts, the Pastoral Letters, the Letter of James, and the Greco-Roman context of early Christianity. He has voiced his disagreements with the Roman church, including its prohibition of same-sex marriage. In his honor, reacquaint yourself with his scholarship!

On **November 20**, the Russian Orthodox Church (recognized by the Ecumenical Patriarch of Constantinople) celebrates the birth in 1946 of **Vladimir Mikhailovich Gundyayev**, who would become Patriarch Kirill of Moscow. In a spirit of ecumenism, pray for him and for the Russian Orthodox Catholics he serves!

Sunday, November 21, 2021
CHRIST THE KING OF THE UNIVERSE
(white)

The Sundays of Summer/Fall Ordinary Time have come to an end: **Decorate your worship space** in white and gold. Be sure your vestments match the environment and are ironed or steamed. Highlight the solemnity of this day with an arrangement of fresh flowers!

The thread in today's scriptures: "The Lord is king" (Ps. 93:1)! Daniel had a vision of the "Son of man" coming on a cloud, receiving dominion and kingship, and served by "all peoples, nations, and languages" (Dan. 7:14). John viewed Christ as "ruler of the kings of the earth," bringing us together into a kingdom (Rev. 1:5-6). When asked by Pilate if he was the King of the Jews, Jesus spoke of his kingdom (Jn. 18:33-37).

Holy humor: Hundreds of years ago, when Timbuktu was nothing more than a large collection of grass huts, the king ordered that a fine collection of thrones be made, so that his young son could choose his throne when he became a man. The craftsmen of the village created an exquisitely-carved ivory throne. They created the loveliest gold throne. They also made a throne covered with diamonds, emeralds, sapphires and rubies. They then locked the thrones inside a grass hut to guard them for the future king. Unfortunately, one stormy night, lightning struck the grass hut, and, to the king's horror, all three thrones were entirely destroyed! And the moral of this story is: People who live in...grass houses...shouldn't...stow thrones! [Segue into the way in which we often tuck away or hide Christ, like the thrones in the grass hut. What good were the thrones locked away in a grass hut? What good is it to say that Christ is king of our lives, if this is not apparent to all?]

Looking for a visual aid for your homily or object lesson? Consider a gold crown! The crown is a traditional symbol of those ruling over others. In a world of increasing democracy, we have less monarchs in our world, with more power wielded by democratically-elected persons, like prime ministers and members of Parliament. The power dynamics have also changed: In the United Kingdom, the queen symbolically wears the crown and gives "royal assent," but exercises no real political power. We say that Christ is the king of the universe, but does he have any power in our lives? Is he merely a symbolic "king," with a fancy crown, or is he also the Prime Minister and Parliament of our lives?

Thanksgiving is this week: Consider hosting a post-Mass **Thanksgiving dinner**, complete with traditional foods!

In preparation for Thanksgiving, consider sharing with each family a laminated card with a beautiful, meaningful **Thanksgiving meal blessing**. Include your community's name and contact information on it. Congregants will use it, then find a special place for it, so that they can use it in future years!

Will your community have an **end-of-year appeal**? After the celebration of Thanksgiving this week, congregants will be receiving end-of-year appeals from a number of non-profit organizations. Consider an appeal, perhaps to launch on Giving Tuesday next week! Also, be thinking about a custom holiday card that you might design and print during the coming days, to be shared during the holidays as a symbol of your appreciation for all who have supported your community throughout this year!

On **November 21**, when it doesn't fall on a Sunday, the Church celebrates the **Presentation of Mary**, a day observed for centuries despite its lack of scriptural basis. Many artists depict her as a three-year old presenting herself to God. If you serve a *Latino* community, be sure to note the tie between this act and the traditional *presentación de 3 años*, in which *Latino* parents present their three-year-old children to the Church!

On **November 21**, we remember the passing of **Jean-Baptiste Henri-Dominique Lacordaire** (1802-1861), the French priest, theologian and political activist who reestablished the Dominican Order in post-Revolutionary France and whose liberal Catholic views were not welcomed by the Roman papacracy. He demanded the separation of church and state, challenging French clergy to embrace apostolic poverty over state salaries, and he attacked conservative, government-appointed bishops as ambitious and servile. He was an early advocate for freedom of conscience and freedom of the press — both of which were condemned by Gregory XVI. In his memory, pause to consider how your own words and actions contribute to and/or limit basic human freedoms!

On **November 21**, the Independent Sacramental Movement celebrates the consecration in 1897 of **Anthony Stanislas Kozlowski**, who organized the Polish National Catholic Church in Chicago for Polish congregants dissatisfied with their mostly-Irish Roman Catholic bishops. Pray today for those unable to identify with the Church's ministers around them!

On **November 21**, the Polish National Catholic Church celebrates the anniversary of the installation in 2010 of **Prime Bishop Anthony Mikovsky**. In a spirit of ecumenism, pray for him and for the 26,000 people he serves!

On **November 22**, the Church celebrates **St. Cecilia**, the third-century matron saint of musicians. She was martyred for refusing to forsake her vow of virginity and sacrifice to pagan gods. Find a small way today to grow in your own musical ability. If you're not entirely confident in your vocal abilities, ask a gifted friend for a brief vocal lessons! Also, if you haven't recognized your parish's instrumentalists and vocalists recently, this is an opportune day to do so!

On **November 22**, we remember the passing of **C.S. Lewis** (1898-1963), the British Anglican writer and theologian whose fiction and Christian apologetics have been read by millions. In his memory, read one of his works and/or consider the written legacy you're leaving!

On **November 22**, we also remember the passing of **Aldous Leonard Huxley** (1894-1963), the English Nobel Prize winning author, philosopher, humanist and pacifist who wrote on mysticism and who illustrated the similarities between Western and Eastern mysticisms. In his memory, reflect on the universality of your own spiritual vision!

On **November 22**, the Greek Orthodox Church of Jerusalem (recognized by the Ecumenical Patriarch of Constantinople) celebrates the anniversary of the installation in 2005 of Ilias Giannopoulos as **Patriarch Theophilus III of Jerusalem**. In a spirit of ecumenism, pray for him and for the 500,000 Greek Orthodox Catholics he serves!

On **November 23**, the Church celebrates **St. Clement I** (c. 35-99), **St. Columban** (c. 543-615), and **Bl. Miguel Agustín Pro Juárez** (1891-1927). Clement I addressed division in the Church and urged Christians to live in love and union. Columban was a monk who urged the Church toward greater holiness. Miguel Agustín was a Jesuit priest murdered by the anticlerical, anti-Christian political regime in Mexico. Consider today your own commitment to unity, holiness and our faith!

On **November 23**, the Assyrian Church of the East celebrates the birth in 1941 of **Warda Daniel Sliwa**, who would become Catholicos-Patriarch Gewargis III. In a spirit of ecumenism, pray for him and for the people he serves!

On **November 25**, the Church celebrates **St. Catherine of Alexandria** (c. 287 – c. 305), a saint removed from the canon of saints for lack of historical evidence—but later restored as a gesture of good will to Orthodox Christians. Consider today what gestures you're making—or could be making—to increase ecumenical relations!

On **November 25**, the Greek Orthodox Patriarchate of Alexandria and all Africa (recognized by the Ecumenical Patriarch of Constantinople) celebrates the birth in 1954 of **Nikolaos Horeftakis**, who would become Pope and Patriarch Theodore II of Alexandria. In a spirit of ecumenism, pray for him and for the 1.4 million Greek Orthodox Catholics he serves!

On **the fourth Thursday of November**, U.S. society celebrates **Thanksgiving**: Find a way to involve your congregants not only in celebrating the abundance they enjoy, but of sharing with others. Encourage a canned food drive to assist those who will hunger during the upcoming holiday season, or volunteer for a community Thanksgiving dinner! For the intellectually-curious, note how the turkey is traditionally a symbol of bounty, a rare treat for early settlers in the New World, and/or point to the nine "turkeys" in today's gospel who lacked an "attitude of gratitude"!

On **November 26**, we remember the passing of **Bernard Joseph Francis Lonergan** (1904-1984), the Canadian Jesuit philosopher and theologian regarded as one of the prominent Catholic thinkers of the 20th century. In his memory, spend a few minutes reacquainting yourself with his life and works!

And with that, we've come to the end of the Year of Mark!

If you have any feedback on how we can improve this text for use by you and your community, please call us at (512) 826-0280 or write us at editor@extraordinarycatholics.faith.

Please know of our prayers for you and your community as you seek to create celebrations that "stick"!

Important Dates to Remember
& Celebrate in Our Community!

December

_____   _____

_____   _____

_____   _____

January

_____   _____

_____   _____

_____   _____

February

_____   _____

_____   _____

_____   _____

March

_____   _____

_____   _____

_____   _____

April

_____   _____

_____   _____

_____   _____

May

_____   _____

_____   _____

_____   _____

Important Dates to Remember
& Celebrate in Our Community!

June

_____   _____

_____   _____

_____   _____

July

_____   _____

_____   _____

_____   _____

August

_____   _____

_____   _____

_____   _____

September

_____   _____

_____   _____

_____   _____

October

_____   _____

_____   _____

_____   _____

November

_____   _____

_____   _____

_____   _____

Our Plan for Creating Celebrations that "Stick"!

November 29 – First Sunday of Advent

_____   _____

_____   _____

December 6 – Second Sunday of Advent

_____   _____

_____   _____

December 13 – Third Sunday of Advent

_____   _____

_____   _____

December 20 – Fourth Sunday of Advent

_____   _____

_____   _____

December 24/25 – The Nativity of Our Lord

_____   _____

_____   _____

December 27 – The Holy Family of Jesus, Mary & Joseph

_____   _____

_____   _____

January 3 – The Epiphany of Our Lord

_____   _____

_____   _____

January 10 – The Baptism of Our Lord

_____   _____

_____   _____

Our Plan for Creating Celebrations that "Stick"!

January 17 – Second Sunday in Ordinary Time

_____ _____

_____ _____

January 24 – Third Sunday in Ordinary Time

_____ _____

_____ _____

January 31 – Fourth Sunday in Ordinary Time

_____ _____

_____ _____

February 7 – Fifth Sunday in Ordinary Time

_____ _____

_____ _____

February 14 – Sixth Sunday in Ordinary Time

_____ _____

_____ _____

February 17 – Ash Wednesday

_____ _____

_____ _____

February 21 – First Sunday of Lent

_____ _____

_____ _____

February 28 – Second Sunday of Lent

_____ _____

_____ _____

Our Plan for Creating Celebrations that "Stick"!

March 7 – Third Sunday of Lent

_____   _____

_____   _____

March 14 – Fourth Sunday of Lent

_____   _____

_____   _____

March 21 – Fifth Sunday of Lent

_____   _____

_____   _____

March 28 – Palm Sunday

_____   _____

_____   _____

April 1 – Holy Thursday

_____   _____

_____   _____

April 2 – Good Friday

_____   _____

_____   _____

April 3 – Easter Vigil

_____   _____

_____   _____

April 4 – The Resurrection of the Lord

_____   _____

_____   _____

Our Plan for Creating Celebrations that "Stick"!

April 11 – Second Sunday of Easter

_____   _____

_____   _____

April 18 – Third Sunday of Easter

_____   _____

_____   _____

April 25 – Fourth Sunday of Easter

_____   _____

_____   _____

May 2 – Fifth Sunday of Easter

_____   _____

_____   _____

May 9 – Sixth Sunday of Easter

_____   _____

_____   _____

May 16 – The Ascension of the Lord

_____   _____

_____   _____

May 23 – Pentecost

_____   _____

_____   _____

May 30 – The Most Holy Trinity

_____   _____

_____   _____

Our Plan for Creating Celebrations that "Stick"!

June 6 – The Solemnity of the Most Holy Body and Blood of Christ

_____   _____

_____   _____

June 13 – Eleventh Sunday in Ordinary Time

_____   _____

_____   _____

June 20 – Twelfth Sunday in Ordinary Time

_____   _____

_____   _____

June 27 – Thirteenth Sunday in Ordinary Time

_____   _____

_____   _____

July 4 – Fourteenth Sunday in Ordinary Time

_____   _____

_____   _____

July 11 – Fifteenth Sunday in Ordinary Time

_____   _____

_____   _____

July 18 – Sixteenth Sunday in Ordinary Time

_____   _____

_____   _____

July 25 – Seventeenth Sunday in Ordinary Time

_____   _____

_____   _____

Our Plan for Creating Celebrations that "Stick"!

August 1– Eighteenth Sunday in Ordinary Time

_____   _____

_____   _____

August 8 – Nineteenth Sunday in Ordinary Time

_____   _____

_____   _____

August 15 – Twentieth Sunday in Ordinary Time

_____   _____

_____   _____

August 22 – Twenty-first Sunday in Ordinary Time

_____   _____

_____   _____

August 29 – Twenty-second Sunday in Ordinary Time

_____   _____

_____   _____

September 5 – Twenty-third Sunday in Ordinary Time

_____   _____

_____   _____

September 12 – Twenty-fourth Sunday in Ordinary Time

_____   _____

_____   _____

September 19 – Twenty-fifth Sunday in Ordinary Time

_____   _____

_____   _____

Our Plan for Creating Celebrations that "Stick"!

September 26 – Twenty-sixth Sunday in Ordinary Time

_____   _____

_____   _____

October 3 – Twenty-seventh Sunday in Ordinary Time

_____   _____

_____   _____

October 10 – Twenty-eighth Sunday in Ordinary Time

_____   _____

_____   _____

October 17 – Twenty-ninth Sunday in Ordinary Time

_____   _____

_____   _____

October 24 – Thirtieth Sunday in Ordinary Time

_____   _____

_____   _____

October 31 – Thirty-first Sunday in Ordinary Time

_____   _____

_____   _____

November 7 – Thirty-second Sunday in Ordinary Time

_____   _____

_____   _____

November 14 – Thirty-third Sunday in Ordinary Time

_____   _____

_____   _____

Our Plan for Creating Celebrations that "Stick"!

November 21 – Christ the King of the Universe

_____   _____

_____   _____

Other Notes on Our Plans for Celebrations that "Stick"...

Index

Made in the USA
Columbia, SC
11 June 2021

39853723R00139